THE LITTLEHAMPTON LIBELS

The Littlehampton Libels tells the story of a poison-pen mystery that led to a miscarriage of justice in the years following the First World War. There would be four criminal trials before the real culprit was finally punished, with the case challenging the police and the lawyers as much as any capital crime.

The story of the police investigation—by a leading Metropolitan Police detective—takes the reader into the emotions and intrigues of neighbourhood life, and into a lost world of everyday language. At a time when universal literacy was still a novelty, the investigation showed in extraordinary detail how ordinary people could use the English language in inventive and surprising ways.

Christopher Hilliard is the Challis Professor of History at the University of Sydney. He is the author of four other books, including *A Matter of Obscenity: The Politics of Censorship in Modern England* (2021), *English as a Vocation: The 'Scrutiny' Movement* (OUP, 2012), about F. R. Leavis and his followers, and *To Exercise Our Talents: The Democratization of Writing in Britain* (2006), which traces a forgotten history of aspiring writers' clubs and how-to-be-an-author magazines.

Further Praise for
The Littlehampton Libels

'*The Littlehampton Libels* is both a gripping read and a sophisticated analysis of class dynamics, notions of respectability, and the weaknesses of the British legal system.'

Adrian Bingham, *American Historical Review*

'The reader's attention is carried partly by Hilliard's infectious pleasure in his story-telling, partly by the barely credible drama of the libels continuing for trial after trial and partly by the thoroughness of the research.'

David Vincent, *English Historical Review*

'Chris Hilliard's *The Littlehampton Libels* ... is a real-crime scholarly history, but Agatha Christie fans should love it. It's Christie's world, and those dogged and courteous police officers turn out to be real.'

Sheila Fitzpatrick, *Australian Book Review: 2017 Books of the Year*

'The tale unfolds with all the fascination of a mystery thriller ... few towns could offer such an extraordinary story, nor hope to find a better qualified chronicler.'

Sussex Life

'As an exciting experiment in merging the genre of the mystery novel with a work of historiography, Hilliard's *The Littlehampton Libels* succeeds in crafting an engaging, pacey, and intellectually stimulating account of an unusual criminal case in 1920s England.'

Eloise Moss, *Journal of Interdisciplinary History*

'Gooding and Swan fell from posterity's view, but thanks to Hilliard we have a well-researched, thoroughly compelling contribution to the scarce library of working-class histories.'

Belinda Webb-Blofeld, *Times Literary Supplement*

THE LITTLEHAMPTON LIBELS

A MISCARRIAGE OF JUSTICE AND A MYSTERY ABOUT WORDS IN 1920s ENGLAND

CHRISTOPHER HILLIARD

OXFORD
UNIVERSITY PRESS

OXFORD
UNIVERSITY PRESS

Great Clarendon Street, Oxford, OX2 6DP,
United Kingdom

Oxford University Press is a department of the University of Oxford.
It furthers the University's objective of excellence in research, scholarship,
and education by publishing worldwide. Oxford is a registered trade mark of
Oxford University Press in the UK and in certain other countries

Published in the United States of America by Oxford University Press
198 Madison Avenue, New York, NY 10016, United States of America

British Library Cataloguing in Publication Data
Data available

Library of Congress Cataloging in Publication Data
Data available

ISBN 978–0–19–879965–8 (Hbk.)
ISBN 978–0–19–890006–1 (Pbk.)

For my father

Acknowledgements

I came across the Littlehampton libel case accidentally. I read through the Metropolitan Police file in the National Archives at Kew, put it aside, and got on with what I was supposed to be researching. But the story stayed with me, and eighteen months later I went back to that file and began working towards this book. I might not have if Shane White hadn't encouraged me to believe that there was a book there. Shane read and improved each iteration of each chapter. I owe him a lot.

Kate Summerscale gave me perceptive advice at a critical stage. I'm grateful to Deborah Cohen for introducing me to Kate, and for her own insights about and support for the book. Peter Robinson's guidance enabled me to work out what I was really trying to do with this story. Penny Russell read the whole manuscript while she was supposed to be on vacation, and has provided advice and encouragement along the way. Warwick Anderson helped me think about the psychological aspects and gave the epilogue a critical reading. Tanya Evans brought her expertise as a social historian and an insider's knowledge of Littlehampton to bear on the manuscript, which benefited a great deal from her sympathetic and probing reading.

Colleagues and friends gave me leads to follow and questions to confront. I am especially grateful to Robert Aldrich, Daniel Anlezark, Tara Aurakzai, Helen Dunstan, Nicholas Eckstein, Andrew Fitzmaurice, Sheila Fitzpatrick, John Gagné, Raewyn Glynn, Philippa Hetherington, Miranda Johnson, Chin Jou, the late Pieter Koster, Jon Lawrence, Sophie Loy-Wilson, Mark McKenna, Kirsten McKenzie, Peter Mandler, Nick Morton, Tamson Pietsch, Anne Rogerson, and Natasha Wheatley. I talked to Matt Houlbrook about the case early on, and his extraordinary work has been a stimulus to my own. Emily Cockayne generously shared material relating to her work in progress on anonymous letters, which includes an account of the Littlehampton case. Susan Pedersen and Guy Ortolano gave me the precious opportunity to test out some of my ideas in a talk at Columbia University's Heyman

Center for the Humanities. I deeply appreciate all that Guy and Susan and Sarah Cole and Alma Igra did to make that visit possible. Thanks also to Roger Luckhurst for his comments on my paper at Columbia, and to Emily Rutherford for putting my work into new frames in the piece she wrote for the *Journal of the History of Ideas* blog.

Robert Faber at Oxford University Press was the champion every author hopes for. OUP's anonymous readers improved the manuscript a lot with their criticisms and suggestions. Robert's successor Cathryn Steele has brought the book through the later stages of the publication process with care and insight. I'm indebted to Cathryn and everyone else involved in the editing and production of the book, especially Mohana Annamalai and Kim Allen. Rhiannon Davis did the index and helped with the proofs and the illustrations with her characteristic precision, ingenuity, and thoughtfulness.

I am grateful to the staff of the National Archives and the British Library, and to the other archivists and curators who have helped me. Jonathan Parrett hunted out wonderful material for me at the Littlehampton Museum. Matthew Jones of the West Sussex Record Office in Chichester negotiated with Sussex Police on my behalf to secure permission to examine police station log books. Philip Barnes-Warden of The Met Heritage Centre in London dug up personnel records for me. Ernestos Karydis, Gillian Collins, and Christopher Boyce of the Arundel Museum went to a lot of trouble over the cover image. Thanks also to Jennie Taylor, Emma Grant, and Alexander Hutton for copying documents in London.

I could not have written this book without a sabbatical from the University of Sydney and a fellowship from the Australian Research Council. I want to express my gratitude to these institutions and to all the individuals who gave up their time to assess applications and serve on awards committees.

This is a very different book from my earlier ones, and in writing it I've been sustained by my family. Sarah Graham's questions and ideas pushed me in new directions, and her faith in me means everything. I'm constantly moved by Rose and Tess's loving enthusiasm. Anne Hilliard and Susan McClennan have been unwavering. John Hilliard has been such a loyal supporter. This book is for him.

Contents

Illustrations

(e) 23rd September, 1921 :-

(1) To fucking old bastard May, 49, Western Rd,
Local. You bloody foxy ass bastard you don't do
Stopped in the Post. your duty or you would find out what old four eyes
brings home in a sack from the Beach hotel.

(2) To the foxy ass whore 47, Western Rd Local.
you foxy ass piss country whore you are a character.

Close-up of a police transcript of offensive letters and cards found in Western Road, Littlehampton, September–October 1921. MEPO 3/380, National Archives

Introduction

Over the spring and summer of 1920 a quarrel between neighbours in a town on England's south coast intensified into a storm of abusive letters. The dispute found its way to the courts and one of the women involved went to prison. She protested her innocence and in time the authorities launched an inquiry into whether a miscarriage of justice had taken place. Before the case was finally over there would be a succession of painstaking investigations, surveillance from sculleries and sheds, and two more trials reported unsparingly in the national press. The Littlehampton libels demanded more from the police and the lawyers than most murders.[1]

Poison pen letters were a common source of intrigue in golden-age English detective fiction. Agatha Christie's *The Moving Finger* even features a Scotland Yard officer who specializes in anonymous letters.[2] The mystery plumbed in this book played out not in a village of eccentrics or an Oxbridge college, but in a working-class street one block back from the hotels on Littlehampton's seafront, home to the cleaners and tradespeople who kept the resort functioning. The conflict broke along divisions between established residents and new-comers, between respectable families and those with damaging secrets. At a time when paid work and the credit needed to keep a household afloat depended on maintaining a 'good name', the libellous letters played havoc with reputations. The question of who made a credible witness before the courts likewise turned on the capacity to project respectability. This is a story that is profoundly social at the same time as it is acutely personal.

The narrative shadows the detective tasked with unravelling the mystery. Historians like to imagine themselves as detectives, but detectives are also historians.[3] They chart relations between people and places over time; they assemble evidence from varied sources. The Littlehampton investigation generated an archive of letters, reports, obscene notes, bits of blotting paper, and scores of statements. This witness testimony enabled the detective to scrutinize events from many angles. The multiple perspectives offer the historian rare access to the psychological dynamics of a group of working-class people— their tangles of devotion and resentment, desire and manipulation. We are used to emotional complexity in books about the privileged, but the archival record is seldom so forthcoming about ordinary people. In the case files on the Littlehampton libels we can catch the accents of the past, come up against the words of forgotten people.[4]

For this was very much a case *about* words. These days we think of libel as a matter of civil law—a person who makes defamatory statements runs the risk of paying damages to compensate for the harm done to another person's reputation, not the risk of going to prison. But until quite recently libel was also part of the criminal law.[5] A written attack on another person could graduate from a civil matter to a criminal one if the libel threatened 'to disturb the peace and harmony of the community', as a judge put it in 1906.[6] Criminal libel charges were regularly used to thwart harassment campaigns conducted through the post.

These events unfolded at a time when it was still common to encounter people who could not read or write. Most of the people involved in the Littlehampton libel case belonged to only the second generation to pass through a system of compulsory elementary education. David Vincent, the great historian of the rise of literacy in England, has shown that learning to read and write was less disruptive than contemporary reformers expected it to be. Literacy did not necessarily prise people loose from close-knit local communities. For most English people of the late nineteenth and early twentieth centuries, Vincent observes, 'reading and writing fostered personal contact, and magnified, rather than stilled, the sound of the human voice'.[7] Yet the written word was far more than a supplement to speech.[8] Letters, postcards, writing pads, account books, and forms all became instruments of everyday commerce. And, as the residents of Western Road, Littlehampton, became only too aware, official letters of complaint and very unofficial denunciations opened up new fronts in community conflicts. The strangeness of the language in the Littlehampton libels is part of their mystery—if not for those at the time, then certainly for anyone reading them now. The outlandish insults form part of a larger story of individuality and originality in unexpected places. Bad language is an unlikely subject for a book about people living creatively in straitened circumstances, but when people make their own history words are often involved.

Prologue
Reopening the Case

Rose Gooding was serving her second prison sentence before anyone thoroughly examined the evidence against her.

The change in her fortunes took place well away from the scene of the crime on the Sussex coast, as officials in London reviewed her trial records and began to question the convictions. Sir Ernley Blackwell was the central figure in this process. A Scot who had made his career in England as a barrister and then as a civil servant, Blackwell was the top lawyer in the Home Office, the government department charged with oversight of criminal justice in England and Wales.[1] Capable of cold ruthlessness, he was not someone predisposed to favour a defendant.[2] All the same, he quickly came to the conclusion that Rose Gooding had been wrongly imprisoned.

As Blackwell told it, the story began in May 1920, when Edith Swan laid a complaint with the National Society for the Prevention of Cruelty to Children. Swan, a woman of thirty who lived with her parents at 47 Western Road, Littlehampton, accused Gooding, from number 45, of 'illtreating a child who was living with her, the daughter of her sister'.[3] The society's inspector called on Gooding and her family. He found the baby well cared for and the small, crowded cottage clean and tidy. After the inspector's visit a 'flood of filthy postcards' started. The first one, Edith Swan later testified, read: 'You bloody old cow, mind your own business and there would be no rows.'[4] The language became worse as the postcards and letters accumulated. The early letters were signed 'R—' and 'R. G.'; one ended 'with Mrs. Gooding's compliments'. 'It seems to have been assumed', Blackwell went on, 'that Mrs Gooding's alleged campaign of scurrilous postcards etc against Miss Swan was by way of revenge upon Miss Swan for having made this complaint to the Inspector.'[5]

Swan went to the police. The officer in charge of the Littlehampton police station, Henry Thomas, had a word with Rose Gooding and her husband Bill. They denied that she had written the letters. Inspector Thomas instructed a constable who lived in the house on the other side of the Swans' to discuss the matter further with the Goodings. The Littlehampton police left it at that.[6] Not satisfied, Swan approached the local justices of the peace. They suggested she see a solicitor.[7] Swan managed to find the necessary money and initiated proceedings for criminal libel. Private prosecutions were a vestige of a tradition that citizens as well as the authorities had a duty, if they could, to enforce 'the king's peace'. By the early twentieth century, most criminal prosecutions were handled by professionals—the police and the staff of the Director of Public Prosecutions. The fact that the first Littlehampton libel case was a private prosecution meant that it went to court without the backing of a thorough investigation.

A warrant summoned Rose Gooding before the justices of the peace, who held a hearing to decide whether there was a case to answer. They concluded that there was and committed her for trial at the next session of the assizes, where criminal cases were heard before a jury and a high court judge on circuit. Gooding was remanded in custody at Portsmouth prison, some thirty miles from Littlehampton—a difficult journey for family members to make. In the event, she had only one visit, from Bill, in the two-and-a-half months she spent in gaol before her case came up.[8] At the assizes a jury found her guilty of criminal libel. Mr Justice Roche sentenced her to two weeks in prison and bound her over to keep the peace for two years after her release.

'Mrs Gooding came out of prison on the 23rd December', noted Blackwell, 'and about the 1st of January, 1921, Miss Swan says she received a dirty message which contained the words, "I hope you get all the bad luck you deserve in the New Year for getting me sent to prison."' This made no sense to Blackwell. 'Now if Mrs. Gooding was the writer of that message we have this extraordinary position; that, having been in custody for about three months and only regained her liberty about a week before, and knowing that she and her husband are under a liability for £40, she deliberately sends Miss Swan a message which she must have known would land her again in prison with the forfeiture of £40.'[9]

More letters followed, increasingly profane. Swan was the most common recipient. Shopkeepers and tradesmen also received letters calling Edith a whore and her family 'a dirty drunken lot'.[10] She launched a new prosecution. Rose Gooding was arrested and committed for another trial. Again a jury found her guilty, and this time Mr Justice Avory sentenced her to twelve months in prison.

Gooding sought to have her conviction reconsidered by the Court of Criminal Appeal. The court's registrar, Sir Leonard Kershaw, read over the records of Gooding's second trial on Easter Monday 1921. Kershaw later told the Director of Public Prosecutions' office: 'I had at first very considerable doubt about the case. My private note was "Query, any ground of appeal.... [Q]uery, is verdict right." ' He then called up the transcript of the first trial. 'I found that Judge Roche complained that no expert evidence of handwriting was called before him but that after the Jury had convicted the appellant he said that he agreed with the verdict. Avory J. at the second trial also agreed with the verdict.... The concurrence by Roche J. and Avory J. in the verdict affected my mind though I did not feel entirely satisfied.' Kershaw nevertheless felt he had to defer to the juries. He 'sent the case on in the ordinary way' to a single judge, who declined to take it up. Gooding appealed, and her application was reconsidered by a bench of three judges. She had no counsel to represent her at the hearing. The three judges dismissed the application. Gooding had exhausted her appeal rights.[11]

The week before the hearing by the full bench of the Court of Criminal Appeal, two new libellous documents came to light. An unknown person claimed to have found a torn tradesman's book on Selborne Road in Littlehampton, several blocks away from the Goodings' and Swans' cottages, and put it in the post to Inspector Thomas. The book contained obscene scribblings in what looked like the same handwriting as the libels for which Rose Gooding had been convicted. Two days later, someone dropped a red exercise book containing 'filthy expressions concerning Miss Swan and in the same handwriting as the torn book of the libels' into the mail.[12] The name of Rose's eleven-year-old daughter Dorothy was, as Blackwell put it, 'placarded all over these filthy books, and in each of them the expression appears,—"Inspector Thomas wants pole-axing for taking my angel mother to prison" '.[13] The red book was 'wrapped in a flimsy piece of paper, unaddressed'. As such it was sent to the General Post

Office in London, which in turn forwarded to the main West Sussex post office at Horsham.[14] The postmaster there alerted A. S. Williams, chief constable of West Sussex. Williams contacted his superintendent at Arundel and instructed him to find out who owned the book.[15] After making inquiries, Frederick Peel replied airily: 'the writing in the book is no doubt the same as was on the postcards that Mrs. Gooding was convicted of sending. Mrs. Gooding could not have written what is in the book unless she did it before she went to Prison, it seems to be a mystery, no information can be obtained as to who posted the book'.[16] Williams enclosed Superintendent Peel's letter with the report he made to the Director of Public Prosecutions, Sir Archibald Bodkin, nearly two weeks after Gooding's hearing at the Court of Criminal Appeal.[17]

Williams was not troubled or apologetic, but the very fact that he was informing the Director of Public Prosecutions was an acknowledgement of the seriousness of the situation. Bodkin immediately grasped the implications. He was a hardened and reflexively suspicious criminal lawyer.[18] As Gooding was in prison in April, Bodkin observed, 'she could not have uttered either the torn book or the red book'. 'The position, therefore, is to raise the question whether this woman, Rose Gooding, was rightfully convicted.' It was possible, Bodkin added, 'that Rose Gooding is an artful woman, in addition to being a foul minded woman, and has so arranged, when imprisoned on the latter occasion, that the torn book, and the red book, should be discovered so as to give rise to the observation that somebody else was responsible and not she herself, as she was in prison, and that the torn book and the red book was part of her stock, so to speak, which she had written before she was arrested on the 15th of February, and that she had arranged for its publication after she was arrested.' Even if something this implausible had occurred, the stratagem would have been counterproductive. It 'would have served her purpose very much better' if the 'so-called discovery' of the two new books had happened 'shortly before her trial on 3rd March [when she was already in custody awaiting trial], thus providing her with a topic for the Jury'.[19]

When the matter came before him in the middle of 1921, Blackwell agreed. 'I have very little doubt that this woman has twice been wrongly convicted', he jotted on the minutes page at the beginning of the Home Office file. 'In any case the finding of these two books uttered weeks after the p[risone]ʳ had been taken into custody & the fact that though the evidence was available it was not brought to the notice of the C^t of C. A. would render it necessary for S of S [the Home Secretary] to refer the case for rehearing by the Court.'[20] Blackwell made some inquiries of his own. He wrote to the governor of Portsmouth prison, who replied that he was very familiar with Rose Gooding's case. The governor said he had 'all along been of opinion that it was a matter for further investigation. I have heard her story over & over again & she has from first to last protested her innocence. It was at first suggested by her own Counsel that she was of unsound mind, but she has shown no trace of it here.'[21] The chief warder was able to confirm that Gooding could not have smuggled any libellous writings out of prison. All her correspondence was read, and 'Owing to the position of the visiting box it would be practically impossible for the prisoner to pass or receive any document whilst being visited'.[22]

Blackwell contacted Williams, the chief constable for West Sussex. Blackwell was implicitly but unmistakably critical of the way Williams's officers had responded to the new libels. 'It seems to have been assumed', Blackwell wrote, that the fragments of a tradesman's notebook posted to Inspector Thomas really had been 'found by some unknown person' on the street. 'The envelope was marked "Contents found in Selbourne [sic] Road", but it appears to me that the handwriting of the address is very similar to the writing of the contents, and I am inclined to think that the author of the previous libels was responsible also for the writing and posting of this packet.' Blackwell said he understood that the West Sussex police were satisfied that the handwriting in the two books was the same as the script in the earlier libels. 'It is difficult indeed to find any reasonable theory on which the writing and publication of these two books within a very few days of the hearing of her Appeal could be ascribed to the prisoner, Mrs Gooding.' Blackwell brushed aside the possibility that the recent libels had been written by Dorothy Gooding or Dorothy's cousin Gertrude Russell. Blackwell had seen samples of the girls' handwriting and ruled out this explanation.[23] The next step was inevitable: 'Has the question whether Miss Swan may not herself be the author of all these libellous writings been carefully considered?'[24]

Rather than the libels being Gooding's revenge on Swan for informing on her to the child protection charity, Blackwell conjectured, 'this apparently ill-founded complaint may have been the first step in a campaign by Miss Swan for some reason of her own to bring about the ruin of Mrs. Gooding'. Blackwell evidently believed that the books distributed (or 'uttered') while Gooding was in prison were enough to exonerate her. He wanted to send the case back to the Court of Criminal Appeal urgently.[25] Bodkin cautioned that first there would have to be a serious police investigation. Unlike Blackwell, Bodkin thought it possible that Dorothy Gooding or Gertrude Russell had written the libels. Others in Littlehampton had their own pet theories about the source of the letters.

Blackwell found it frustrating that a fresh inquiry would delay the court hearing, but he realized it was important to find out who the culprit was if it was not Rose Gooding. 'It is quite likely', he wrote, 'that if or when Mrs. Gooding is released the libellous writing will begin again. That would not, to my mind, necessarily mean that Mrs. Gooding was at it again, but a difficult situation would be created!'[26] Given that the local police still doubted she was innocent, and could not believe that Swan was capable of writing the insulting letters, the new investigation would have to be led by someone from outside the West Sussex police.[27] Although large cities had their own investigative units, a third of county police forces in England had no trained detectives.[28] Under an arrangement made by the Home Office, a chief constable outside London could request the assistance of the Metropolitan Police's Criminal Investigation Department 'to unravel any serious crime committed in his area without any cost to the local authority'. The opportunity was not always taken up, in part because of pride on the part of local forces.[29] In the Littlehampton case, of course, the West Sussex police were not asking for help but having it imposed upon them. Bodkin wrote to the head of CID asking him for the loan of an experienced detective.[30] Later the same day, the assistant commissioner nominated a suitable officer: Inspector George Nicholls.[31]

Nicholls was forty-four and had served in the Metropolitan Police since 1898. When he joined, practically all recruits were drawn from the ranks of manual workers.[32] Nicholls came from a working-class Islington family, but he had had much more formal education than most working-class Londoners, becoming proficient in French and German. He worked as a clerk at a securities firm in the City before joining the police at the age of twenty-one.[33] Nicholls spent several years as a uniformed constable before securing a place in CID (all Metropolitan Police detectives served an apprenticeship in uniform).[34]

He won fame in 1912 when he caught the international fugitive Charles Wells, the swindler who 'broke the bank at Monte Carlo', hiding in a yacht in Falmouth harbour.[35] Nicholls's facility with languages led to assignments in Paris, Berlin, and Hamburg; during the First World War he kept tabs on potential spies in London.[36]

Nicholls's post-war duties were less dashing and cosmopolitan, but not necessarily less complicated. Several months before he took on the Littlehampton case, the Metropolitan Police had lent him to another force outside London. The Carmarthenshire police needed help investigating a baffling murder in the coal-mining town of Garnant. The manager of the Garnant branch of the Star Supply Stores, 'a bachelor ... of regular and simple habits and of a studious nature', was alone in the shop one winter's evening when an intruder robbed him of the day's takings and killed him. A shop assistant found his body behind the counter the next morning. Lying near his head was a broken set of dentures, the upper jaw's teeth covered in blood-stained cheese. Evidently the assailant had rammed a whole cheese into the victim's mouth to gag him before he stabbed him.[37] Despite Nicholls's best efforts, the identity of the killer was never fixed, and the Garnant murder remains unsolved.[38]

A criminal libel case was an altogether different proposition. Yet before the mystery was solved the Littlehampton libels would tax Nicholls's considerable expertise and patience. Nicholls met Bodkin for a briefing about Rose Gooding's case on Wednesday 15 June 1921.[39] He left for Littlehampton on the Friday.[40] His investigation would range further than Western Road, but not much further. The Goodings and Swans lived intensely local lives. Rose and Edith in particular spent most of each day within the bounds of the district known as Beach Town, or simply the Beach.

.

I

Beach Town

Littlehampton was not a storied place. In the early 1920s it was a middling town with a population of just over 11,000.[1] Yet like other small ports dotted along the southern coast of England, the town at the mouth of the river Arun was connected to a wider and various world. Ships from Normandy and the Channel Islands brought fruit, butter, barley, and potatoes. Vessels sailing from Sweden, Denmark, and Latvia unloaded grain and timber at Littlehampton's Baltic Wharf.[2] Sweden even maintained a vice-consulate in the town.[3] Shipyards lining the river repaired these vessels and the fishing boats that took lobster, crab, skate, sole, and mullet in the spring and prawns just outside the harbour in the autumn.[4] Littlehampton's workshops were part of the timber ship-building industry long established in a number of Sussex ports, using Wealdon oak floated downriver.[5]

Wood and sail continued to predominate at Littlehampton as steel and steam became the norm elsewhere. The port lost business to Portsmouth and Newhaven, which had deeper water and better rail links, and after the First World War the coastal freight business as a whole began to be supplanted by lorries.[6] As maritime trade declined, tourism became increasingly important, though the two engines of the town's economy were not in direct conflict. Unlike their counterparts in other seaside towns, Littlehampton's leaders do not appear to have attempted to drive messy maritime industries away from the tourist zones.[7] The pier that was an essential part of any British seaside resort extended from the eastern bank of the river, so those promenading could watch the ships gliding up the narrow channel. In postcards and photographs from this time, deck chairs and cranes occupy the same frame. The combination of port and resort was part of Littlehampton's charm.[8]

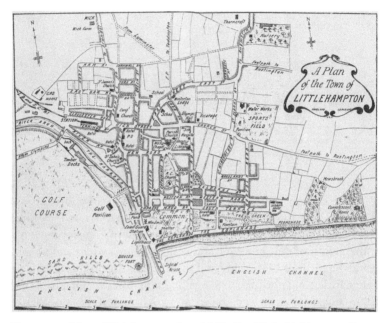

Figure 1.1. Map of Littlehampton from M. Dudley Clark, *Littlehampton, Sussex: With Its Surroundings* (London: Homeland Association and Frederick Warne and Co., n.d. [1915]), 14–15

Littlehampton became a seaside retreat long before the age of piers and fun fairs. Sea-bathing for health and pleasure brought members of the gentry as early as the 1770s. A local notable established a characteristic eighteenth-century institution, a coffee house, close to the sea and three-quarters of a mile from the village. The coffee house grew into the Beach Hotel, and in the 1790s the earl of Berkeley built a villa five hundred yards to the east. Other local landowners invested in accommodation, and the resulting settlement became known as Beach Town.[9] Though clearly for the well-heeled, Beach Town and other small seaside resorts provided an economical alternative to the competitive social scene of spa towns such as Bath.[10] As seaside holidays came within reach of more and more people in the Victorian period, Littlehampton expanded and the land between the sea front and the original village filled up. The result was 'pleasant but exasperatingly disjointed', in the judgement of Pevsner's *Buildings of England*. There was

Figure 1.2. Postcard of Littlehampton beach and pier, 1927. Ph 1396, Littlehampton Museum

the old town on the bank of the Arun, 'a familiar small-scale affair of hard-bitten flint cottages', and there were the more recent products of the 'seaside fever'. Littlehampton became 'a rather bewildering mixture of Old Hastings and Bournemouth'.[11]

Bournemouth was the work of aristocratic landlords, who were often the driving forces behind fashionable resorts in the late nineteenth century. Landowners were expected to improve their estates, and in an age of urbanization such as the Victorian era there were strong incentives to increase the returns on land. A family that controlled the freehold of a town's lands was in a strong position to direct the design of a resort. Moreover, the infrastructural needs of a coastal town, such as sea walls, could be beyond the means of lesser property developers.[12] In smaller resorts, however, aristocratic demiurges were less in evidence: in such towns, cooperation and rivalry between local interests propelled development. Littlehampton falls into this latter category even though it did have aristocratic patrons. The town stood on the estate of the duke of Norfolk. The Norfolk trustees commissioned a succession of planners to develop the area between the town centre and the Beach, and the fifteenth duke paid for the construction of the esplanade in 1868.[13] He declined a later request to extend it eastwards and to finance the building of the pier. Owning much of Sheffield's land, successive dukes had other claims on their improving energies. Since Sheffield's somewhat shambolic development has been blamed partly on the dukes' languor, it is not surprising that they did not play a very active role in Littlehampton.[14] Indeed, they progressively disengaged from the town. The Norfolk estate transferred the esplanade and other waterfront property to the municipal authority in the 1890s. The council now became actively involved in promoting the resort, sponsoring guidebooks and borrowing a local filmmaker's footage of Whitsun holidaymakers to show to potential visitors from London and the Midlands. With donations from the public, the council built a bandstand on the common behind the esplanade.[15]

Performers and small-scale entrepreneurs laid on the kinds of light entertainment expected at the English seaside in the late nineteen-teens and -twenties. 'Concert parties' performed comic and sentimental songs and sketches.[16] Variety artists such as Freddie Spencer delighted crowds with songs and impersonations, complete with costumes, including drag. Dr White Eye's black and white minstrel group took their act round different parts of Littlehampton in the 1920s but played most often on the groyne closest to the pier.[17] Pierrots in white makeup and clown costumes performed songs and sketches and told jokes suitable for adults and children. Pierrot troupes were fixtures at smaller resorts that bigger players in the entertainment industry passed over.[18] Harry Joseph's troupe was a Littlehampton institution from the late 1880s through the 1920s.[19] Joseph tried his hand at a variety of entertainments. One August he organized a 'Grand Bicycle Gymkhana and Evening Fête', the climax of which was a parachute jump from a hot-air balloon.[20]

And then there was the beach itself. The shore was sandy and the sea calm, safe for children and cautious bathers. By the early twentieth century, swimming or paddling about in the shallows was more about exercise and fun than about the medicinal qualities of salt water. Beach culture also became more relaxed. Littlehampton had tolerated mixed bathing, men and women swimming together, since before the war.[21] The council provided tents for beachgoers to dress and undress in before walking down to the water's edge.[22] Bathing machines—small enclosed carriages in which swimmers could get changed and be wheeled into the sea without onlookers seeing them in their bathing costumes—were still available, but they were used less and less. They were a gesture demonstrating the town's propriety rather than facilities everyone was expected to use.[23] Judging by photographs of the beach in the first few decades of the twentieth century, many people were unperturbed at being seen in a swimming costume.

In the early twentieth century most of Littlehampton's beachgoers were middle class.[24] The week-long summer holidays enjoyed by the northern working classes at booming resorts such as Blackpool took much longer to become common in the south of England. The northern practice of taking a week's vacation had its origins in local customary holidays such as the Lancashire Wakes. In the midlands and the south, prosperous workers were unable to get away from their jobs for so long, and vacations tended to take the form of long weekends, either on the 'Saint Monday' principle (where workers took Monday off and made up time by working longer hours the rest of the week), or taking advantage of the August bank holiday, introduced in 1871.[25] Thousands who did not take a long weekend's vacation nevertheless made day trips to the seaside. Here Littlehampton's distance from London counted against it. For working-class Londoners, the smaller and less accessible Sussex seaside towns provided little competition for the resorts of East Kent and Essex.

Littlehampton held a number of attractions for more affluent visitors. It was a good spot for recreational yachting. As the port declined, builders of timber ships retooled for the growing market in pleasure craft. Any seaside resort courting a middle-class clientele needed a golf course, and guidebooks to Littlehampton talked up the links on the western bank of the Arun.[26] 'The course of eighteen holes is one of the best in the country and full of interest throughout. It is situated on sandy and gravelly ground, with hazards of sandhills, furze, ditches and other water, with rushes, etc., and the greens are good.' The golf club had an all-male membership but women were allowed to play under certain conditions, a concession to the vogue for mixing in leisure activities favoured by the post-war middle classes (tennis being another example).[27]

Littlehampton also continued to cater to that comparatively well-off type, the convalescent. One of those who visited the town for health reasons was D. H. Lawrence. 'It is a grey day with many shadowy sailing-ships on the Channel, and greenish-luminous water, and many noisy little waves', the novelist wrote to a friend in 1915. 'It is very healing, I think, to have all the land behind one.'[28] In an advertisement one landlady advised: 'Nursing attention given if necessary to permanent guests. Medical References.' Another promised special attention to nurses accompanying guests. As a destination for invalids, Littlehampton hosted visitors in the off-season as well as the hectic weeks of late summer. 'It is particularly recommended as a winter resort', declared an advertisement for one lodging house.[29]

Like many others, this lodging house stood 'facing sea and common' on South Terrace. A long stretch of large nineteenth-century houses running roughly parallel with the esplanade, South Terrace was Beach Town's premier street. There were several hotels on South Terrace (and the Beach Hotel was in front of it, jutting onto the common), but the main source of accommodation was private houses taking in paying quests. Guidebooks and directories described the accommodation on offer as 'apartments'. This meant private rooms and board rather than self-contained flats.[30] Married or widowed women and a few single women and pairs of sisters would offer rooms and meals. The prominence of landladies led one contemporary to pronounce that the typical seaside resort was 'a woman-run town'.[31] This is an exaggeration, as the all-male lists of office holders in the town directories make clear: but seaside resorts certainly were notable for the number of women running small businesses.

Beach Town's apartment houses and hotels were provisioned by shopkeepers and their porters; maintained by builders, plumbers, and painters; and kept ticking over by a host of live-in and live-out domestic servants. Like every genteel town, Littlehampton was a working-class one as well. The 1920s were a pivotal moment in working-class history.[32] The exit from the First World War caused enormous economic dislocation, and deflationary policies pushed a disproportionate burden onto waged workers and their families. The protest and militancy of the decade was fanned by the revolution in Russia and uprisings elsewhere, and by the structural troubles of the great Victorian industries of textiles, steel, and coal. At the same time, 'new industries' such as pharmaceuticals and electrical appliances began to form the basis for comparatively prosperous working-class communities in the south of England. The best vantage points for observing these transformations were the embattled industrial towns of Scotland and the north of England; the South Wales coal field; the hubs of the new industries, like Banbury and Luton and parts of west London; or much-maligned Slough, whose enormous trading estate, established at the end of the

Figure 1.3. Western Road, Littlehampton, *c.* 1920, by an unknown photographer. Ph 3455, Littlehampton Museum

decade, was the first durable industrial park in Britain. In contrast, Littlehampton was a site of very small-scale industry, residential construction, and the hospitality and service sectors. Littlehampton in the 1920s bears more resemblance to many towns in contemporary post-industrial Britain than it does to a classic factory town.

The main working-class districts were Wick, north of the town centre, and the area around Norfolk and Western Roads in Beach Town. Western Road ran parallel to South Terrace and the seashore. The street mixed housing with business premises. There was a butcher, a grocer, and Boniface's Fish Stores, a local business of long standing. The Victoria Dairy, which is visible in several photographs from this period, sold milk to locals, landladies, and the nursing home at the Beach (specialty: 'Nursery and Invalid Milk from own Alderney Cows').[33] William Leggett was a partner in the farm that supplied the Victoria Dairy. His wife Kate managed the shop, another of the small businesswomen in evidence in the town.[34] Further up Western Road, the Misses Thomson ran a dining room. There were three pubs: the large New Inn, run by a couple named Bedford; the Prince of Wales, which Frank and Emma Reeves managed in conjunction with livery stables, hiring horses out and accommodating visitors' animals; and the intimate Surrey Arms.[35] Alice and Henry Twine had taken on the

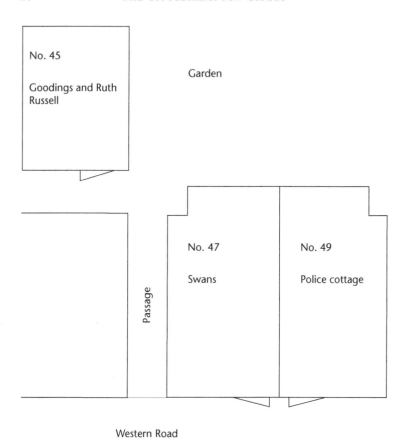

Figure 1.4. Plan of the houses in Western Road

Surrey Arms' licence together, and after her husband died Alice continued on her own.[36]

At the centre of this story are three houses on Western Road: numbers 45, 47, and 49. Like the majority of urban working-class dwellings in England at this time, they were rented from private land-lords.[37] The houses dated from the early nineteenth century, and were built of flint cobble with red brick dressings and quoins.[38] Numbers 47 and 49 were side by side, part of a terrace. The house at 45 Western Road was set back from the street, down a passage that led past number 47 to the garden behind the terraced houses: number 45 was, in effect, a cottage built in the garden.[39] It and number 47 were owned by the same landlord, who held them under a combination of leases from the Norfolk estate granted in the 1830s. The two houses were sold together at the end of the First World War, and the auction catalogue survives. Number 47 consisted of 'Two bed Rooms, Sitting Room, small Kitchen, Outside Wash-house, and W.C. Small Garden at rear.' The house behind was smaller: 'Entrance Passage, with Sink, Sitting Room, Scullery, large Store Room, Two Bed Rooms, and Outside W.C.'[40]

The auction catalogue indicates that the garden belonged to number 47, but the front door of the cottage down the passage also opened onto the back yard; who was entitled to use the garden was a question that stoked resentment. Neighbours further up the road had access to the yard too. Lavatories and washhouses stood part of the way between the backs of the houses and the garden gate. The garden was also the site of a motley collection of sheds and home to the residents' rabbits and chickens (working-class people fortunate enough to have access to a back garden often kept rabbits, chickens, or pigeons).[41] At the end of the block was the drying ground, a patch of grass where women from the neighbourhood hung out laundry.

The longest-standing residents of this part of Western Road were the Swans, at number 47. They were natives of the Littlehampton area. Edward Swan was born in the town and his wife Mary Ann in the village of Climping, less than two miles away across the river. Both were now in their early seventies. Mrs Swan was a quiet and unobtrusive person. Her husband, in contrast, was quick to involve himself in other people's business. When Inspector Nicholls met them, he found Edward Swan 'an irritable and excitable old man, who would not be very difficult to upset'. Mr Swan was a retired house painter and sign writer.[42] Littlehampton's private residences, apartment houses, and hotels generated enough work to sustain a number of construction firms and painting businesses. In this respect Littlehampton was not unlike the fictional south coast town in Robert Tressell's novel *The Ragged Trousered Philanthropists*, in which a small army of painters and decorators—some of them old, others irritable and excitable—scrambles to renovate a sprawling mansion.[43]

The Swans had had nine children, three of whom currently lived with their parents. 'The others are scattered', Nicholls wrote, around England and overseas. One of the scattered children was a son who, Mrs Swan told Nicholls, 'suffered from Epileptic fits' and 'had a mania for writing letters to himself'.[44] Like a difficult relative in a nineteenth-century novel, he was now living in Australia, with one of his brothers.[45] This son was probably John, listed in the 1911 census as a grocer's porter.[46] Edwardian social reformers cited porters' work as a 'blind-alley job' that exemplified the problem of boys leaving school and getting stuck in unskilled casual labour, unable to move up to an apprenticeship.[47] The Swan brothers living at home were Stephen, aged 40, and Ernest, 39. Stephen too had got stuck in the unreliable market for unskilled labour. He had been a fishmonger's porter, working for Boniface.[48] During the war Stephen served in the Middlesex Labour Corps before being discharged as medically unfit.[49] When Nicholls called in 1921, he found that Stephen Swan had been on the dole 'on and off for the past two years ... but occasionally does some gardening work'. 'He does not strike me as being mentally strong', Nicholls wrote. 'His brother Ernest Walter is a painter, and appears to be a hardworking man.'[50] Despite having a trade, Ernest too was often out of work.[51]

The Swan brothers shared a bedroom; their sister slept in the same room as her parents. Edith, called Edie by her family, was a tall, thin woman of thirty. Nicholls's initial appraisal was devastating in its measured syntax: 'Edith Swan is a person who from the stony expression of her face, and peculiar stare in her eyes struck me as being, possibly wrong in her head.'[52] Nicholls spoke to her old teacher from East Street School, another Boniface. 'There was in her, Miss Boniface says, something that made her think she was different from the other girls.' Boniface remembered Edith as 'very clever at Essay writing, and a good penman'.[53] The formal, carefully weighted letters she wrote in adulthood bear out this judgement. Edith appears to have been one of those many working-class children good with words who might have stayed at school longer or gone into an office job had their family circumstances been different.

Nicholls found further evidence of Edith Swan's character in her employment history. 'Some years before the war and during the early part of the war, Miss Swan used to go out to work daily, at Apartment Houses.' The word 'daily' signalled not only the frequency of the work, but its type: Swan was a live-out domestic servant. She 'appears to have given satisfaction for a time, but the people who have employed her do not appear to have been very favourably impressed with her'. One of these employers was Jane Gibbs, who kept an apartment house on South Terrace. 'Miss Gibbs says that on one occasion Miss Swan brought a sixpence to her and said, "I have found this on the stairs. I thought it

my duty to bring it to you.'" Later this happened again in front of
guests. 'On another occasion she went to a lady visitor with a brooch
she said she had found under a bed. This lady was quite positive that
she had left it on her dressing table, and had seen it there only a short
time before.' Eventually Swan was accused of stealing some children's
clothing belonging to a visitor. Gibbs sacked her but did not report
Swan to the police.[54]

During the war, another employer suspected her of dishonesty. In
1915 Swan worked for Snewin's, a local construction firm. With many
working men away in uniform, Snewin's hired women to take on jobs
normally done by men. Snewin's won the contract to renovate The
Hillyers, an imposing Regency house on South Terrace converted to a
hotel.[55] Swan spent six months there distempering and whitewashing.
One day at The Hillyers she fell off some steps. Swan made a claim for
compensation and the insurers paid out £20, though Snewin's manager
regarded the whole affair as highly suspicious.[56]

Swan's wartime job distempering was unusual, as was the way with
wartime jobs. Otherwise, the pattern of her employment was quite
conventional. Domestic service, whether live-in or 'daily', was still the
most common type of paid employment for women in Britain at this
time.[57] Edith's movement from one job to another was also consistent
with the informal nature of labour in many parts of Britain up to the
1920s (it was only later, with the administrative requirements of the
emergent welfare state, that employment became more formalized and
regular). This relative casualness made paid work feasible for many
working-class women, since, as the sociologist and historian Mike Savage
explains, 'a woman's participation in paid employment... depended
on the informality of her participation, so that she could "slip" back
into domestic labour whenever this was a pressing need (for instance,
due to family illness)'.[58] As the only young woman in her household,
Edith shouldered domestic responsibilities that typically fell to eldest
daughters.[59] At the time of the libels, she was earning some money by
taking in laundry, something many women did to supplement their
household's earnings.[60]

The money Edith brought in must have helped in a family without
a real breadwinner. That said, the Swans did not live hand-to-mouth.
They belonged to one of the savings clubs common in English working-
class communities. Savings schemes (and, for some working-class families,
investments in property) were strategies for coping with fluctuations

in the labour market and the unexpected events of family life.[61] Work
was especially insecure in a seaside resort, even one that attracted visitors all year round.[62] Edith Swan belonged to the 'Tontine Club' that
met at the Surrey Arms.[63] In a classical tontine, investors contribute
to a fund that pays an annuity to all the living investors. As each
investor dies, the annuities increase, and the capital ultimately passes
to the last surviving member—making a tontine a useful plot device
for authors of murder mysteries. In Britain, though, the word was
often used loosely to refer to various forms of organized thrift.[64]
Some publicans ran savings clubs for their customers, putting money
aside for a Christmas goose, for instance.[65] What was going on in
Alice Twine's pub may have been something along these lines, but it
was more likely a general-purpose thrift club. The Swans certainly
had enough money put aside to pay the legal bills from Edith's pursuit
of Rose Gooding.

None of the Swan children living at home socialized much.[66] Edith
did, however, have a fiancé. Bert Boxall was a Horsham man several
years her senior. He had worked as a bricklayer's labourer and a
groundsman at a cricket club before becoming a soldier. Boxall enlisted
in the Royal Sussex Regiment a year into the First World War and was
deployed to India. He later joined the East Kent Regiment, the Buffs,
and served in the 1919 conflict in Afghanistan.[67] By the time the libels
began, he was a lance corporal with the British forces in Mesopotamia.[68]
Although he and Edith corresponded, the couple obviously did not
see much of each other. While Edith stayed close to home, she was
eager to gossip with a few other women in the surrounding streets,
such as Kate Leggett from the dairy. She was also keen to befriend
new neighbours.

The house on the eastern side of the Swans' was rented by the West
Sussex Constabulary, which sublet it to police officers and their
families.[69] When the libels started flying, the tenants were Constable
Alfred Russell, his wife Edith, and their six-year-old son. They lived
next to the Swans for seven and a half years. 'I knew the Swan family
and was friendly with them', Mrs Russell recalled. She was in and out
of hospital; when she was at home she was often laid up in bed, 'and
consequently did not see much of my neighbours'.[70] Asked about the
Swans, Alfred Russell said he 'knew the family well as neighbours', the
last two words quietly indicating the limits of the relationship. In
crowded streets it was common for neighbourliness to 'stop at the

doorstep', as the historian Ben Jones puts it.[71] The threshold between being friendly and being friends was monitored carefully.

It was harder for the neighbours to the rear of the Swans' house to keep their distance. '[O]wing to the peculiar situation of the Goodings' cottage in relation to the Swans' cottage', Nicholls observed, 'everything that went on in the Goodings must have been known in the Swans and vice versa'.[72] Although the two houses did not share a wall, the Goodings' front door and sitting room were very close to the Swans' scullery, and a person standing in the passage could eavesdrop on conversations in the Goodings' cottage. Edith knew both houses well: at one stage her parents had rented both of them and taken in lodgers.[73] In subsequent years, number 45 had been let to various unsatisfactory tenants. A man named Horner rented it in the days when number 45 and number 47 shared a lavatory. One day, Edith recalled, Horner asked Mr Swan to come down and take look at the toilet, 'as the seat was filthy. My father went with him to the lavatory, there was nothing the matter with it and Horner stabbed my father several times with a pen-knife.' Later, she went on, a cab driver named Patrick Kinsella occupied the cottage. 'He had a young woman living with him who was supposed to be his daughter.' Kinsella may have been a pimp: the woman 'encouraged men there all hours of the day and night'. The Swans complained to Ellen Skinner, the owner of both number 45 and number 47 at the time. She evicted Kinsella. The Goodings and Rose's sister and her family moved in next, just before Christmas 1918.[74]

Unlike the Swans, the Goodings were not from Littlehampton. Bill Gooding grew up in Kent. He was born in 1879 and spent his childhood on a barge—not a floating platform that needed towing, but a flat-bottomed sailing ship built to negotiate rivers and canals.[75] When he was old enough, Bill worked on barges as his father had, transporting coal, cement, lime, and bricks. He enlisted in the army in 1904 and stayed for three years, discharged as medically unfit after developing an abscess in his jaw. He went back to manning barges owned by firms based in Maidstone and Gravesend, sailing the waterways of Kent, Essex, and Sussex. Plying the river Ouse between Newhaven harbour and Lewes, he met Rose Russell. Some of those who knew her attested to her kindness. A few found her idiosyncratic in manner and dress. 'Mrs. Gooding was rather an eccentric woman', Constable Russell thought. 'I have seen her come out into the yard and go into the Street with her hair down her back, and wearing a thin frock, no stockings, and white shoes.'[76] Nearly everyone found her hot-tempered. After several months' courtship, she and Bill Gooding married at the Lewes registry office at the end of 1913.[77]

When they married, Rose was twenty-two, twelve years younger than Bill.[78] She was the mother of a baby girl, Dorothy. The social stigma of illegitimacy forced many unmarried mothers from middle-class families to give their children up for adoption. Working-class families, however, were extremely reluctant to surrender children to what they feared would be a life of drudgery, either in institutions or as second-class children in adoptive families. The usual place to abandon an infant was the workhouse, and the working-class revulsion for the workhouse was so fierce that even the very poor would 'absorb' illegitimate children into their own families if at all possible.[79] Rose Russell kept her daughter and lived under her parents' roof. After Rose and Bill were married, the three of them stayed on with the Russells.

Bill told Nicholls that his step-daughter 'passes under the name of Gooding all'tho. registered in the name of Russell'.[80] It seems that the Goodings moved to Littlehampton to pass more effectively as a legitimate family. The move makes little sense on other grounds. Littlehampton offered a seaman fewer opportunities than the Lewes–Newhaven axis. (The tonnage of ships entering Newhaven port was more than twenty times greater than the total for Littlehampton.)[81] And in leaving Lewes Rose was cutting herself off from her existing support networks. She had spent all her life in Lewes. Her parents were born there, her grandmother lived there, her cousins lived in the same street.[82]

They made the move early in 1916, after two profound changes in the life of the family. In November of the previous year, Bill Gooding and his father-in-law William Russell were both crew members on the steam ship *Nigel*. The ship had spent most of its life as a passenger vessel shuttling between Leith and the Netherlands, and then carrying cargo between Tyneside and London. In 1915, the *Nigel* was refitted as a military stores carrier, steaming back and forth over the English Channel.[83] On one such voyage the ship struck a mine near the entrance to Boulogne and sank. Bill Gooding escaped uninjured; Mr Russell was killed. As a fireman, stoking the engine, he had been in the most dangerous place on the ship.[84] Shortly before she lost her father, Rose gave birth to a boy, William Henry Victor Gooding.

The Goodings moved around a lot in their first year and a half in Littlehampton. Nicholls interviewed their various landlords. As Edith Swan's employment history was made to disclose weaknesses in her character, so did the Goodings' record as tenants bring to light the tensions in their marriage. When they lodged with Ellen Gamman, 'a good many rows occurred between Mr. and Mrs. Gooding. Mrs. Gooding was in the habit of swearing and on one occasion Mr. Gooding accused Mrs. Gooding of being intimate with a local Pilot named Short.' Bill was still away at sea a lot, on another military transport. Nicholls took care to add that Mrs Gamman described Bill as 'a sober, hardworking man, who was, on one occasion only seen the worse for drink'. The next family they lived with had no complaints until they went away for six weeks, during which time 'Mrs. Gooding let the place get into a neglected and dirty state'.[85] They left in June 1917 to rent a furnished bungalow near the disused Arun windmill.

At this point Rose's younger sister Ruth Russell came to live with them, bringing her daughter, Gertrude, and her son, named William Henry like his cousin (one went by 'Willie' and the other by 'Billy'). The emotionally and economically interdependent household they formed with the Goodings was a creative response to the challenge of raising two children without a husband.[86] Ruth received maintenance payments from Billy's father, a crane driver at Newhaven port, after Rose and their mother shamed him into it.[87] Ruth does not appear to have been in contact with Gertrude's father.[88] Perhaps Ruth too had left Lewes in the hope of concealing her past. At work she 'passed ... as Mrs. Russell'.[89] Several neighbours reported that Rose told them Ruth was a widow, informing one that Ruth's husband had been killed in the war.[90] It was not unusual for unmarried mothers to describe themselves as widows.[91] Ruth later asserted that she never told anyone she was a widow and nor, to her knowledge, did her sister. However, Ruth admitted that she 'allowed people to think that I was a married woman'.[92]

If Leila Streeter, who owned the bungalow and lived nearby, knew more, she did not bar Ruth and her children from her property. Streeter did think, though, that Ruth was the reason for the 'frequent rows' between the Goodings: 'So far as Miss Streeter could gather the trouble arose through Gooding's alleged attentions to Miss Russell'. On one occasion, Rose left the bungalow 'and went to Miss Streeter for protection from her husband, who had been assaulting her. She shewed Miss

Streeter a number of bruises which she alleged her husband had caused, and she stayed with Miss Streeter two or three days and nights.'[93] Nicholls must have confronted Bill Gooding with this story, for in a follow-up statement he made at Littlehampton police station he admitted: 'It is true that while we were living at the Bungalow I turned my wife out owing to an allegation made against her that she had been going about with a Pilot named—Jack Short. My wife went to Miss Streeter's Bungalow and 3 nights afterwards, I took her back again. I admit that I denied this at first, but I did not like to let anybody know about it.'[94]

Domestic violence was widely condemned in the press, and had been since the middle of the Victorian era. On occasion, neighbours would take punitive action themselves. A Lancashire man recalled coming home one evening around the beginning of the twentieth century and finding his father pinning another man on the floor. 'My father had him by the throat as this neighbour had come home drunk and turned out his wife and kiddies in their nightclothes. My father reprimanded him and he struck at my father and my father retaliated.'[95] It is telling that this anecdote concerned a violent drunk. If a man had a reputation for self-control—as Bill Gooding did—this sort of vigilante action was less likely. Neighbours often treated husbands' and fathers' violence as legitimate discipline if the injuries did not seem excessive by local standards and if they thought the woman might have 'deserved' the beating.[96] (And juries in domestic violence cases tended to treat a male defendant leniently if the victim was said to have 'nagged' or otherwise failed in her performance as a wife.)[97] Leila Streeter did not evict her tenants after Rose was 'turned out'. But the arguments wore on, and eventually she gave them notice to quit. They took rooms with another family for six months. 'There were one or two rows between the Goodings here, but otherwise there was nothing to be said against them.'[98]

Their next home was 45 Western Road. The seven of them shared a two-bedroom house. It was common in small working-class dwellings for children and adults to share bedrooms, and beds. '[T]he four in a bed arrangement is common enough to need attention', wrote the Fabian reformer Maud Pember Reeves in the light of investigations in south London.[99] At the cottage in Western Road, Rose and Bill probably slept in one bedroom with their children, and Ruth with hers in the other.[100] The house soon became even more crowded. Ruth fell

pregnant again and gave birth to another boy, Albert Edward Russell.[101]
Bill Gooding told Nicholls he did not know who the father was but
Rose did. Bill supposed that Rose and her mother were going to try to
extract financial support from Albert's father, as they had from the
father of Ruth's other son.[102] In fact, Ruth's mother did not 'know
anything about the father of the third child', though Ruth had told
her that 'she had been going out with a soldier'.[103]

For all the drama, the Goodings and Ruth Russell got by. The mass
of information collected about them during the ordeal of the libels
contains the rudiments of a household budget. When Nicholls began
his investigation, the rent on the furnished cottage was 13s. 6d. a week,
which was on the high side.[104] The Goodings and Ruth Russell were
subletting from a Mrs Hopkins. At the time the two houses went up
for sale in December 1918, just as the Goodings moved into 45 Western
Road, Hopkins paid only 3s. 9d. per week in rent (and paid the district
and water rates herself). Even allowing for inflation between 1918 and
1921, the Goodings were paying Hopkins a hefty premium, and far
more than the Swans paid.[105] Were they paying more because they had
a record of causing trouble? In any case, they could afford it. Ruth
Russell received thirty shillings a month in compensation for the loss
of her father.[106] The father of her second child sent her 7s. 6d. a week.[107]
Bill Gooding worked in shipyards and had done since he 'gave up the
sea on the signing of the Armistice in 1918' (the words have the ring of
a phrase Bill had honed for years).[108] He worked for two years at
Harvey's shipyard, a fitting employer for someone who had served his
apprenticeship on the rivers of Kent: the original Harvey hailed from
Rye, which was known for its barges, and in Littlehampton he and his
sons built and repaired craft that sailed coastwise or up and down
rivers.[109] When Nicholls first interviewed Bill, he had recently moved
on to another boatbuilding firm, Osborne's.[110] There he earned £2
18s. a week as a rigger. As a baseline, therefore, the household's weekly
income was three pounds and twelve shillings.

The findings of the contemporary social statisticians A. L. Bowley
and Margaret H. Hogg help put this figure into context. Working with
prices of coal, food, and clothing, as well as data on dietary needs, such
as average caloric intake, Bowley and Hogg updated and refined earlier
definitions of the so-called poverty line. According to their figures,
which are from 1924, the weekly cost of living at the 'minimum standard of expenditure' for a household consisting of a man, two women,

four children aged between five and fourteen, and one under five was £2 7s. 9d. The price of coal varied from place to place. If we take Reading, one of Bowley and Hogg's case studies, rather than the northern towns where coal was cheaper, as a proxy for Littlehampton, the fuel bill would add another three shillings to the week's expenses.[111] So to live at 45 Western Road and maintain the three adults and five children at a level above the poverty line required £3 4s. 3d. a week. The Goodings' and Russells' regular income exceeded this figure by 12 per cent.

They were thus able to save some money. Rose joined the tontine club.[112] Ruth said that her child support money was 'spent on the home and insurances'. That could have meant the burial insurance that many working-class families bought, or it could have meant the tontine or some other savings scheme.[113] (A study a generation later treated 'insurance' as a synonym for 'saving': 'Our informants, time after time, say that if they wish to save they have to take out some policy. These policies range from ones taken with big insurance companies to informal "clubs" run by someone in the street, called tontines.')[114] The household could also afford modest but up-to-the-minute luxuries. They had a gramophone.[115] Rose went to the cinema.[116] Their diet included fish as well as meat (more readily available in a coastal town, of course, fish that did not come from a fish-and-chip shop was not a significant part of most British working-class diets), and Rose had a sizable repertoire of desserts and baking.[117]

One thing that did not siphon money away from the family budget was alcohol. Alice Twine of the Surrey Arms backed up other reports that Bill Gooding did not drink heavily: 'Mr. Gooding has only been in my house very occasionally; he was always sober.' She added that Ruth Russell sometimes popped into the Surrey Arms 'for supper beer'.[118] In contrast, a budget study in a poor quarter of London in 1915–1916 defined a moderate drinker as a man who consumed two pints a night with an extra one on Saturdays and Sundays. The bill for that level of alcohol consumption came to nearly three shillings a week—a sum that would cover meals for a family of five or six for at least two days.[119] Bill Gooding's sobriety also meant that he was at home most evenings. He did not conform to the stereotype of the working man who came home for dinner, returned to work for the afternoon, and then put in an evening shift at the pub. The home at 45 Western Road was a man's place as well as a woman's, and the three adults spent a lot of time together in the downstairs sitting room.[120]

Much of the time either Rose or Ruth was earning wages that supplemented Bill's income and Ruth's maintenance and compensation payments. The sisters appeared to have 'slipped' back and forth between paid employment and housewifery. In November 1919 Rose became a daily servant at the house of a family in Norfolk Place, just around the corner from the Goodings'. Her employer managed a boutique publishing company in London.[121] When he and his wife went up to London for a few days each month, Rose looked after the house and children, sleeping over. She got the sack after three months because of her 'habit of making horrible accusations particularly about her husband and sister...that her husband was sleeping with her sister, he treated her as his wife, that he took no notice of her (Mrs. Gooding) when she was in the room and if she made a remark she was told to shut up. Mrs. Gooding would become excited and work herself up into a temper and would come next day with her head tied up in a big white cloth soaked in vinegar.' Like the Goodings' former landlord, the publisher testified that he judged Bill 'a very straight, honest and hard-working man'.[122]

Several months after Rose lost her job at the publisher's house, she and her sister seem to have come to an understanding that Rose would look after Ruth's baby and the house while Ruth went out to paying jobs. Ruth did housework for several women in the town, including the Misses Langfield at Groombridge School, one of a number of small private schools in Littlehampton.[123] She was there 'off and on for 4 or 5 months'. She worked for a while at the restaurant in Western Road and then as a domestic servant to a solicitor on South Terrace.[124]

Ruth unburdened herself to her employers in the same way her sister did. Richard Sharpe, the solicitor, reported that Ruth 'frequently mentioned that whereas Mrs. Gooding took no interest in her husband's discourses on sea-faring matters, she, Miss Russell was extremely interested, and Mr. Sharpe gathered that Miss Russell and Mr. Gooding were on excellent terms'. The mock-heroic register of 'discourses on sea-faring matters' cast the Goodings and Ruth Russell as comic plebeians, unaware of their ridiculousness. Still, they were not too ridiculous to be worthy of a middle-class professional's curiosity. Sharpe said that he often noticed Ruth 'going in the direction of the ship-yard where Mr. Gooding was employed, at knock-off time'.[125]

Whatever was really going on between Ruth, Bill, and Rose, none of them could have afforded to break with the others if they had wanted to.

The care of the house and children depended on Rose; the composite family needed the money Bill and Ruth brought in. The relationship between the three adults was at once the basis for the household's existence and a threat to its viability. Rose's complaints about her husband and sister cost her a job. The 'rows' turned landlords against them. The fighting also had the potential to alienate neighbours.

2

Easter and After

Relations between the Western Road neighbours began well. Only a little while after Rose Gooding moved in next door at the end of 1918, she and Edith Swan were friends. This was a neighbourliness that did not stop at the doorstep. 'I was friendly with them and went in and out', Edith told Inspector Nicholls. 'Mrs. Gooding came into our house once or twice. I have taken the children out for her.'[1] Edith drew Rose into community institutions, encouraging her to join the tontine. Although Rose did join, she avoided the club's social side and got Edith to take her subscription payments to the meetings at the Surrey Arms on her behalf. (Rose spoke to the club's hostess only once, when she went to the pub 'to sign for her Tontine money'.)[2] Rose lent the Swans her family's bath and Edith lent Rose clothes pegs, patty pans, and a suet scraper. 'About 18 months ago', Edith recalled for Nicholls, 'I gave Mrs. Gooding a Star Cookery Book which contained a recipe for Marrow Chutney as my father had given her a large marrow. Later I gave her a Weldon's knitting book containing instructions for making socks as she kept on sending in to know how to do them.'[3] Thus did the police investigation incidentally assemble an inventory of domestic objects. The chutney recipe and the sock pattern would later become points of contention in Rose Gooding's case.

The statements that Bill Gooding, Ruth Russell, and Stephen Swan provided to Inspector Nicholls give the impression that the only personal connection was between Edith and Rose. Old Mr Swan would occasionally engage the Goodings, but usually to complain about something. A common source of friction was the back yard shared by the Swans, the Goodings, and the tenants of the police cottage. '[I]t appears that the Swans consider the Goodings have no right in the garden, and that has undoubtedly been one cause, at any rate, of a good

deal of ill-feeling between the two families', Nicholls noted.[4] At one
point Bill Gooding put a padlock on a shared store in the yard, pro-
voking an indignant letter to the landlord from Mr Swan.[5] The smell
of the Swans' rabbits, Alfred Russell's chickens, the Goodings' dustbin,
and everyone's drains all caused irritation. When asked at her second
trial why they had fallen out, Rose said she thought the Swan family
'seemed to turn against her ever since one Saturday afternoon, when
she was unable to lend Mrs. Swan her flat irons'. There was laughter in
the court.[6] No doubt the matter seemed less trivial to Mrs Swan, who
supplemented her old age pension by doing ironing for others.[7] But
this was not an accurate explanation of the breach between Rose
Gooding and the Swans.

The turning point was Easter Sunday 1920. Until then, Edith told
Nicholls, there had been no 'serious quarrelling' between Rose and
Bill, though there was certainly a persistent hum of conflict. Rose had
'a violent temper', Edith claimed. 'I have noticed it by the outbursts to
her husband when he came home from work. She would not have his
meals ready. He was always complaining about this. I have heard him
say to her "No bloody tea ready again, not even the kettle on".'[8] The
Swans' neighbour in number 49, the confusingly named Edith Russell,
gave another account of Rose's temper, describing arguments with her
sister and the children rather than with Bill. 'My first impression of
Mrs. Gooding was that she was not right in her head, but as I got to
know her, I found out that she was a woman of a very bad temper, and
I frequently heard her shout at her children, and quarrelling with her
sister, generally because the work was not done to her satisfaction.'[9]
The constable's wife went on: 'In conversation with me she used to
talk about her husband. She said, "You do not know the life I have to
lead with him. I don't like it at all. You don't know what I have to put
up with. When he is in a temper he calls me a rotten cow, and a bloody
sod." She told me that at least twice, and was usually crying.'[10]

What happened the afternoon of Easter Sunday was of a different
order. Edith Swan told George Nicholls her story:

He [Bill Gooding] took the baby away from her because she had been beating
her sister's baby with the cane. He said he would not allow her to hit it with
the cane. She accused Mr. Gooding of being the father of her sister's last baby.
    She said 'I know more about you and Ruth than you think I do, you always
take the baby's part because you know you are the father of it.'

He said:—'You can say just what you like Rose, but what are you under the doctor for now? Your guts are bloody rotten through going with other men while I was risking my life at sea.'[11]

The rumours that Rose had been involved with other men during Bill's spells at sea circulated widely. Constable Russell stated: 'The Goodings used to live in a cottage near the harbour mouth and it was said that she, Mrs. Gooding, used to lie about on the common with different sea-captains, while her husband was on a transport trading to France from Littlehampton.'[12]

Nicholls found another witness to the Easter dispute, a neighbour from further down the street. William Birkin was a bathing machine proprietor whose house at 51 Western Road backed onto the communal yard. Birkin said he overheard an argument that Sunday when he went into the garden to feed his rabbits. 'I heard Mr. Gooding shout to his wife "You bloody rotten cow—You rotten buggar". I had seen him previously in the Surrey Arms where he had one pint of Stout.' The Goodings were using 'the filthiest language I had ever heard'. Birkin did not wait around to hear any more. (Later on, Mr Swan was eager to fill him in on what he had heard, including the detail that Bill had said 'that Mrs. Gooding's guts were rotten'.) On Easter Monday, Birkin 'saw Mrs. Gooding standing at the passage way leading up to their house with her eye bandaged and I surmised that Mr. Gooding had struck her'.[13]

Bill Gooding and Ruth Russell denied that an argument had even taken place. Nicholls put Edith Swan's allegations to Bill and he replied: 'It is untrue that I came home on any occasion and swore because my tea was not ready, and that there was a row between me and my wife at Easter, 1920.'[14] Ruth said she did not 'remember a big row between Mr. and Mrs. Gooding during Easter 1920, nor any bad language being used'. Nicholls pressed her, but she stuck to her story and offered an alibi: 'I was out to work at Miss Langfields, Groombridge House, on Easter Sunday, Monday and Tuesday, 1920.'[15] Nicholls judged Ruth 'untruthful', and believed Alice Morgan when she said that Ruth had been present during the dispute on Easter Sunday.[16]

Morgan was a single woman in her late thirties.[17] She met Rose Gooding when they both worked in the publisher's house in Norfolk Place. When Rose discovered that Morgan, a Londoner, did not know anyone in Littlehampton, she invited her home. Morgan became a regular visitor, going to 45 Western Road every Thursday and Sunday evening. 'Mr. and Mrs. Gooding and Miss Russell were always there. They were friendly together, but occasionally Mr. and Mrs. Gooding quarrelled.' When Morgan arrived on Easter Sunday, 'Mrs. Gooding was lying in front of the fire and Mr. Gooding was lying in a deck chair. They did not speak to one another and at tea time Mrs. Gooding went upstairs, and we had tea without her.' Ruth put the children to bed. 'Mrs. Gooding came downstairs and told Mr. Gooding that he was always carrying on at Dorothy. He . . . called her a bloody liar. She used some foul expressions to him which I cannot remember and he called her a dirty rotton cow. They were carrying on for some time and I left.'

The following day, Bill Gooding returned to the pub and this time drank a lot more than usual. Ernest Swan attested that 'Mr. Gooding came home drunk', and the following exchange ensued:

I heard him say 'You ought to be bloodywell strung up, you old fucker.'
    'I ought to be?'
    'Yes. And you ought to be bloodywell shot.'

'That's all I heard', Ernest concluded, 'and I went out'.[18]

Alice Morgan confirmed that Bill Gooding had been drinking on Easter Monday. When Morgan arrived back at 45 Western Road that afternoon, she found Bill lying drunk in front of the fire. Rose was sitting at the table crying. After a while Bill got up and said: 'If I were you Alice, I would not stay here. You do not want to be brought into anything. I shall smash the home up and go away.' Morgan replied: 'You must not do that.' She left, 'and later in the evening met Miss Russell standing in Western Road. She asked me to go back to the house. I did so and there saw Mrs. Gooding crying. Mr. Gooding had gone out and Mrs. Gooding and Miss Russell said he was in the Public House, drinking. Mrs. Gooding asked me not to stay away from the house and I promised that I would not.'[19]

After relating all this to Nicholls, Morgan addressed Edith Swan's allegations: 'I do not remember Mr. Gooding taking the baby away from Mrs. Gooding, because she was beating it with a cane, nor Mrs. Gooding accusing Mr. Gooding of being the father of Miss Russell's child; nor do I remember Mr. Gooding saying anything about Mrs. Gooding being rotten through going with other men. Mrs. Gooding told me on one occasion that Dorothy had told her that she had seen her Aunt Ruth in bed with Mr. Gooding. She also told me that she had to undergo an operation for womb trouble, and Mr. Gooding had said she would not have been in that state if she had not been going with other men.'[20] Bill's interest in Ruth, his suspicions that Rose had sex with other men, and his folk diagnoses were all clearly part of the stock of grievance in the Gooding–Russell household, and it is possible that they were raked over later on Easter Sunday 1920 after Alice Morgan had gone.

On the Monday, according to Edith Swan and her mother, Rose repeated some of the things her husband had said during the row, including his claim that promiscuity was the cause of her medical problems. Mrs Swan told her: 'If my husband had spoken to me like that I should have packed up and gone away.' The older woman was more affronted by Rose's passivity in the face of Bill's accusations than by the accusations themselves. The Swans appear to have paid no more mind to Bill's violence against his wife than any of the others who witnessed it over the years the family lived in Littlehampton. Mrs Swan said that this was the last time she ever spoke to Rose Gooding.[21]

Maintaining any privacy was always a struggle in a street of crowded houses jammed in against each other, and Rose herself appears to have decided that the neighbours knew too much about her business.[22] Shortly after their final conversation, Mrs Swan said, she overheard Rose warning Alice Morgan not to have anything to do with the Swans: 'Beware when you come up here, for Mrs. Swan is a bloody old cow and a crafty old mare.' Both Mrs Swan and her daughter were in their washhouse and could make out Rose's words. Edith claimed to have heard Rose deliver the same message to her sister in even more insulting terms.[23] While Ruth was talking to Mrs Swan in the passage, Rose sent one of the children out to fetch her sister. When Ruth entered the house, Rose is supposed to have said, 'Ruth I won't have you out there talking to bloody old Mrs Swan—Creeping up old mother Swan's arsehole.'[24] 'Ruth was afraid of her sister and said nothing', Edith added.

At the beginning of the following week, Rose asked Edith to accompany her to the doctor. Robert Going was a surgeon and it was presumably he who performed Rose's operation. His regular fees would surely have been beyond the Goodings' means, and he may well have treated Rose pro bono; he held a number of public service roles, including those of medical officer to the workhouse and public vaccinator.[25] Edith refused to accompany Rose and told her that 'she was not to ask me to do anything again until she had apologized for what she had said about my mother. Mrs. Gooding said:—"Yes, I did say Creeping up mother Swan's arsehole and—Out there talking to bloody old mother Swan."' Abruptly, Rose then said: 'My sister is not a married woman, I do not know if you know it or not.' Up to this point, Swan had 'always thought Miss Russell was a widow, as Mrs. Gooding had said to my mother and Mrs. Russell the Policeman's wife and me that her sister was a widow, her husband having been killed in the war'. Though clearly interested in this news, Edith reproached Rose for changing the subject: 'I am not talking about your sister, I am talking about what you said to my mother.' Edith was not completely sure, but thought that this was the last conversation she had with Rose.[26] She spoke to Rose's sister at least one more time, telling her that she had resolved to write to the National Society for the Prevention of Cruelty to Children.[27]

Historians of philanthropy and welfare have emphasized that charity is not simply something the poor receive, but something they can bend to their own purposes.[28] The National Society for the Prevention of Cruelty to Children and later the Littlehampton sanitary inspector and ultimately the court system were drawn into the quarrel in Western Road, as both the Swans and the Goodings manipulated systems of philanthropy and government in pursuit of personal agendas. The inspector the NSPCC sent over from Chichester was A. C. Bailey, a senior figure in the national organization who had been awarded an OBE for his charitable work.[29] He met with Edith Swan before visiting the Goodings' house. Rose was sitting in the garden and heard him and Edith Swan talking in the passage. Bailey then called upon Rose, saw baby Albert, and spoke to Bill as well. Though the accusation concerned her child, Ruth was out at work for the duration of the visit.[30] Rose was suffering the ultimate indignity for a working-class housewife—having an outside authority intrude into her home to pass judgement on her parenting and her care of the house.[31] All the same, she made a sympathetic connection with the inspector, telling Bailey that 'she suffered terribly with her head at times, and that made her irritable'.[32] Later, in her petition from Portsmouth prison, Rose told the Home Secretary about Bailey's visit in language that was uncharacteristically broken for her but still articulated her pain and pride: 'he gave me a good name and credit how all the fine little children looked after for a poor person he told me not to brood over it as the person

who wrote him had no cause whatever'.[33] According to Nicholls, who
was not one for exaggeration, Bailey 'found the home to be spotlessly
clean and the children in a perfect state in every way'. Nicholls
suggested that Edith Swan's letter of complaint to the NSPCC was
suspicious in its level of detail.[34] No one whom Nicholls spoke to
corroborated Edith's claim that Rose had beaten her nephew and that
Bill had taken the baby away from her.

Although he took many statements about the events of Easter 1920,
Nicholls did not attempt to explain the breach between the two families in the long report he wrote at the end of his time in Littlehampton.
Perhaps the mysteries of relations between women were not his kind
of mystery. From the suddenness and severity of the Swans' break with
Rose Gooding, it seems clear that after the Easter row the Swans
decided that she was a woman of bad character and that they should
not associate themselves with her. If Edith made up the story of Rose
hitting her nephew with a cane, she undoubtedly heard things that
disturbed her on that Sunday afternoon and the days that followed.
Whatever currents of revulsion or desire or both that Edith Swan felt,
her initial action in shunning Rose Gooding followed a recognized
social logic. By the early 1920s, theatrical forms of shaming, such as
burning effigies of adulterous women (seldom of adulterous men), had
given way to ostracism, 'the silence of disapproval and rejection', the
historian Melanie Tebbutt writes.[35] In cutting Rose off, Edith and her
parents were administering a standard sanction used against women
who were judged immoral. They were also protecting themselves from
the sort of gossip—another community sanction—that they themselves engaged in.[36]

The need to maintain a 'good name' weighed heavily on working-
class women. It guided their interactions with men, their comport-
ment in public places, the strenuousness with which they cleaned their
homes. The obligation to uphold standards of cleanliness is a recurring
theme in working-class autobiographies.[37] It was on display every
morning in the ritual of ostentatiously whitening the front step at the
same time as the neighbours.[38] A bad name not only made a woman's
dealings with other people in the community miserable: it also threatened her ability to manage the household. 'The whole structure of
social life in working class districts', Ben Jones concludes from interviews with Brighton residents of the 1920s and 1930s, 'depended both
upon "being known" and upon...knowing how to manage relations

with kin, neighbours, traders, shop-keepers, and outsider figures such as policemen, rent collectors and the "relief men".' Managing these relationships typically fell to mothers or to those daughters, like Edith, who acted in their mother's stead; and managing them successfully depended on 'being known' in a good way, of course, as upright and trustworthy. A bad reputation weakened a woman's position when she negotiated with a landlord or rent collector. It made it harder to get credit.[39] The judgements involved were moral as well as actuarial. Delinquent debtors no longer went to prison, but the association between creditworthiness and morality, between credit and credibility, remained embedded in popular culture and everyday economics. Credit in one form or another—from pawning goods to having a tab with a shopkeeper—was, like 'insurance', a means of smoothing out the volatility of employment and earnings. Another historian, Ross McKibbin, goes as far as to say that in this period 'working-class life without access to credit was almost impossible'.[40]

Here lies one of the puzzles of the scurrilous letters and postcards that began flying shortly after Easter 1920. The libels denounced Edith Swan as a whore and her family as drunken and dirty. They denounced them to people who were economically important to them—Edith's laundry clients, Ernest Swan's employer, 'tradespeople, Wooley & Over, Selbourne [sic] Rd., Miss Sands at Caffyns the Butchers, Mr. Boniface, Fishmonger in Western Rd., Mrs. Knight, General Stores, Norfolk Rd. and Mrs. Leggett at the Dairy. We dealt with all these people...'[41] Sir Ernley Blackwell thought it made no sense for Rose Gooding to start writing libellous postcards as soon as she had been released from prison after her first conviction. It would get her sent away again, and as such was implausibly self-destructive behaviour. If Edith Swan wrote the libels, she was not only framing Rose Gooding, but tearing at the fabric of her own daily life.

3

A Craze for This Sort of Thing

The most destructive letter went all the way to Iraq, where Edith Swan's fiancé was serving with the British occupying forces. In August 1920 Bert Boxall received a letter purporting to be from Edith Russell, the Swans' neighbour at 49 Western Road. The writer informed Boxall that Constable Russell had 'gone away with Miss Swan who was expecting a baby by him'. Boxall's letter was written in the same hand as the libels circulating in Littlehampton. The writer claimed to have found Boxall's address on some old envelopes that Edith Swan had given to the children of 'my friend Mrs. Gooding' to play with, thereby dragging Rose into the matter.[1] Boxall believed the story and wrote to Edith breaking off their engagement, though within a few months it was back on.[2]

Other libels targeted more workaday aspects of Edith Swan's life. Kate Leggett from the dairy on Western Road received an anonymous letter 'to the effect that I should not send my washing to Miss Swan'.[3] Swan also did laundry for the households of Charles Haslett and William Corse, who were partners in a photographic studio on Western Road for less than a year before moving on, Corse to South America and Haslett to Fulham. At the beginning of September 1920 they received a letter 'purporting to be signed by Mrs R. E. Gooding and about Miss Swan'. The gist of the letter was that 'if the people knew what the Swan's were, they would not let them have their washing'.[4] The day the photographers received their letter, Edith dropped by to ask 'if a slanderous letter had been received from Mrs Gooding who was trying to get her work'. Edith hoped Haslett and Corse would stick with her.[5]

Struggling to remember the details, Haslett said he thought the letter was left at the studio rather than sent through the post. Though many of the libels were mailed in the ordinary way, others were hand-delivered and some posted without stamps, obliging the addressee to pay to receive them. Sometimes the abuse and denunciation came enclosed in an envelope and sometimes on the back of a postcard. With a postcard there was the danger that other members of a household, whether family or servants, would see the message before the intended recipient did. This had been one of the objections to postal cards when they were introduced in 1870. Who, wondered a contributor to *Chambers's Journal*, would write 'private information on an open piece of cardboard that might be read by half a dozen persons before it reached its destination'?[6] '[T]he post card, p.c., half-private half-public, neither the one nor the other', wrote the philosopher Jacques Derrida a century later, conjuring with the postcard as a metaphor for the ways writing cannot always be tied to its origin or destination.[7]

Edith Swan's brother Ernest was defamed on postcards that most likely passed through several hands at the Beach Hotel before they reached its manager, Ernest's employer at the time. 'Mr. Stacey, Manager of the Beach Hotel, received three postcards, all within a week, accusing me of stealing things. The first one he tore up, and the others Mr. Stacey handed to me.' After an obscene postcard turned up in the Swans' washhouse, Ernest 'sat up all night in the wash-house' in case Rose Gooding put another one there ('We thought it was Mrs. Gooding who was doing it, because they were signed, "R.G."').[8] A subsequent letter taunted the Swans that they would not catch the culprit even if they sat up all night.[9]

The libels attacked the Swans selectively—Edith's father never received one himself and none of them mentioned him specifically.[10] All the same, the whole family became consumed by the affair. When Mr Bailey of the National Society for the Prevention of Cruelty to Children made a follow-up visit to the Swan household on Monday 7 June 1920, after Edith had lodged a fresh accusation against Rose Gooding, 'he was received with complaints about a number of anonymous letters that had been sent to the Swans; to Miss Swans brother's employers, and to the Police'. The state delegated some powers to NSPCC inspectors, but abusive letters between neighbours fell outside Bailey's remit. This was apparently the occasion, Inspector Nicholls recorded, 'when old Mr. Swan broke in the conversation and said that Mrs. Gooding was a whore, and that her sister's children were bastards'.[11] Perhaps he did not know that Bill Gooding was not Dorothy's father.

Edith's father took on the responsibility of confronting the Goodings about the letters. He went to see them the day the postman delivered the first libel, an unstamped letter calling Edith a 'bloody old cow' and telling her to mind her own business.[12] Mrs Swan recalled: 'My husband took it to Mr. Gooding, and shewed it to him and asked him what he thought of it. Mr. Gooding said that no one in his house wrote it, and he said that neither he nor his wife had written it, and said, "Do you think that we should let the children do it." '[13] Edward Swan retorted: 'If you didn't write it, you knows who did.'[14] One evening later the same month, Mr Swan knocked on the Goodings' door and handed Bill a letter that he said had been wrongly delivered to the Swans. On looking at it more closely, Bill realized that the letter was indeed addressed to the neighbours and took it back to Mr Swan, who said: 'Your wife knows all about it, I heard your wife dictating the words to your daughter.' Bill confirmed that Rose had been dictating a birthday note for her grandmother in Lewes. (Given that Rose wrote many letters herself, it is odd that she was dictating this one. She might have had one of the headaches she suffered from.) Bill Gooding did not ask Mr Swan what was in the offending letter 'and He did not tell me'.[15] And then, on an evening when all the adults were in the front room of 45 Western Road with the door open, Mr Swan threw a letter in over the doorstep. Bill was lying down while Ruth Russell bandaged his ulcerated leg, a chronic affliction for him. Bill told Rose to throw the letter back into the little courtyard where the passage opened out onto their house. She tossed it out and closed the door. Mr Swan was still outside and slid the letter under the door. Bill went to the police station to complain about his neighbour's behaviour.[16]

After he returned home, Bill got ready to go out again, this time with Rose and Ruth. At this point Alfred Russell weighed in.[17] The constable was at home at number 49, not on duty, though his authority as a policeman did not leave him when he hung up his uniform. He called out to Bill, who went to hear what he had to say. Russell told him he knew that offensive letters were going about and that Mr Swan accused Rose of writing them. Bill denied it. Russell 'wanted to draw Gooding. I said, "If anyone accused my wife of writing these letters I should go for him," and that if he did not it would shew guilty'.[18] Bill declined to take the bait. He took his leave of Constable Russell and headed out with Rose and Ruth. In the street they encountered Mr Swan yet again. 'I told him I did not want to be accused or my wife or anyone concerning me.' 'That's the one who's doing it', said Mr Swan, pointing at Rose.[19]

Mr Swan gossiped to other neighbours and family friends about the plague of letters. Reuben Lynn, a painter whom Mr Swan had worked with off and on over many years, eagerly became a party to the intrigue. 'The Swans showed me 2 or 3 letters and I came to know the handwriting', he recalled. Lynn needed little persuading that the letters signed 'R. G.' really were the work of Rose Gooding. 'I was at Beach Post Office on an occasion in June or July 1920, posting a paper to my daughter in Durham when I saw the little girl'—he said 'Rosie Gooding', but he was talking about Dorothy—'at the post box. She came up and posted a letter and as she put it in the box I saw the name "Swan" on the letter...I saw Stephen Swan just afterwards in Norfolk Road and said to him:—"There will be another letter for you in the morning. I have just seen the little girl post one."' The following day Lynn ran into Steve Swan again and Steve told him they had indeed received another insulting letter.[20]

The Swans and their supporters appear to have been unaware of other embarrassing letters and postcards circulating at the same time. Rather than attack the Swans in the name of Rose Gooding, these cards and letters attempted to stir up conflict between the Goodings. Bill received two letters at Harvey's shipyard a week apart. One of them accused Rose of 'having men' at the publisher's house while she was working as a domestic there. The second letter read 'Ask your wife who she was with on Tuesday afternoon on the Common.' It bore the initials 'V. G.' and gave Pier Road as the sender's address.[21] A different kind of mischief arrived in the form of a postcard from Worthing at the end of August. Though it was addressed to Bill at 45 Western Road, he was unlikely to be the one who saw it first, given that he was out at work six days each week. 'From your darling Sweetheart Philis' was the entirety of the message.[22] The front of the card depicted a woman in a bathing costume or a skimpy dress sitting on a rock, with the caption 'Some of the birds down here are going about half plucked.' The painter was W. Stocker Shaw, who provided the artwork for many of the suggestive postcards that were as much a part of the British seaside experience as rock and donkey rides.[23] As 'Phyllis' was misspelled, it seems unlikely that the card was actually sent by a girlfriend of that name. It could have been

Figure 3.1. Postcard sent to Bill Gooding on 30 August 1920. MEPO 3/380, National Archives

the work of the Littlehampton libeller or a prank by a workmate. This card and the two letters Bill received at the shipyard were never accounted for in the investigation into the Littlehampton libels.

Apart from these anomalous pieces of mail, the offending letters, postcards, and fragmentary notebooks that circulated in the spring and summer of 1920 all led plausibly back to Rose Gooding. The signatures and initials were not the only identifying features. The libels included words and phrases that the Goodings were alleged to have used and their neighbours not. 'I have heard them use the language that was on the postcard', Edward Swan told the police.[24] Edith claimed that she had heard Rose Gooding use the phrase 'bloody old cow' about her the day before it showed up in that first letter. Edith was in her wash-house while Rose was repeating her injunction to Alice Morgan not to talk to Edith or her mother: 'they are a thorough bad lot, they are bloody old cows and crafty old mares'.[25] Interactions with Rose Gooding had libellous sequels. In August 1920 Littlehampton's sanitary inspector, Reginald Booker, received a letter 'purporting to come from Mrs R. Gooding complaining of Mr. Swan's rabbits and P.C. Russell's fowls'. Booker paid them a visit and after inspecting the yard told Alfred Russell that he had too many chickens. He thought he told Mr Swan to take the rabbits away, but was not absolutely sure.[26] (The rabbits stayed.) The way Russell remembered the encounter, the inspector examined the dustbin under the Goodings' window and said: 'If there is anything unsanitary here, it is that dustbin.' Booker did not see the Goodings or Ruth Russell, but their children were leaning out the window taking in the proceedings.[27] The following day, the sanitary inspector received 'a letter containing abuse signed "R. G." Western Rd'. He went to confront the Goodings. Booker told Bill he had 'made investigations on the letter from his wife and that it was not fair that I should receive this abusive letter'. Bill assured him that Rose was not the writer. 'Old Mr. Swan came out and there were a few words between Gooding and Swan.' Booker said he was not there to get involved in a neighbours' quarrel. He informed them that he would report the matter to his committee, 'with a view of the Town Clerk writing a letter to the Goodings reprimanding them'. The next day he received a letter signed 'R. G.' that declared: 'I don't care for your Fucking Committee.'[28]

An officer in the West Sussex police summed up how it looked: 'Any Person who went and saw Mrs Gooding on any Subject the next day received a post card referring to the subject they had called on her about.'[29] Constable Russell's wife Edith registered a variation on this theme: 'Mrs Gooding on several occasions sent in some cakes to my boy, and on one occasion a piece of fish. She always wrote a nice little note asking me to accept them, and the curious part about it was that on each occasion we received cake or fish, [it] was followed by one of these offensive letters or cards to my husband.'[30] Practically all these dealings with Rose Gooding, however, could have occurred within earshot of Edith Swan. (And the Swans had more reason than Rose Gooding to abuse the sanitary inspector after his first visit.) Constable Russell, who was firmly of the view that Rose was responsible for the libels, told Nicholls: 'I spoke to Mr. and Mrs. Gooding separately about the letters…Mr. Gooding in my garden, and…Mrs. Gooding at the door of her house. The Swans could easily have heard our conversation. About a week later, postcards began to reach me through the post, in dirty abusive language.'[31] The witness statements read like monologues, but they are really one side of a dialogue, with the interviewer's questions left out. The unexpected reference to the chance that the Swans overheard is a sign of Nicholls interrupting Russell's story to confront him with a possibility that Russell had refused to entertain.

It was not just circumstances that counted against Rose Gooding: there was also the presumption that her family belonged to 'a slightly rougher class than the Swans, Miss Swan in particular'.[32] Frederick Peel of the West Sussex police elaborated with revealing artlessness on his reasons for thinking that Rose Gooding and not Edith Swan must have written the libels. 'I have made enquiries respecting the character of Miss Swan and find that she bears a very good character, She is a very hard working woman, and what I have seen of her I do not Think that she would write such things about herself and send them through the post on post cards for every one to see, Mrs Gooding and her sister…have both had Illegitimate Children.'[33]

Peel, a Londoner long resident in Sussex, was the police superintendent at Arundel. The Littlehampton police reported to him (though it was much smaller, Arundel was more established, and Littlehampton was subordinate to it for some administrative purposes). Peel made his inquiries into the character of Edith Swan, Rose Gooding, and Ruth Russell after the Home Office reopened the case. At the time of the first libels, he and the rest of the West Sussex police force kept their distance. At least, this was their official policy: while the senior officer in Littlehampton, Inspector Henry Thomas, chose to handle the matter through conversations with the Goodings, Alfred Russell went further.

Russell was an interested party: both he and his wife received obscene letters ostensibly written by Rose Gooding. Some time after the Russells began receiving them, Alfred paid a visit to the photographers Haslett and Corse. Haslett recalled Russell's suggesting 'that Mrs Gooding should be brought to our premises by letter and that he should be behind a curtain and when Mrs Gooding arrived, we should produce the letter and ask her whether she knew anything about it'. The photographers 'refused to have anything to do with this matter'.[34] Their defiance suggests they suspected that Russell did not speak for Inspector Thomas when he proposed setting this trap. Russell later approached the same solicitor as Edith Swan about the letters he was receiving, though he opted not to join Swan's private prosecution.[35]

The Goodings took the libels seriously even before Edith Swan engaged her lawyers. As new people received inflammatory letters, Bill Gooding went to see them and protest his wife's innocence.[36] Rose confided to Alice Morgan that 'letters were being sent about to different people in her name, calling them awful names'. Morgan got the impression Rose 'suspected Miss Swan of writing them, although she did not say that Miss Swan had been doing it'.[37] When Bailey called on 7 June in response to the second complaint of cruelty to baby Albert (whom Bailey found 'happy and cheerful'), Rose 'was in a dressing gown, with no shoes or stockings on, and was somewhat strange in her manner, and she told him she had been accused of writing anonymous letters, but had not done so'. Ruth Russell spoke to her employer, the solicitor Richard Sharpe, about 'the unpleasantness with her neighbours...owing to their, the Swans, receiving abusive communications'. Sharpe gathered that 'the Goodings were very worried about it and appeared anxious to find the author of the letters'.[38]

Their anxiety deepened in July. At the beginning of the month Edith Swan received two postcards that must have been exceptionally offensive: although at least twenty-six pieces of mail were admitted as evidence in Rose Gooding's first trial, she was convicted on only two counts of criminal libel, one for each of these two postcards to Swan.[39] On 5 July, Swan went with her mother to seek advice from the local justices of the peace, who convened in the Littlehampton council building every second Monday (in alternate weeks they met in

Arundel). The justices advised Edith to consult a solicitor. That afternoon she met with Arthur Shelley at his office in Beach Road. Shelley was a prominent Littlehampton citizen, serving as clerk to the urban district council and the poor law guardians, among other things.[40] After his interview with Edith Swan, Shelley wrote a warning letter to Rose Gooding and began to lay the foundations for a prosecution.[41]

Shelley dispatched his managing clerk, a Mr Weir, to interview people who had received insulting letters and postcards, and, if possible, collect the libels.[42] Ruth Russell asked Richard Sharpe for help. Sharpe agreed to try to sort the matter out informally. He met with Weir and together they went through the accumulated letters and postcards. Sharpe's guess was some of the children in the house wrote the libels. Ruth Russell refused to believe this, though she confronted the children about it later the same day. The following morning she told Sharpe that all the children denied it.[43] Although the Goodings and Ruth Russell felt shaken by the involvement of lawyers, the offensive letters and postcards continued to circulate. Shelley and his client continued to collect fresh libels from their recipients, but otherwise bided their time. Now that Shelley was involved, he started receiving obscene mail.[44]

In the distant past, most libel cases were criminal matters. Over the course of the nineteenth century, prosecutions declined, as the misdemeanour of libel was displaced by the tort. Paying damages to the victim, rather than going to prison or paying a fine, became the usual sanction the courts imposed on a person who defamed someone else. The decline of criminal libel was part of a general contraction in the scope of the criminal law in the nineteenth century, as Victorian liberal norms of self-government and self-restraint became a social reality.[45] By the latter decades of the Victorian era, for an insult or allegation to warrant criminal charges rather than a civil action for damages it had to involve public order in some way. 'There ought to be some public interest concerned', explained Lord Coleridge in the most authoritative statement of the law, 'something affecting the Crown or the guardians of the public peace (likely to be broken by the alleged libel), to justify the recourse by a private person to a criminal remedy by way of indictment. If, either by reason of the continued repetition or infamous character of the libel, breach of the peace is likely to ensue, then the libeller should be indicted; but, in the absence of any such conditions, a personal squabble between two

private individuals ought not … to be the subject of a criminal indictment.'[46] In 1906 Lord Alverstone reiterated the point to a grand jury
in Somerset: 'if it is only of a private character, and there is an absence
of circumstance which would show that the publication of the libel
would disturb the peace and harmony of the district, the parties
should be left to their civil remedies, and should not institute or pur-
sue criminal proceedings for libel'.[47]

It was a long way down from these general principles to the nitty-
gritty of prosecuting. In practice, criminal libel cases could be sorted
into three categories. The ones with the highest profile were the also
the most exceptional. Oscar Wilde's prosecution of the Marquess of
Queensberry and the dancer Maud Allan's prosecution of Noel
Pemberton Billing after Allan became caught up in the MP's crusade
against a supposed conspiracy to subvert the British state both turned
on imputations of homosexuality.[48] The circumstances were not substantially different from those in which an award of damages would be
an appropriate remedy, but in these cases the 'infamous character' of
the libels made them worthy of the sanction of the criminal law.[49]

The second kind of criminal libel case involved public institutions
and their integrity—'something affecting the Crown', in Coleridge's
usefully loose phrase. Here criminal libel shaded into the territory
covered by the law of sedition. People who denounced judges or made
allegations about police misconduct could find themselves charged
with criminal libel.[50] A long disciplinary saga within the Metropolitan
Police reached its climax when the former officer at the centre of it,
John Syme, attacked the commissioner in a pamphlet, whereupon
Syme was charged with criminal libel. Giving evidence at Bow Street
Police Court, the commissioner stated that insofar as the defamatory
statements affected him personally, 'he would have been quite ready to
ignore them, but in view of the mischievous tendency of the statements and of the apprehension that they might, if continued long
enough, affect the efficiency and discipline of the force … it would
become necessary to put an end to their further publication'.[51] Courts
also entertained criminal prosecutions for libels with implications for
the smooth functioning of commerce and the professions. Stockbrokers
and solicitors accused of corruption prosecuted their critics.[52] Even
impugning the probity of an electrical engineer or the creditworthiness of a labourer was sufficiently 'public' to justify a prosecution for
criminal libel.[53]

The last type of criminal libel proceeding, and the one relevant to the matter of Edith Swan and Rose Gooding, involved harassment. These were libels that 'disturb[ed] the peace and harmony of the district', in Alverstone's phrase: writings that caused a 'breach of the peace' in a more figurative way than a brawl or a rowdy gathering.[54] It was the nuisance the writing caused, not its falsity or its effects on the victim's reputation, that mattered.[55] Late one winter's evening in 1932, a dock labourer named William Shepherd removed the plugs in the thin wooden partition between his family's room in a Holborn tenement and that of their neighbour, Wilhelmina Flanagan, who was living apart from her husband. Shepherd 'played at peeping Tom', watching her have sex with a young man. The following day he wrote her a letter beseeching her to let him play with her breasts and lick her 'giggly ball'. Shepherd's wife would be out until 11 p.m.; if Flanagan was interested, she was to tap three times on the dividing wall. The letter ended: 'Please burn this.'[56] Shepherd delivered the letter in person, saying, 'Take this & read it & see what you can make of it.' 'He went away, back to his room', Flanagan recalled. 'I picked the letter up, I started to read it. That was enough for me. I went to a friend & then to the police.'[57] Shepherd was charged with criminal libel even though he had not defamed Flanagan (though he had certainly written explicitly about her body) or published it to a third party: his letter was disturbing and invasive, and that was what made it a libel. Shepherd pleaded guilty, saying, 'I must have been mad.'[58] He wrote to the clerk of the Central Criminal Court—the Old Bailey—begging for mercy. 'I plead ignorant of the law of libel. I never knew how serious it is.'[59]

In another case from the 1930s, the fact that the defamatory statements were not without foundation proved no bar to a conviction. In *Rex v. Gray*, the 'continued repetition' of the libels was a factor in the decision to prosecute: Charles Gray wrote serially to the victim's husband, in-laws, neighbours, and golf club. Gray worked in the hosiery trade, and on his travels he met Florence Browning, a buyer for a large firm of drapers. Browning earned a good salary and stayed in her job after marrying a stockbroker and settling in Surrey. She and Gray began an affair, staying together in hotels during business trips. Then Gray lost his job and Florence Browning began giving him money to tide him and his family over. Browning left her husband and went to stay with a friend, while still seeing Gray. After a month she returned to her husband. Gray was incensed and began threatening to disclose their affair if she did not keep giving him money. Gray waited for Browning near her home and accosted her at Victoria Station as well as sending threatening letters. She was frightened and took out a loan to pay him off. All up, she gave him around £200, which proved insufficient to ward off the letters detailing their affair.[60] And they were detailed: Gray listed the dates and locations of their 'misconduct'— hotels in London, Nottingham, Wendover, Aylesbury, Amersham; Hampstead Heath, Wimbledon Common, on trains.[61]

The letters Gray wrote to Browning's husband and then to others 'grossly exaggerated' the affair, but Florence accepted that there was a kernel of truth to his claims. This could well have derailed any civil action for compensation for the damage to her reputation, but it did not prevent the police charging Gray with criminal libel. 'Mrs Browning brought this trouble on herself', Chief Inspector John Sands noted at the foot of a police report, 'but the position has now arisen that we must endeavour to protect her from this obvious blackguard'. Gray was arraigned and pleaded guilty, receiving a sentence of nine months' imprisonment. Chief Inspector Sands described the result as 'a satisfactory conviction for criminal libel on what was really— unfortunately the documentary evidence had been destroyed by complainant—a case of demanding money with menaces'.[62]

The defendant in a criminal libel case was often a former lover, or someone who had hoped to become a lover. A man who failed to strike up a romance with a woman at the printing firm where they both worked ended up charged with criminal libel after he wrote anonymous letters to their co-workers accusing the woman of sluttish behaviour, and to the wives of other men at the works claiming that they were having sex with her (when caught in the act of mailing a letter, he shoved it into his mouth, 'tore a piece off and threw the remainder over a fence').[63] Rivalries and resentments in other institutions, not just workplaces, boiled over into harassing letters and criminal libel proceedings: local councils, branches of political parties, church congregations, even the Workers' Educational Association ('I still say your W.E.A. is a brothel').[64] Neighbourhood grievances, too, were fertile ground for letters that disturbed 'the peace and harmony of the district'.

In September 1920, the Director of Public Prosecutions was called upon to rule whether there was sufficient 'public interest' at stake in the Littlehampton libels to justify criminal charges. Shelley wrote to

Sir Archibald Bodkin asking him to take up the case. Bodkin replied that 'as the libels complained of were private libels and the matter was not of general or public importance, the Director did not feel, in view of the limitations under which he acts in prosecutions of this nature, that he would be justified in undertaking the prosecution'.[65] Bodkin's response was ambiguous: the letters to and about Edith Swan were too 'private' to warrant a public prosecution, but were they so private that they did not amount to criminal libels at all? Shelley clearly judged that the letters and postcards disturbed the peace enough to call for criminal sanctions. He and his client went ahead with a private prosecution.

This was an extraordinary step for someone from an underemployed working-class family to take.[66] The legal bills could easily run to £30, a sum equivalent to more than two years' rent for Edith's family.[67] The Swans had clearly saved a considerable amount through the tontine club and maybe other schemes, for there was no prospect of public funding to support Edith's legal campaign. There was little in the way of legal aid available in England at this time. The provisions of the Poor Prisoners' Defence Act of 1903 were circumscribed and unclear, and some judges simply bypassed them, relying on the old 'dock brief' system, whereby a judge could compel a barrister who was hanging around the court robed and ready to work to represent an impoverished defendant for a fee of one guinea. And neither the 1903 act nor the dock brief regime provided support for poor *prosecutors*.[68] They were on their own, or dependent on the charity of lawyers.

With Shelley's assistance, Edith applied for a warrant, and Rose Gooding was summoned to a police court hearing. A police court, also known as a magistrate's court, was presided over by a stipendiary magistrate or by several justices of the peace, as was the case in Littlehampton. The justices—also, confusingly, referred to as magistrates—would determine whether there was a case to answer.[69] After being served with the warrant, Rose Gooding called on Richard Sharpe 'in a state of nervous excitement'. She insisted she was innocent and said 'that she was distracted at these letters'.[70] For whatever reason, Sharpe did not represent her.[71] Two days before the hearing in front of the justices was scheduled to take place, Bill Gooding walked into the offices of another solicitor, Edward Wannop. He took the case on and instructed the barrister John Flowers, a Hove native who regularly appeared in Sussex courtrooms as both a prosecutor and defence counsel.[72] Flowers had a reputation as a cricketer and had been good enough to play for Sussex in his youth, though he enjoyed little success at county level.[73] Flowers would represent Rose Gooding at both the police court and any subsequent trial. Wannop must have believed that Gooding needed a barrister's firepower, because it was possible for a solicitor, who could not argue cases in court, to outline the case at the preliminary hearing before the magistrates.[74] The hearing was set for the second Monday in September of 1920. That morning Rose Gooding went to her solicitor's office saying she was unwell and could not attend.[75] The justices postponed the hearing and arranged a special sitting the following week. On Wednesday 22 September 1920 Rose Gooding appeared in the Littlehampton council chamber before a bench of three justices of the peace chaired by William Rawson Shaw, a former Liberal MP.

Swan's solicitor, Shelley, presented the prosecution's case. Outlining the background to the matter, he mentioned that he himself had 'received a most abusive and filthy letter from the defendant. Why he should receive such a letter he did not know, for he had never seen the defendant before she appeared in the Court that morning.' Shelley called Swan to the witness box to tell the story of her complaint to the NSPCC, the subsequent note warning her to mind her own business, and the flood of letters containing repellent expressions that she had overheard Rose Gooding use when telling family and friends to stay away from the Swans. Edith wrote the phrase 'bloody old cows' on a piece of paper as she sat in the witness box and gave it to the magistrates rather than have to say the words aloud. Edith evoked the menacing feel of the libels when she described the time someone pushed a letter under her front door. It read: 'I know I am watched by the Post Office, but there are more ways than that.'[76] She told of receiving another at the end of July that warned, 'You won't frighten me with your solicitor's letter', as well as many unstamped letters that she refused to accept from the postman. Shelley called Charles Haslett and Kate Leggett as witnesses. Reuben Lynn testified that he had seen 'the little girl Gooding come up to the box and post a postcard. He allowed her to post the card first, while he put on his stamp. He saw the postcard was addressed to Miss Swann.'[77] Lynn 'had seen similar postcards sent to Miss Swann, and that was why he noticed this particular one'. Reginald Booker gave evidence about the letters he had received 'containing phrases similar to those in the postcards received by Miss Swann'.[78]

Alice Morgan also testified. She had unexpectedly become a focus for suspicion and someone whom both sides at once mistrusted and courted. The day Rose Gooding received her court summons, she sent her son Willie to the restaurant on Western Road where Morgan now worked to ask her to come to the house at once. Morgan was surprised because Gooding had been shunning her. Morgan's employers allowed her to take a break and go out to see Rose. She apparently did not detect any lingering hostility on Rose's part. Ruth Russell was at home too, and the three of them talked about the summons. Rose said Morgan would probably have to attend the hearing too. Morgan replied she would not unless ordered to.[79] This, at least, is how Morgan described the conversation. Edith Swan told Nicholls she had overheard something very different: Rose telling Morgan to deny knowing 'anything about the letters and cards'. If she informed on her, Rose reportedly threatened, it would 'be the worst day's work you have ever done'.[80]

A week later Morgan had another visitor at the restaurant: Constable Russell. He showed her a letter with her initials on it. 'The letter said that Mrs. Gooding had written the letters and I had posted them; and also that P.C. Russell was carrying on with Miss Swan, while his wife was ill.' Next she had a visit from Weir, bearing a letter addressed to Shelley, levelling the same allegations and signed 'A. Morgan'. She furnished Weir with a sample of her handwriting. Rose commiserated with her, saying that 'they' had finished with her and were now targeting Morgan. By this time Morgan and Rose Gooding were back spending a lot of time together. Yet there are signs that Gooding or others in her family harboured suspicions about Morgan, which may explain why Rose sent for her the day she received the court summons. The two women sat down and wrote out 'A. M.' together so that each could see how the other formed the letters. Before the police court hearing, Rose's mother, visiting from Lewes, asked Morgan straight out what she had against her daughter.[81]

Morgan had been subpoenaed by the prosecution. On the morning originally set for the pre-trial hearing, the morning Rose stayed away unwell, Morgan encountered Edith Swan, her mother, and Reuben Lynn waiting outside the council building. Edith later asserted Morgan had told them all 'that she knew that Mrs Gooding had written the letters and that she—Miss Morgan—had posted them...and that she would give her away at the following Weds. week at the hearing'.[82]

Morgan strongly denied this claim when George Nicholls put it to her the following year.[83] Even if Edith was lying about Morgan's confession, Shelley must have thought that Morgan's testimony could damage Rose somehow. Morgan's conversation with Rose Gooding in the washhouse and the appearance of the same words used on that occasion in the offensive letter that followed were crucial to Edith Swan's explanation of why she was sure Rose Gooding wrote the libels. At the hearing before the magistrates Shelley attempted to get Morgan to corroborate this story, but to no avail. Morgan said that she could remember 'the interview with the accused that took place in the wash house, but she could not swear what the conversation was that took place. She was positive, however, that Miss Swann's name was not mentioned.'[84] She would later tell Nicholls: 'It is untrue that Mrs. Gooding ever told me that I was not to talk to Mrs. Swan or her daughter, or that she ever said the Swans were a thorough bad lot, and bloody old cows, and crafty old mares. This was put to me at the Police Court, and I denied it.'[85] Confronted in court with the letter to Shelley repeating the allegations that Rose Gooding wrote the libels and Morgan posted them for her, Morgan said that the letter was not in her handwriting, and reiterated what she had said to Rose on the subject: why would she 'write letters to a gentleman she knew nothing of'?[86]

Gooding's barrister did not call any witnesses; Flowers announced that Rose would reserve her defence.[87] It was routine for defence counsel to decline to disclose their strategy in front of the magistrates and wait until the trial proper, though senior legal figures were heard to say that innocent people should reveal their defence right away, so that it could be investigated (and defendants had to do so if they wanted legal aid).[88] All the same, in his cross-examination of the prosecution witnesses, Flowers tried out some lines of attack. He stressed that the handwriting was in dispute and attempted to have some pieces of evidence, such as the letter to Shelley, excluded on that ground. He even asked Edith Swan if she had written any of the documents herself, though when she answered no he did not press further.[89]

The magistrates committed Rose for trial. They offered her bail if she could find two sureties of £50.[90] A carpenter who worked alongside Bill at the shipyard was willing to stand as one guarantor. Appropriately for an upstanding working man born in the nineteenth century, he bore the same name as the Free Trader Richard Cobden.[91] (While Cobden's name is inseparable from Lancashire radicalism, he

was born in Sussex and was buried in the churchyard at Midhurst.)[92]
Bill could not find another person to vouch for his wife, so she spent
the twelve weeks until her trial in Portsmouth prison. Her solicitor's
clerk, William Smith, consulted Rose's doctor, Robert Going, and came
to the conclusion that this was not necessarily a bad thing. It would
give the prison doctor an opportunity to see 'whether there was anything mentally wrong with her'.[93] This was not unusual. Two contemporary critics of the prison system noted that defendants in criminal
cases were regularly 'placed on remand in order that their mental condition may be observed', and a committee appointed to look into
insanity and crime reported to Parliament that 'In many cases of poor
persons charged with crime there is no known medical history and the
opportunity of judging his state of mind comes when he is placed in
prison on arrest or committal.'[94] Generalist medical officers, not psychiatrists, made the judgements about prisoners' mental health; only in
a few places, such as Birmingham and Bradford, did prisons and local
magistrates approach mental health 'on the most enlightened lines of
modern criminology'.[95] Smith duly asked the governor of Portsmouth
prison, Ernest Hall, to keep Rose Gooding under medical observation.
Hall acceded, and in mid-November Smith heard from the prison's
medical officer, who 'could find no mental disease in the woman'.[96]
The governor would later second this judgement in his letter telling
Sir Ernley Blackwell that Rose Gooding had 'shown no trace' of insanity in her time at Portsmouth.[97]

Rex v. Gooding was placed on the docket of the assize court convened
at Lewes, Rose Gooding's hometown, in December 1920.[98] Outside
London, jury trials took place in courts that sat—the word 'assize'
derives from the Old French for 'to sit'—four times a year. Assize courts
dealt with civil cases as well as criminal prosecutions, and they were
presided over by high court judges on circuit. The south-eastern circuit's second half was a favourite among the judges. As one of them
reminisced: 'All the four towns are within easy reach of London; it is
throughout a single Judge circuit; the work is seldom heavy until Lewes,
the last town, is reached, and there are many worse places in which to
spend three weeks than in the lodgings at Lewes with a good garden
[and] a view right over the valley of the Ouse to Newhaven.'[99] The
trials took place in the County Hall, erected in 1812.[100]

The judge on duty in the winter of 1920 was Alexander Roche.
Born in Ipswich in 1871, Roche had proceeded from a local grammar

school to Oxford and on to the bar. His early experience was with maritime commercial cases, especially in the north-east of England. He accepted some criminal briefs as well as shipping cases, but the criminal work quickly fell by the wayside. By the time Roche was appointed King's Counsel in 1912, his practice was exclusively commercial. When he became a judge five years later, he balanced hearings in the commercial court in London with assize work, which he preferred. Roche believed strongly in the value of the circuit system, and, being a lover of country sport, he appreciated the opportunities circuit work afforded for hunting, shooting, and fly-fishing on non-sitting days.[101] He was not the ideal judge for a criminal libel case arising from a dispute between neighbours.

Flowers represented Rose Gooding once more. Shelley had instructed a barrister from Shoreham, Thomas Gates, to present the prosecution's case. Roche faulted Gates for not providing any expert evidence about the handwriting of the libels.[102] Such expertise was not new. The forensic scrutiny of handwriting stretched back to ancien régime France, and its exponents became visible in Britain and the United States in the last third of the nineteenth century.[103] Handwriting experts had deployed their skills in English criminal libel cases well before Rose Gooding's. In 1903, when a publican and his wife prosecuted an acquaintance for criminal libel over anonymous letters, one of which insinuated that the couple were not actually married, they secured the services of a handwriting expert who had been in the business for twenty years.[104] Although Roche thought that expert testimony about the handwriting was desirable, he let the charges go to the jury anyway.[105]

Why did Roche wave the prosecution's case through? He may have decided, over-cautiously, that if he did not he would be violating the rule that whether a libel had been committed was strictly a question for the jury, not the judge. This principle held a special place in the folklore of civil liberties in Britain, at least among lawyers.[106] It dated back to the eighteenth century. Lord Mansfield, the dominant judge of the era, insisted that whether a publication constituted a libel—and he used the term in its old, capacious sense: a document that should be outlawed, whether because it was defamatory or because it was seditious, blasphemous, or obscene—was a question of law, and as such a question for the judge and not the jury, who were to confine themselves to questions of fact.[107] It was up to jury to decide whether the prosecution had proved that the accused did in fact publish the alleged libel, but the main question—was this pamphlet seditious or defamatory?—was out of their hands. Mansfield's position was intolerable to many, and in 1792 the Whig leader in the House of Commons, Charles James Fox, successfully introduced a bill 'to remove doubts respecting the functions of juries in cases of libels'. Fox's Libel Act stipulated that in any trial for libel (again, in the widest sense) 'the jury sworn to try the issue may give a general verdict of guilty or not guilty upon the whole matter put in issue upon such indictment or information; and shall not be required or directed, by the court or judge before whom such indictment or information shall be tried, to find the defendant or defendants guilty, merely on the proof of the publication by such defendant or defendants of the paper charged to be a libel, and of the sense ascribed to the same in such indictment or information.'[108] The principle was summed up in the textbook formula: 'Libel or No Libel a Question for the Jury'.[109]

In Rose Gooding's, case, though, there was no disagreement about the libellous nature of the insulting letters: it was the fact of authorship and publication, usually a formality, that was the crux of the case. The prosecution adduced no evidence that 'fixed' Gooding as the author of the libels: she was convicted 'mainly on the evidence of Miss Swan and Reuben Lynn'.[110] In what the defence regarded as a misdirection, Roche told the jury that if Gooding had not written the letters, Swan must have.[111] Asked which woman they trusted more, the jury gave the same answer as the local police.

Roche acknowledged that Gooding had already spent two and a half months in prison awaiting trial. But he thought she must stay locked up a little longer because 'she needed frightening so that she did not do the sort of thing, of which she had been found guilty, with impunity'.[112] He sentenced her to fourteen days' imprisonment. She would be bound over to keep the peace, and would lose £20 if she failed to do so; Bill Gooding would have to stand surety for another £20.[113] Speaking to her husband before addressing the prisoner herself, Roche asked Bill Gooding if he could stop his wife writing such letters. Bill said yes. 'She seems to have a craze for this sort of thing', Roche mused. He turned to Rose. Was she content to be bound over? Rose 'replied in a firm voice: "Yes, sir, I am quite content, as I have always been."'[114]

4

Will You Let Me Have
That Letter

H.M. Prison Portsmouth housed inmates of both sexes. Women were a minority of British prisoners, and Holloway in London was the sole woman-only prison in the country. Most female prisoners were held in smaller provincial prisons such as Portsmouth, in wings separate from the buildings for men. Every prisoner had to do physical work, despite the confusing way the phrase 'with hard labour' was appended to some defendants' sentences and not others'.[1] Nearly all the labour assigned to female prisoners was indoor work. Women did laundry, cleaned, delivered food, carried coal, and, above all, sewed. Rose Gooding took in needlework from clients in Beach Town, and it would be no surprise if she had been set sewing in prison. Although one British prison provided sewing machines with which the inmates ran up dresses for the female warders, a huge amount of needlework was done by hand, mostly in poorly lit spaces. Complaints of eye strain were common. The inmates worked alongside each other, but they were not supposed to talk. There are indications that warders in the women's wings enforced the 'silence rule' less strictly than they did with the men. All the same, prison was an isolating experience. On Sundays there was no work and the prisoners remained in their cells. Every day the evening meal concluded before five and a long stretch of dreary solitude began.[2]

Rose Gooding's first spell in Portsmouth prison ended just before Christmas 1920. In the three months she had been away, no one had complained of receiving obscene postcards or letters.[3] Within two weeks of her return to Littlehampton, the libels started again. This time Edith Swan did not wait. In the first few days of January she went to

the police about the resumption of the wounding letters.[4] The police
telephoned Rose Gooding's solicitor.[5] Wannop's clerk, William Smith,
who seems to have had far more invested in the case than his employer,
phoned Harvey's shipyard immediately and left a message asking Bill
Gooding to call by his office on the way home.[6] Smith had a plan.

Bill Gooding arrived at the offices of Wannop & Falconer around half
past five. He 'knew nothing about the letters going about again' until
Smith told him. Smith's idea was to get Rose out of Littlehampton and
have her stay with her mother. 'I advised Mr. Gooding to act in a manner
which would make the neighbours believe that Mrs. Gooding was still
in the house.'[7] Whoever was writing the letters would go on sending
them, trusting that the blame would fall on the convicted libeller.

They acted quickly. Rose was on a train to Lewes less than two
hours after her husband walked into Smith's office. She cannot have
had much to pack. Rose's mother, Barbara Russell, was at the house in
Western Road that evening. Dorothy Gooding had spent the Christmas
holidays at her grandmother's house and had overstayed; Ruth Russell
sent a postcard summoning Dorothy back to Littlehampton to resume
school, and Barbara Russell accompanied her home that day.[8] Smith
walked with the Goodings and Barbara Russell to Littlehampton station. On arrival they caught sight of Reuben Lynn on the platform.[9]
In an attempt to avoid alerting Lynn to the plan, Bill got on the train
too, travelled one stop to Ford Junction three miles away, and then
doubled back to Littlehampton by himself.[10]

For the next two weeks, Bill Gooding, Ruth Russell, and the children
made a show of calling out to Rose as if she were in the house some-
where out of sight. In the statement she gave to Nicholls, Ruth said that
she accepted deliveries from the baker and explained to him that her
sister was in bed with a headache. 'I did that to mislead the Swans, so that
they would think my sister was still there.'[11] According to Bill, when the
baker's roundsman called, Ruth would shout out to her absent sister
asking how many loaves she should buy.[12] The children would yell goodbye to Rose as they left for school.[13] One morning Dorothy went upstairs
to the bedroom to 'ask her mother to come and meet her coming out of
school', again to fool the Swans, if they happened to be listening—an
indication of the extraordinary acoustics of the cluster of houses.[14]

Rose was also instructed to write to her family regularly so as to
build up a collection of letters with Lewes postmarks that would help

prove that she had been away from home those two weeks. One of
these letters survives in the police files. Though addressed to Ruth and
Bill both, it was mostly directed at Ruth:

Dear ruth i have got a suit fore your Billie and one fore Little Willie and a
Dress fore your Gertie and one fore Dorie and some stockings for them and
a Black skirt fore you to wark aboute in a Disent one Dear ruth i am coming
nix wensday in the afternoon same time so Dear ruth Be on the Look out fore
me i dont think i have any more fore to say this time so i will close with Best
Love from your mother and also Grandmother Mr hawlkins sends his Best
respects to you both fore the Dear children xxxxxxxxx
                                        xxxxxxxxx
Dear ruth coming nix wensday with out fail[15]

It is hardly possible now to read such a letter neutrally, independent
of a literary tradition of non-standard spelling. For centuries, novelists
have used phonetic spellings to indicate lack of cultivation. When a
character's use of the word 'business' is rendered 'biz'ness' on the page,
we know he is 'rude' or 'vulgar', in spite of the fact that *business* and
biz'ness represent identical sound patterns...in the realities of direct
speech'.[16] Rose Gooding's spelling marks her as the creature of another
age even more vividly than her domestic arrangements do. Novelists'
use of so-called 'eye dialect' does not only suggest social status, of
course: it is also meant to capture regional variations in English.
And the phonetic spellings of Rose's letter ('wark' instead of 'walk',
'hawlkins' instead of 'Hawkins', 'nix' for 'next') convey something of
her accent.[17] The content is less expressive. The social critic M. E.
Loane (in fact the pen name for a team of two sisters, one a writer and
the other a pioneering district nurse, and thus professionally judge-
mental in complementary ways) was familiar with letters like this.[18]
'The poor are as a rule strangely incapable of the art of letter-writing.
A mother will correspond for years with a son in America, or a married daughter "in the north," and neither will succeed in giving the
other more than the haziest and most incorrect ideas of situation and
surroundings.' This was not simply a function of the 'mechanical diffi-
culties of writing and spelling': 'many of the baldest and emptiest epis-
tles look like the original of a lithographed circular and are faultless in
spelling'.[19]
    If Smith's plan was to succeed, someone needed to receive an insult-
ing letter or postcard sent locally while Rose Gooding was holed up in

Lewes. On the eleventh or twelfth of January, Smith was at the Town Offices and bumped into Reginald Booker, the sanitary inspector. They got talking and the libel case was mentioned. Booker said that his wife 'had been foolish enough to pay two pence for one of these disgusting letters which came through the post for him unstamped'. That letter never found its way onto the official record.[20] Either the same day or the next Smith saw a chance to get his hands on another letter—one with the potential to incriminate Edith Swan as well as exonerate Rose Gooding.

Ruth Russell had sent her daughter Gertrude up to Groombridge School to collect some wages owed to her. On the way, Gertrude saw Edith Swan post a letter at the Beach post office. When he heard this news, Bill went straight out to fetch Smith. Together they went round to the sorting office. The staff allowed Smith to look through the mail, and he found a letter addressed to Constable Russell's wife in the hospital. Smith was able to get a hold placed on the letter so it was not forwarded until the next day.[21] He was desperate to see the letter and managed to intercept Alfred Russell on his way to the hospital to collect it. The envelope must have borne the distinctive features of the abusive letters, as the hospital had alerted Russell's superior officer, Henry Thomas, who told Russell to go and retrieve it. In the street Smith asked Russell if he had picked up the letter yet. Russell said no and pressed on. He took the letter back to the police station and opened it in Thomas's presence.[22]

Later in the day, Smith saw Russell in Beach Road and called him into his office. Russell claimed that the exchange unfolded this way:

He said, 'Will you let me have that letter'
    I said, 'No.'
He said, 'Mrs. Gooding, you know, is away. She went to Lewes last Friday. I saw her off by train last Friday morning.[23] How could she write that letter?'
    I said, 'Quite an easy matter for her to write the letter. It does not matter Mr. Smith. It ought to have been tried before. This is the second event.' What I meant was they ought to have got Mrs. Gooding away during the period of the first letters.
    I said 'Look here Mr. Smith. This case won't do you any good. There is nothing to be got out of them. We know very well that the woman is not away.'
    'Well' he said, 'It's like this. I went to Gooding and I said to him "The best thing you can do is to get her away to Lewes for a week". Gooding said, "Why should I send my wife away from them" (meaning the Swans) I could not

persuade him to get his wife away, so I said, "Well, Get her upstairs. She must be ill for a week."' I was at the office for about 2 hours and I gathered from his demeanour that Mrs. Gooding was not away.[24]

What made Russell so certain that Rose Gooding was still in Littlehampton? Somehow Edith Swan's solicitor Arthur Shelley learned of Smith's trick only two days after Rose took the train to Lewes. Shelley informed Russell, apparently in his capacity as one of Shelley's clients rather than in his capacity as a police constable. Russell told Swan that evening. Edith insisted that she had seen Rose that morning, crossing the yard to the lavatory. Russell encouraged her to keep a record of every sighting of Rose Gooding. It was not only Edith who claimed to have seen Rose: so did Edith's mother, whose honesty no one seems to have questioned. 'I saw her on one day when she was supposed to be away, coming from the drying ground. That was a Friday... I cannot say the date... I was sitting near the window and she passed with some clothes in her hand.'[25] (When this story was put to Rose's sister she denied it emphatically.)[26] Constable Russell was persuaded that Rose Gooding had not gone to Lewes—or that she had not stayed there more than a few days. He believed the Swans and took their side, as Reuben Lynn did. The Gooding camp was smaller, but from the middle of January it was strengthened by the addition of Maurice Blackman.

Blackman was a former police sergeant who retired in 1913, shortly after moving to Littlehampton.[27] Then, a month after Britain declared war on Germany, he re-joined the West Sussex police as a special constable. He now worked for the council as a beach inspector.[28] When Smith put Bill Gooding in touch with Blackman, Bill was keeping watch on the Norfolk Road post office. Blackman took over surveillance of the post office and Bill kept observation on the pillar box on South Terrace. He did this for several hours each day after knocking off at the shipyard, until the last mail collection.[29] 'The idea', Blackman explained to Nicholls, 'was to see whether the Swans, or a daughter of Mr Spicer, of Western Road, was posting the letters'.[30] The Spicers, a hackney carriage driver and his wife, had five daughters aged between ten and fourteen.[31] One of the Spicer girls 'was said to have been frequently over at Swan's house, and to have been called there by Miss Swan'.[32] The youngest Spicer, Marjorie, apparently knew Gertrude Russell.[33]

Blackman and Bill Gooding did not make any discoveries in the time they staked out the post office and the pillar box. As that threatening note boasted, there were more ways of delivering a letter than though the post. According to Swan, the libels that precipitated the second prosecution were thrown down at her back door and into her kitchen. Edith retold the story for George Nicholls four months later. 'Nothing more occurred with regard to me until the 10th Feb. 1921 when my father and mother and two brothers were having dinner with me and I heard the children go out to school. Miss Russell's boy . . . ran back as far as our back door and shouted out:—"Oh Dorrie, look where you have throwed it," Dorothy said "Never mind leave it where it is and come on." I afterwards went to the back door and there picked up a folded paper which I opened and found was two notes, one addressed to "Bloody old whore Miss Swan" the other was addressed to "Bloody buggering old Russell." I took Mr Russell's note into him and the same day I took mine into Mr. Shelley.'[34]

Two days later, on a Saturday morning, Edith watched Rose Gooding farewell Bill as he left for work. 'Mrs Gooding came out with her husband said goodbye and kissed him, waved her hand to him up the road, and as she went back into her house she deliberately threw a piece of paper in my back kitchen, she was dressed in a white jumper and a grey skirt. The note fell at my feet, I picked up the note which read: —"We have as much right in the garden as you you bloody old cow, carrying on with old Russell while his wife is away in the hospital, Sergt. Goodwin is on the look out for you." I posted that to Mr. Shelley the same day with a letter and on the Monday I went to the Bench with Mr. Shelley and applied for the warrant.'[35] Inspector Thomas arrested Rose Gooding on the Tuesday and at a special sitting later that day the magistrates committed her for trial at the March assizes in Lewes.[36] She was refused bail.[37]

Bill Gooding could no longer afford Wannop's fees, and the solicitor told him he was dropping the case. Again, a sympathetic working man with savings stepped in to help. Maurice Blackman 'told Mr. Gooding that I would guarantee him a Counsel up to £50 which he could re-pay me when he was able to do so'. He was content to trust Bill and did not put the agreement in writing. Blackman said he knew Rose Gooding only by sight and 'knew nothing against the Swans'. 'I have no interests in any of the parties and did what I did as it seemed to me that Mrs. Gooding was innocent.' The solicitors agreed to brief

Rowland Harker, but at the last minute Harker sent word that he could not attend the hearing. They managed to retain Eustace Fulton, an experienced but still rising barrister active at the Old Bailey and on the south-eastern circuit.[38]

This time the presiding judge was Horace Avory, who had been a legendary criminal advocate before he took his seat on the bench and was an altogether more formidable presence than Mr Justice Roche.[39] Admittedly, he was not physically imposing. When the young Patrick Hastings first met him, he found Avory 'small, almost insignificant in appearance': 'but he had a personality which could look infinitely forbidding'. Hastings survived an uncomfortable job interview and became Avory's understudy.[40] A future Attorney General, Hastings was one of several notable barristers who got their big break working for Avory. They and others who crossed his path all had Avory stories to tell. These accounts match genuine awe with backhanded compliments.[41] The most sparkling (and devastating) portrait comes, surprisingly, from the memoirs of Sir Chartres Biron, who is now remembered, if he is remembered at all, as the judge who condemned Radclyffe Hall's novel *The Well of Loneliness* as an obscene publication.[42] Avory, wrote Biron, 'liked law for itself, and the more repellent the matter the greater his enthusiasm. Such a question as whether a sewer was a drain would give him a pleasure almost sensual in its intensity.... Nor was he a man of any distracting interests; after he left Cambridge I do not believe he ever read anything but law, and not too much of that.... He had a mind like a circular saw: through the intervening matter, however tough or repellent, it drove straight to the point.'[43]

There was only a light calendar of six cases at the winter assizes.[44] Among the other defendants to be tried were a man accused of wounding his wife with intent to murder and two labourers indicted for trespassing 'with a gun and bludgeon for the purpose of taking game'. There was an alleged bigamist represented by Rose Gooding's former counsel, John Flowers. A woman charged with murdering her infant daughter had been brought up with Rose from Portsmouth, accompanied by the prison's medical officer, James MacGregor, who would testify that she heard voices and was not fit to stand trial. Rose Gooding's was the first case the court heard that morning after the church service that traditionally marked the beginning of the Lewes assizes. Avory joined the mayor and other civic officials in St Michael's

Church before walking two hundred yards down High Street to the County Hall.[45]

That morning was the first time women had been called for jury duty at the Lewes assizes. One woman and eleven men were empaneled to hear Rose Gooding's case. Thomas Gates, Edith Swan's barrister, prefaced his opening speech by saying 'that several of the letters in the case were of an obscene nature, and he wondered if his Lordship would like to make an intimation to the lady present'.[46] Under the Sex Disqualification (Removal) Act, which made women liable for jury duty, a judge had the discretion to exempt a woman 'from service on a jury in respect of any case by reason of the nature of the evidence to be given or of the issues to be tried'.[47] Avory would exercise this discretion in a gruesome murder case several years later.[48] That morning in Lewes, he said that it would not be necessary to read the letters aloud in court, but the jury would have to see them. 'If the lady on the jury objected he would entertain the objection.' She replied that she would rather not hear the case, but would remain if it was her duty. Avory said that reading the letters was 'one of the unpleasant duties which must fall upon women if they are called to serve upon juries'.[49]

Gates invited Edith Swan to run through the story of the NSPCC complaint and the abusive letters that ensued. The barrister passed a bundle of letters to the judge. Avory kept them for the jury, and spectators in the gallery learned nothing of their specific contents. Under cross-examination, however, Edith revealed that one of the letters had read: 'I hope you get all the bad luck you deserve in the New Year for getting me sent to prison.' Edith testified that on 12 February Gooding ran past the Swans' back door 'and threw one of the notes into the kitchen. Another note was picked up near the back gate of witness's house.' Gates added that other letters had been stopped in the post. Reuben Lynn returned to the witness box, testifying that he, like Swan, had received a note cursing him for his part in sending the anonymous writer to prison. Lynn was the only other libel recipient to appear in court, even though the photographer Charles Haslett and Kate Leggett from the Western Road dairy, both of whom testified at the first trial, had received fresh abuse in January of 1921.[50] The first prosecution was some time in the making and drew in the wider community of Beach Town; the second prosecution moved quickly and focused intensely on Swan herself.

Defending Gooding, Eustace Fulton made much more of the question of handwriting than Flowers had at the first trial. Fulton handed Swan several documents and asked if they were in her handwriting. These items were not libels, but their handwriting must have borne some resemblance to that of the libels. Swan denied that she had written these documents, and while Gooding testified that Swan had handed them to her she conceded that she did not see Swan actually write them.[51] Recalling this moment in her petition to the Home Secretary later in the year, Gooding stated: 'Miss Swan disowned her handwriting in the year 1919 Christmas she gave me pattern of sock and a recipe for marrow chutney which in Court said was not hers but disguised writing by myself which she knew to be false.'[52] Fulton attempted to turn the tables on the prosecutrix (as she was often called) in the witness box. He handed her a pencil and asked her to write out the text of the note that was the basis for the warrant ('carrying on with old Russell'). This paper took its place alongside the other exhibits.[53]

Fulton sought to disrupt assumptions that Swan was the only woman of good character. He induced Inspector Thomas to concede that aside from 'the present and previous charges, prisoner was quite a respectable person'.[54] While Bill Gooding was in the witness box, Fulton let him wander from the subject at hand to paint his wife in a sympathetic light. Bill told the story of the time Rose accompanied him on a pleasure cruise on the barge *Edith and Hilda* years beforehand (on their first wedding anniversary). They were shipwrecked. Rose suffered badly from exposure—this was in the middle of winter—and she was traumatized by the experience.[55]

Fulton also called witnesses to show that Rose had been out of Littlehampton while the libels continued to circulate. Here the defence ran into trouble. Some of the witnesses they enlisted, such as the postman, were vague about the dates. In one instance, the effort to prove that Rose had been in Lewes backfired. A lodger in Rose's mother's house, Fred Hawkins—the 'hawlkins' of Rose's letter—prepared a document for the neighbours to sign, attesting to Rose's presence there between the sixth and the twentieth of January.[56] Winifred and William Upton signed it even though they remembered seeing her only on the fifteenth and sixteenth. When they realized their mistake, they felt they were being tricked into perjuring themselves. They 'sent for Mrs Russell and told her they could have nothing to do with the case'.[57]

The morning of the trial, Bill Gooding visited Mr Upton at his job at the Lewes gas works and appealed to him to testify:

I said 'No as I have only just started work'.

He said, 'Well if it is the money I will pay you for your days work' and he gave me 6d to get a shave. He said 'it's too late to subpoena you to attend otherwise I would.'

I said 'The reason I don't want to come Bill is because Mrs. Russell told my wife to swear that she saw Rose Gooding on the 7th January, 1921.'

He said 'Take no notice of the old lady at all but come to Court and keep to those two dates—the 15th and the 16th January.'[58]

Bill was unable to persuade Upton. The defence mustered five witnesses to speak to Rose's whereabouts in January: Bill, his sister-in-law, his mother-in-law, her lodger, and the postman.

The deficiencies in the evidence for the alibi could well have lost the case for the defence. Sir Archibald Bodkin commented after reviewing the trial notes that juries commonly 'decide the guilt or innocence of the accused... according to their view of whether... an alibi is satisfactorily proved or not. Logically it is not proper to do so, but that it happens is within the experience of everyone' who was involved in criminal cases.[59] It may also have been risky to run the alibi alongside another defensive strategy, the insinuation that Swan wrote the libels herself. A contemporary legal textbook warned that running incommensurate defences in tandem undermined the prisoner's credibility: 'Jurymen are very apt to think that it shows a want of confidence in each branch.'[60] As a more recent authority notes, 'Alibi has been described, not without justification, as an "eggs in one basket" defence. A defendant pleading alibi cannot launch a vigorous attack on the commission of the offence itself, for fear of exciting suspicion in the minds of the jurors as to why he concerns himself with this aspect of the case if he has the support of the brute geographical fact of alibi.'[61]

In his summing up, Avory declared that he 'did not think much' of Rose Gooding's alibi.[62] The jurors did not accept the alibi, and Fulton's dictation exercise did not do enough to shift suspicion away from Rose to Edith Swan. Yet the jurors evidently began their deliberations with doubts about whether the prosecution had met the burden of proof. The jury returned to the courtroom eight minutes after withdrawing to ask for a sample of Gooding's handwriting. Avory told them they could not see one at this stage.[63] The jurors conferred further and returned their verdict of guilty. Before sentencing Rose Gooding, Avory heard further testimony about her character. Frederick Peel, the police superintendent at Arundel, said that 'previous to the conviction in December last prisoner bore a good character'. The sentence for the first conviction, he added, had been a light one.[64] Avory then passed sentence. He had a history of imposing severe sentences in criminal libel cases.[65] According to the *Sussex Daily News*, 'his Lordship remarked that the extremely lenient course adopted towards her in December was evidently misplaced. He was satisfied that she had been convicted rightly, and she must be prevented for some time from repeating that abominable system of persecution of Miss Swan. The sentence was that she be imprisoned with hard labour for 12 months.'[66]

Rose was taken back to Portsmouth prison. Bill was able to visit her a week later, and once again at the end of March. After that she did not have a visitor until June.[67] Bill Gooding owed £30 to Blackman and the household had lost a wage-earner. With Rose away, her sister slipped back out of paid work to look after the house and the children.[68] Meanwhile, the family and their supporters tried to get Rose released. One legal avenue remained open to her: the Court of Criminal Appeal.

This court, which sat in London, had been in place since 1907. For much of the nineteenth century, advocates of criminal law reform had pressed for the establishment of a court that could review sentencing and order retrials on points of law, or if new evidence came to light. The judiciary and much of the legal profession fiercely resisted these proposals. Opponents argued that the volume of appeals would overwhelm the judicial system; the costs to the state would be excessive, since most prisoners would not have the money to pay their own legal bills; granting rights of appeal would weaken the deterrent value of swift and final justice; and surely the system worked fairly most of the time. After a spectacular miscarriage of justice in the early twentieth century, this position became politically untenable, and the Court of Criminal Appeal was established. Judicial opposition did not dissolve, however: the judges who now sat on the Court of Criminal Appeal took a very narrow view of its role. They scrutinized disparities in sentencing but seldom overturned convictions. Judges' continuing aversion to questioning jury verdicts largely thwarted the legislature's purpose in setting up the court.[69]

When Smith consulted Fulton about the prospect of an appeal, the barrister considered it at some length and eventually decided that there were insufficient grounds.[70] Rose applied to the Court of Criminal Appeal anyway, without legal representation. The court's response followed the familiar course of deference to jury verdicts. The registrar, Sir Leonard Kershaw, made some preliminary judgments, which he set out in his briefing for the court. He recommended letting the conviction stand.[71] This conclusion did not flow from the body of the report, which spelled out his doubts: 'It seemed to me a case for the Jury though, as I pointed out in my confidential report to the Court, though it was suggested that the writer of the letters and postcards, &c., had taken care to disguise the handwriting the subject matter in the body of at least five of the letters or cards was such as to cast suspicion on nobody except the appellant.' Kershaw passed the file on to a single judge, who refused Rose Gooding leave to appeal on 5 April. She asked for a full bench of the court to reconsider, 'and the application was finally dismissed by the Chief Justice, Darling and Salter J.J. on the 18th of April'. The hearing was over quickly: Rose was not present and no one appeared on her behalf. 'The appellant was not represented by counsel at the hearing of the appeal but applied for legal aid, which was in the ordinary course refused with the other applications', Kershaw wrote.[72]

The Goodings did not give up. Rose protested her innocence to the prison governor, Ernest Hall, and repeated her story to him many times. Hall felt that something was amiss with her conviction. He was also personally sympathetic, 'as my relatives at Lewes know her family quite well'.[73] Bill Gooding wrote periodically to the Home Secretary, beseeching him to reopen the case and offering 'fresh information concerning these Swans who prosicuted the wife and this man Reuben Lynn'. It was not unreasonable to think that Edith Swan wrote obscene letters to herself: 'I have been told that the youngest Swan boy used to write letters to him self and tear his clothes up and knock his self about and say other people was doing it.' Bill also questioned Lynn's credibility: 'A sargent who was in the police'—Blackman, undoubtedly—had informed him that Lynn had failed to 'pay his Rates & Taxes they used to take him to prison every time they was due'.[74] 'Gooding did his utmost to get his wife out of prison', Sir Ernley Blackwell remarked.[75] But the campaign to free Rose made little headway until a battered notebook was 'found in Selbourne Road'.

5

A Case of Handwriting

Two months after the notebook filled with obscene writings about Edith Swan was purportedly found on a Littlehampton street, George Nicholls arrived in the town to begin investigating the libels in earnest.

The detective's first stay in Littlehampton lasted a week. Arriving there on a Friday afternoon in June 1921, he met with Inspector Thomas to discuss the case. After getting all the information he needed from him, Nicholls telephoned Thomas's commanding officer in Horsham to request the assistance of a policeman 'who had had nothing to do with either of the cases against Mrs. Gooding'.[1] The chief constable of West Sussex sent a promising twenty-six-year-old constable from Midhurst on the South Downs. Leonard Lewis had worked alongside his father as a butcher until he was old enough to join the police.[2] Lewis made the journey to Littlehampton, some twenty-two miles, in time to help Nicholls as he began his inquiries on the Saturday morning.[3]

Between then and the following Sunday, Nicholls and Lewis spoke to a great many people connected to the case. The testimony they elicited is the basis of the story pieced together in the preceding chapters. Nicholls took detailed statements from twenty-nine people: family members, neighbours, recipients of abusive postcards—every relevant witness other than Rose Gooding herself. Nicholls interviewed Edith Swan, Bill Gooding, Ruth Russell, and two of the children living at 45 Western Road more than once, returning to confront them with allegations others had made. He also spoke to others without taking statements. Richard Sharpe, Ruth Russell's sometime employer, talked to Nicholls about his association with the family and his efforts to mediate with Edith Swan's solicitor. Even though Sharpe had never officially represented Rose Gooding, it is not surprising that the lawyer did not make a formal statement to the police. William Smith, Rose's solicitor's clerk, gave a statement to Nicholls but no barrister or solicitor went on the record.

Most of the interviews took place at houses and shops along Western Road and South Terrace. For a few, Nicholls went further afield, speaking to the photographer Charles Haslett in London, where he was then living, and calling on Alfred and Edith Russell in Worthing, where they had moved upon Alfred's retirement from the police the previous month. Nicholls also went on the road to resolve the question of whether Rose Gooding had or had not been at home in January 1921.

'I proceeded with P.C. Lewis to Lewes on the 24th. June', Nicholls reported, 'and took statements from Fred Hawkins, a lodger in Mrs Gooding's mother's (Mrs Russell) house, from a Mrs Alice Newnham who lives opposite, from William James Upton and his wife Winifred (relatives of Mrs Russell), Charles Parsons, a postman, and Charles Christopher Weller. I also took a statement from Mrs Gooding's mother.... From the point of view of speaking of particular dates not one of these persons is reliable.' Weller did not know which day he had seen Rose Gooding, despite the fact that he had signed the letter Hawkins prepared for the second trial, vouching that he had seen her 'from the 6th. to the 20th. January'. As Bill Gooding found out the morning of the second trial, the Uptons took against Barbara Russell after they realized that they should not have signed the blanket statement about Rose's alibi. When they spoke to Nicholls the Uptons 'accuse[d] Mrs Russell of asking them to alter the date and to swear to something that was not correct'. Nicholls believed that they had misjudged the situation, and that Mrs Russell, or Hawkins, had made an honest mistake. Though Hawkins had shouldered the responsibility of documenting Rose's presence in Lewes, his memory proved erratic. As Nicholls wrote, 'Mr Hawkins starts his statement by saying that he received a letter from Mrs Russell saying that she was coming home to Lewes with her daughter. That is obviously incorrect in the light of events as they happened. Mrs Russell and Mrs Gooding had only a couple of hours notice that they had to leave Littlehampton for Lewes and could not have written.'[4]

Nevertheless, Nicholls thought that Hawkins 'did see Mrs Gooding about the house at Lewes for a fortnight'. The detective also believed Mrs Newnham: 'She cannot fix the dates but says Mrs Gooding was at

Lewes at least a fortnight and she seems a sensible honest woman.' Nicholls acknowledged in his understated way that Constable Russell's statement 'threw some doubt on the veracity of Mr Smith, Messrs. Wannop's clerk, and suggests that Mrs Gooding[was not sent away', but Nicholls was satisfied that Rose had indeed stayed away from Littlehampton for two weeks. It had to be admitted, though, that there had been 'a good deal of bungling over getting the evidence to prove that Mrs Gooding was at Lewes'.[5]

If Rose Gooding was not responsible for the libels, who was? Various candidates had been put forward. Nicholls set no store in the theory that the abusive letters and postcards were the work of Dorothy Gooding or her younger cousin, Gertrude Russell, and he does not appear to have checked out Maurice Blackman's theory that the youngest Spicer child was involved. Reuben Lynn was another possibility. The Goodings suggested that Lynn was not merely an ally of the Swans and that his handwriting bore a resemblance to the script in the libels.[6] Nicholls discounted Lynn as a suspect, though not before vetting him. The detective contacted Lynn's employers to inquire about his character. Lynn had worked 'on and off for years for Messrs. Snewin', like several members of the Swan family. Snewin's verdict on Lynn was that 'although he is lazy they do not think there is any vice about him'. After spending time in his presence, Nicholls concluded that Lynn's eyesight was too weak to see much at a distance. It was unlikely that he could have made out the name 'Swan' on the card he claimed under oath to have seen Dorothy Gooding posting. What convinced Nicholls that Lynn could not have written the libels were 'the great efforts which he had to make to do some writing in my presence'.[7]

That left Edith Swan, her father, and Ruth Russell as possible authors of the libels. Edith Swan was under suspicion before Nicholls was even dispatched to Littlehampton, whereas the other two names on this list scarcely registered with Sir Ernley Blackwell and Sir Archibald Bodkin when they reopened the case. In his long report detailing the investigation, Nicholls never explained his attention to Mr Swan. Presumably Nicholls's suspicions had something to do with his diligence in recording the older man's various outbursts about Rose's morals. Nicholls did elaborate on his reasons for suspecting Ruth Russell. He called her 'untruthful' on account of the way she 'denie[d] persistently that at Easter, 1920, there was quarrelling going on in the house'. 'That Miss

Russell is immoral goes without saying', Nicholls declared, going down
the same path as the West Sussex police, for whom having an illegitimate
child indicated the likelihood of other transgressions. He added: 'I had
it from Mrs Sharpe (the Solicitors wife) that although she makes no
allegations she got rid of Miss Russell because she (Mrs Sharpe) was
missing things.' Nicholls 'should have felt impelled to say that Miss
Russell . . . was the most likely person doing these writings' were it not
for the other evidence he uncovered—evidence to do with writing.[8]

Police work required a command of literacy unusual among occu-
pations filled predominantly by working-class men.[9] Aspiring West
Sussex constables had to show that they knew how to address a duke,
marquess, or bishop in a letter, and what i.e., e.g., p.m., OBE, MA, and
PC stood for.[10] All police officers had to report in writing to their
superiors and compose statements to deliver when giving evidence in
court. They had to learn shorthand and deal with card indexes.[11]
Detectives also had to take notes in interviews, manage case files, and
write and edit longer narratives of events and analyses of evidence.[12]
Nicholls's reports in the Littlehampton investigation were confident
performances, mixing the formal with the colloquial. They contrast
sharply with the halting syntax and spelling errors in the communications of the uniformed West Sussex police. Investigating a case where
the crime was libel made special demands on an officer's command
of language: the evidence itself, not just the final report, called for a
mistrustful sensitivity to words.

Nicholls took handwriting samples 'from all the persons likely to
have had anything to do with the writing of these indecent letters and
postcards'. Nicholls, Constable Lewis, and Inspector Thomas also
retrieved the wartime National Registration forms completed by the
Swans, the Goodings, and the rest, to obtain more neutral specimens of
their handwriting.[13] Nicholls was unable to match the handwriting of
the libels to any of the samples he collected. However, the writing
exercises that he made his interviewees complete did turn up a point
of what might be called orthographic evidence, and it reinforced his
suspicions about Ruth Russell. 'She makes the mis-spellings of "business" and "their" appearing in the indecent letters and postcards and
neither Miss Swan nor Mr Swan upon whom strong suspicion also
rests makes those errors.'[14]

The decisive evidence pointed in another direction, however.
Nicholls and Lewis retrieved it when they searched the cottages in

Western Road. It was the first time such a search had been made—a reflection of the fact that both Rose Gooding's trials were the results of private prosecutions, not public prosecutions emerging from police work. The Goodings' house was first. On the morning of Saturday 18 June Nicholls sent for Bill Gooding at work. Gooding came to Littlehampton police station and Nicholls and Lewis questioned him at length.[15] When the interview was over, Nicholls informed Gooding of his intention to search his house. Nicholls and Lewis accompanied Bill home. 'Mr Gooding invited me to go anywhere I wished in the house and offered me every facility.' Nicholls and Lewis searched all the drawers and looked through the correspondence kept in the house, but they found nothing incriminating. They did, however, take away a small piece of blotting paper.[16]

A blotter used to absorb the excess ink from a note made with a fountain pen could sometimes preserve a mirror image of the writing. Blotting paper was part of the stock in trade of the fictional detective. In 'The Adventure of the Missing Three-Quarter', Sherlock Holmes uses a blotter to conjure up the words of a telegram sent by the missing man he is tracking. Holmes realizes that the man has used a quill pen, and announces: 'I can hardly doubt that we will find some impression upon this blotting-pad. Ah, yes, surely this is the very thing!' Holmes tears off a strip of the blotting paper and shows Watson the 'hiero-glyphic' of words written backwards. 'Hold it to the glass!' cries the detective's client. 'That is unnecessary', replies Holmes. 'The paper is thin, and the reverse will give the message.'[17]

The blotting paper recovered from the Goodings' cottage yielded no such breakthrough. It was a different story at the Swans' house the following morning. The Swans do not appear to have expected their house to be searched, or did not think the house contained anything suspicious. Nicholls took a statement from Edith and then announced his intention to examine the writing table in the room. There were several pieces of blotting paper on the table, some of it bought from Frank Barnard, the newsagent and tobacconist on Norfolk Road.[18] The officers took it away to examine. Back at the station, Lewis was able to make out the word 'Local' in 'the same big handwriting as in the indecent letters and postcards'.[19] Nicholls therefore returned to the Swans' cottage the following morning to ask Edith for an explanation. 'She without the slightest hesitation said that Mrs Gooding had bor-rowed her blotting paper, pens ink and pencil, that her sister Miss

Russell had also borrowed them, that Dorothy Gooding always came for these things.' Noticing that Nicholls was examining the empty covers of a writing kit of the Britishers' Own brand ('Notepaper and Envelopes for Home and Foreign Correspondence'), Swan volunteered that she had also lent that to Rose Gooding.[20] She added that Bill Gooding had asked her for the covers of old writing pads for use cleaning windows. Edith said she had not lent the Goodings any blotting paper after June 1920 and nor had they returned any to her since then.[21]

Nicholls took his leave so that the Swans could have their tea. When he returned to their house in the evening, Edith was out but had left a letter for him. It read:

Sir,
I wish you to know that I read in the newspapers three or four weeks ago that there is now a scientific instrument by which anybody's handwriting can be found out, however much disguised I trust it will be used in this case. I am not ashamed for anyone to see my writing and I have nothing to fear.

Edith Emily Swan.

In Edith's absence, Nicholls asked her father if he could explain the writing found on the blotting paper. Mr Swan replied that the handwriting was not his, but conceded that it might have been his daughter's. Both Mr and Mrs Swan declared that the Goodings had borrowed blotting paper, pens, ink, and pencils. Mr Swan said that Rose Gooding had tossed a quantity of blotting paper through the open door of their house. 'I asked him whether he saw her do it and he said "No," "But it must have been her", and it was apparent that he was obsessed with the idea of Mrs Gooding being responsible for everything.' Edith's brother Ernest was at the house on this occasion, and he backed up the claim that Rose Gooding had borrowed blotting paper. Nicholls did not 'give much weight to their statements', knowing the Swans had discussed the matter among themselves. The detective followed up with the neighbours. 'Mr Gooding, Miss Russell, Dorothy Gooding and Gertrude Russell questioned separately on this point declare that no blotting paper, pens or ink were borrowed from the Swans but Dorothy Gooding admits borrowing a pencil. They all said that they had not seen the "Britishers Own" writing pad before.'[22]

There is more than a little comedy in Nicholls's solemn report on the comings and goings of pencils and paper, but the surprising amount of writing paraphernalia needed by the inhabitants of number 45 and number 47 Western Road points to profound social changes. The Swan children and Rose Gooding, her sister, and her husband all came of age at a time when practically every English child learned to read and write. (None of the Swans or Goodings appears to have had any more formal education than what elementary schools provided.) Working-class parents in the nineteenth century would try to teach their children at home and scrimp to send them to precarious private day schools. The efforts of working people themselves meant that literacy levels were rising even before extensive state and church school systems were in place and well before the Education Act of 1870 made elementary schooling virtually compulsory.[23] The Registrar General of Births, Deaths and Marriages published tables of literacy rates using data extrapolated from the marriage registers every bride and groom had to sign or mark. In the earliest tables, dating from the 1830s, 67 per cent of grooms and 51 per cent of brides in England and Wales were able to write their names. In successive decades, the percentage of signatures increased and the gap between men and women closed. By the beginning of the First World War nearly every person who married met the Registrar General's minimal criterion of literacy.[24]

Families, the church, and the state put children through school to prepare them for work in an advanced industrial nation. And, in some quarters, education was promoted as a necessary accompaniment of citizenship, in an age when the franchise was being extended to more and more working-class men and women's suffrage loomed over the horizon. Historians and social scientists have long recognized how important writing was to the emergence of the modern state, especially its routine functions.[25] Scholars such as Jane Caplan have pointed out how much a state's legitimacy inheres in quotidian transactions involving paper.[26] The historian Patrick Joyce rather wilfully puts the Post Office and everyday writing practices—rather than the franchise or free trade—at the centre of his interpretation of Victorian and early twentieth-century liberalism. The capillary extension of the postal system enabled workers to send letters and money orders to family back in another corner of the country, thus making labour more mobile; the mail knitted individuals together in a connected economy.[27]

The uses working-class people made of their literacy varied wildly. At one end of the spectrum were the autodidacts who devoured Carlyle and Dickens, John Stuart Mill, and treatises on engineering.[28]

At the other were people who read or wrote only when they had to, using their education in the utilitarian and joyless spirit with which many schools offered it. The diversity of people's engagement with the written word was captured well in the notes Florence Bell made as she surveyed the workers at her husband's iron foundry in Middlesbrough in the first decade of the twentieth century. Bell made impressionistic but often perceptive comments on the reading that went on in each household, bringing out the contrasts and tensions in couples or across generations:

1. Husband and wife cannot read. Youngest girl reads the paper to them sometimes, but 'she has a tiresome temper and will not always go on.'

2. Does not care very much for reading—'just the newspapers'.

3. Fond of reading.

4. Tries to teach himself German.

5. Husband reads newspapers only, particularly racing news. Wife spends much time in reading penny dreadfuls, illustrated papers which she considers 'thrilling, as they give such a good account of "high life and elopements."' Husband disapproves of his wife's tastes.

6. Wife very fond of reading, particularly children's books. Husband dislikes reading anything.

7. Likes reading the Parliamentary news, and doesn't approve of 'local nonsense'. Wife fond of reading stories of country life.

And so on.[29] Like other commentators on 'what the masses read' (there were many articles with titles like this in the late nineteenth and early twentieth centuries), Bell noted that working-class people tended to read only weekly papers, not dailies, which were more 'serious' in the main.[30] 'The Sunday papers are a very special feature in the literature of the working classes. They are provided in view of the fact that the Sunday is the principal day on which both men and women are likely to read. And they consist of special papers, such as *The Umpire*, *The People*, *Reynolds's Weekly*, *Lloyd's News*, *Weekly Despatch*, *News of the World*, *The Sunday Chronicle*. And it is interesting to note that, even in households where each penny is an important item of expenditure, 1d., 2d., 3d., and sometimes as much as 6d., is set apart for this delectable Sunday reading.'[31] The Swans conformed to this pattern. The boy who delivered newspapers on Sundays brought them copies of the *People*, *Lloyd's*, and the *News of the World*.[32] Mr Swan told Nicholls about news he had read in the Brighton *Argus*.[33] The note Edith left for Nicholls urbanely referred to reading about the handwriting device 'in the newspapers', plural.

If the Goodings read newspapers at all, they bought them over the counter from a newsagent. To many people, 'books' meant fiction magazines or paperbacked 'novels' and 'novelettes' that were seldom reprinted in hardcover or found in libraries.[34] Newsagents sold this fiction, and so did corner shops, tobacconists, and confectioners, all of which sometimes lent out books as a side-line.[35] 'In suburban side-streets and even village shops', wrote a disapproving observer, 'it is common to find a stock of worn and greasy novels let out at 2d. or 3d. a volume'.[36] Where 'proper' booksellers insisted that books were not simply a commodity and that they were not mere shopkeepers, in working-class neighbourhoods they were part of the run of everyday commerce.[37]

Contemporary critics often expressed disappointment (or told-you-so satisfaction) with what they saw as the underwhelming results of popular literacy.[38] Sympathetic reformers and unsympathetic conservatives alike thought that a crabbed elementary schooling left working-class people with little sense of ownership of the written word and its resources. Yet the Goodings and Russells held onto letters they had received; the Swans kept an exercise book that their youngest son had filled with religious lyrics copied from the Salvation Army periodical *All the World*; and both families routinely committed information and sentiment to writing.[39] The blotting paper that Nicholls took away from the Swans' house preserved the residue of a number of personal letters. There is the address of a relative living in Berkshire and part of a sentence about not hearing from an aunt since Christmas and supposing she had not received their letters. The blotter shows the beginnings of a letter to Edith's fiancé, only his name, unit, and service number legible above the crisscrossed smudges in the centre of the paper.[40] Nicholls was able to make out further fragments, nearly all in Edith's hand: 'heard from', 'Edie', 'God bless you', 'some tea', 'as obstinate as', 'A line soon', 'Yours affectionately', and 'He sent me some cards two lovely handkerchiefs'.[41] The fact that these phrases are so mundane only makes them more poignant: the feelings could have been as commonplace as the words standing in for them, or they could have been beyond Edith's power to express with due precision and distinctiveness.

Writing was both a vehicle for individuality and an engine of conformity. This was the case not just with the words people put together, but also with the marks they made on paper. By admitting the testimony of handwriting experts, British courts accepted that handwriting was personal and could identify the person behind it. The idea of handwriting as powerfully individual had some purchase in popular culture, as the newspaper story about that 'scientific instrument' attested. Yet writing was also a standardized means of communication: generations of English school children were drilled in the proper execution of Looped Cursive, a hand developed to improve the legibility of civil service documents.[42] The paradoxical qualities of handwriting were at work in the investigation of the Littlehampton libels: Nicholls was able to match marks on the blotting paper with words in the libellous letters and cards, but the hand was also wholly conventional.

The tell-tale marks on the blotting paper were fragments of addresses, such as the word 'Local' that Constable Lewis noticed on both the blotter and the libels. Nicholls identified the mirror image of another part of the blotting paper several days after searching the Swans' cottage. He took a statement from William Smith, and at their meeting the solicitor's clerk handed him several documents that he had gathered in the course of preparing Rose Gooding's defence. They included a letter addressed to the photographer Haslett—'12, Western Road, Local'—and postmarked 1 January 1921. When he compared the envelope with one of the pieces of blotting paper taken from the Swans' house, Nicholls found that it 'corresponded exactly with the name Haslett and address'. The same scrap of blotting paper matched the 'Miss' and the street number on the envelope of a letter posted to Edith Swan the same day as the other letter was sent to Haslett. That letter to Swan became Exhibit 1 in Rose Gooding's second trial (Figure 5.1).[43] It was written six months after the Goodings last borrowed any blotting paper from the Swans.[44]

Another sheet of blotting paper was even more incriminating. Methodically comparing the markings on it with the exhibits from the two trials, Nicholls was able to identify matches with three different documents adduced as evidence in Rose Gooding's first trial; with two of the exhibits, there was more than one match (Figure 5.2). Nicholls did the painstaking work of comparing the blotting paper with the letters

Figure 5.1. A piece of blotting paper found in the Swans' house in June 1921. MEPO 3/380, National Archives

and envelopes before a police photographer had made the copies reproduced here, which are marked up in Nicholls's handwriting. When he made the initial identifications, Nicholls had to hold all the details in his head.

Nicholls visited the Swans once more and 'put it to Miss Swan and Mr Swan again as to whether they had anything further to say about the blotting paper and showing them the Haslett letter of 1st. Jan. and they said they had not'. Edith referred Nicholls to the note she had left for him, about the device capable of penetrating disguised handwriting. She declared again that she had 'nothing to fear'. Nicholls reported that 'Old Mr Swan became excited and said that I had had a very good innings in his house and he went on to declare that he had given the Goodings all sorts of things, vegetables etc. and he was now giving them to other people'.[45]

By this point Nicholls doubted anything Edith Swan said. He told his superiors in the Metropolitan Police: 'It will be found that Miss Swan's statement is very remarkable in detail and I am forced to think that she could not have possibly heard all she says she has', notwithstanding the way the layout of the Swans' and Goodings' houses facilitated eavesdropping. If Edith really heard everything she claimed to have, then she had an 'extraordinary memory', Nicholls observed

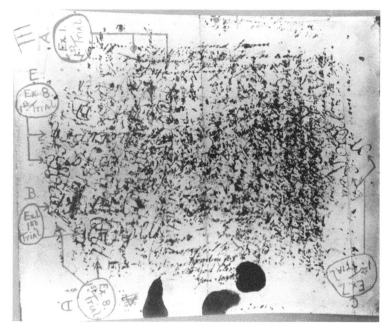

Figure 5.2. A second sheet of blotting paper from the Swans' house. MEPO 3/380, National Archives

sceptically.[46] Edith had an explanation for one conversation she claimed to recall verbatim five months later: 'I made notes of all this at the time and I copied these notes out and took them to the trial at Lewes. I destroyed the original notes a few days ago.' The conversation in question took place on Friday 21 January 1921. According to Edith, Rose was writing an offensive note to PC Russell with help from family members:

Mrs Gooding, Mrs. Russell [Rose and Ruth's mother] and Miss Ruth Russell were all in the kitchen with the door open and the gramophone going, it stopped and I overheard Mrs Gooding say:—'There is an old buggar named Russell who ought to be living in hell'; and it went on 'The shit from his closet.' I heard Miss Russell saying to Mrs Gooding:—'You musn't put dirt, you must put shit.' After that Mrs Gooding said to her mother and sister:— 'One day in the town I saw Mr Russell outside Cocksedges, the Bakers, talking to a girl, Bill was with me and I said to him "What do you think of that ... he will bloody soon be up her."'

Edith said she was in the lavatory the next morning when she over-heard Rose telling one of the children to post the note in the town and make sure Constable Russell did not see her. Edith also claimed to have heard the child return half an hour later and tell Rose that she had not needed to go into the town to mail the card because 'nobody was watching' the nearby pillar box on South Terrace.[47] Nicholls must have put these stories to Rose and Ruth's mother, who denied it: 'The day after I came the children put the gramophone on. I did not hear my daughters talking about Mr. Russell—the policeman—except that they said that Mr. Russell had come to the back door on Christmas day to complain of the drains being stopped up. Neither Rose nor Ruth used filthy language. I did not hear Mrs. Gooding tell Gertrude Russell to take a letter up to the town to post, and not to let old Russell see it.'[48]

Nicholls was blunt about the mischief-making note sent to Edith's fiancé in Iraq. That letter, Nicholls remarked, was 'a concoction that I should expect from Miss Swan herself'. In relation to the incident where the children were supposed to have thrown two folded-up notes in front of the Swans' door, an allegation that Dorothy Gooding and Gertrude Russell denied, Nicholls decided that 'the children are as much to be believed as Miss Swan'. The detective also found 'great similarities' between two of the libels submitted at the second trial and Swan's initial letter of complaint to the National Society for the Prevention of Cruelty to Children.[49]

Yet Nicholls held back from recommending that Swan be charged with any offence. He said that his inquiries had not 'resulted in fixing definitely who the author of the obscene writing is'. (As a subsequent Home Office document put it, Nicholls's investigation 'showed...that Miss Swan was probably the guilty party, but the enquiry was far too stale for a complete case to be then made against Miss Swan'.)[50] However, Nicholls ventured, his investigation had at least 'helped to clear Mrs Gooding'. Nothing in Gooding's handwriting connected her with the libels. It was, Nicholls added, 'perhaps a little point in her favour' that in three of the exhibits from the second trial the writer spelled 'prison' correctly. Rose Gooding always spelled it 'prision' in the letters she wrote her husband from Portsmouth (Nicholls had read a packet of twenty-seven letters Rose had sent to Bill).[51] Once more, spelling provided clues about an individual's guilt or innocence.

For Nicholls, the writing itself was the crux of the case. In contrast, the West Sussex police and the prosecuting lawyers had concerned themselves largely with judgements about character and circumstances. The Director of Public Prosecutions concluded as much after reading Nicholls's report and the shorthand notes of the trials.[52] Tall, lean, and driven, Bodkin was notorious for not delegating work (the legend that 'one Christmas evening he was seen leaving his chambers with a bundle of papers', his biographer remarks, 'is probably true'), and he gave Rose Gooding's case his close attention.[53] In his brief to counsel, evidently dictated to a secretary and marked by the repetitive rhythms of someone thinking out loud, Bodkin spelled out the syllogism that had deprived Rose Gooding of her liberty:

The case seems to have proceeded upon the inferences which ought to be drawn from certain things happening in the little group of houses occupied by the Swans and the Goodings, and that as in the libels references are also made to those occurrences a kind of circumstantial case was built up, the inference ... from which was that the person who might have heard, or might have known of those occurrences, was the person who incorporated references to them in the libels, and therefore that as Mrs Gooding was a person who had an opportunity of knowing of these occurrences, she was the person who wrote the libels.[54]

This circumstantial case had comparatively little use for analysis of the physical evidence—or even the recovery of all of it. A senior officer at Scotland Yard scribbled on the file containing Nicholls's report: 'It is somewhat striking that it should have been left to us, at this stage, to discover the blotting paper, by far the most important piece of evidence.'[55] Bodkin was staggered to find that Mr Justice Roche had not directed the jury 'to compare the proved or admitted handwriting of Mrs Gooding with the handwriting of the libels'.[56] Bodkin was if anything more scathing about Avory, with whom he had a long though not close history: Bodkin had been one of Avory's three serious rivals at the criminal bar.[57] Using lawyerly phrasing that always sounds comically insincere to non-lawyers, Bodkin wrote of Avory's conduct: 'with the deepest respect for the learned Judge, it is again difficult to discover whether the real issue in the case which was, did Mrs Gooding write and publish these libels, was ever put to the jury or their attention invited to Mrs Gooding's handwriting and the writing of the libels'. It was, Bodkin said, 'astonishing that the jury should leave the box at 4.32, come back at 4.40 and ask to see the prisoner's writing, and the learned Judge told them they could not get that now'.[58]

Bodkin went as far as to pronounce that this was 'a case which, from its commencement to the end of it, was a case of handwriting'. When Nicholls collected samples of handwriting from those connected with the case, he did so at Bodkin's instruction. Bodkin was satisfied that the handwriting in the books that came to light in April 1921 was identical to that in nearly all of the libels for which Rose Gooding had been convicted. It was a quite orthodox kind of script: 'They are in a round, bold and well formed writing such as, if Counsel's memory serves him, he used to find at the top of school copy books with nicely looped Y's, G's and H's, well formed, and to the Director's eyes, not studied or unnatural.'[59] Rose Gooding, in contrast, had a very distinctive style of writing.

One of her handwriting's 'chief features', Bodkin noticed, was the 'extraordinary manner in which she makes a "Y" and the loop of a "Y" or a "G".' Her writing had 'other peculiar features' besides. It was significant that not a single tic of this style appeared in any of the dozens of libels written over a period of eight months. How remarkable it was, wrote Bodkin, 'that a woman of that class whose handwriting presents marked and well formed and constant characteristics, never once allows anyone of them or any portion of any one of them to emerge into the libels she is accused of writing'. In the same paragraph Bodkin described Rose Gooding's hand as 'a well formed and apparently educated and very characteristic writing'.[60] Bodkin spoke with the confidence of his class and gender, but it is easy to miss that there was something more unusual and humane at play in his discovery that Rose Gooding wrote above her station. His surprise that her handwriting gave the appearance of education *and was very much her own* mixed predictable condescension with an openness to the quiet ways in which a working-class woman might be her own person, not simply a type.

The idiosyncrasies of Rose's handwriting—the loops, the extravagant Ys, the use of stylized capitals for some letters, such as D and P—were in full bloom in the pencilled notes she sent to her sometime employers in Norfolk Place, the publisher George Rose and his wife. (One of the confusing quirks of this story is the way many of those involved shared a small pool of names: Ruth Russell, Alfred Russell, Edith Russell, Edith Swan, Rose Gooding, George Rose.) Two exchanges between Rose Gooding and Mr and Mrs Rose survive—the first a negotiation over pay for work, the second a dispute over needlework that Gooding had held onto (undergarments and children's pyjamas) after getting the sack. In each case, letters went back and forth over the course of a single day. It is striking that Rose Gooding, a citizen of what is often thought of as an overwhelmingly oral working-class culture, should transact her business in writing when less than a hundred yards separated her house and the Roses'.

The prose style was not as flamboyant as the script, but in these letters Rose Gooding used words far more assuredly than she did in the stilted letter she wrote to her sister and husband from Lewes. Dorothy delivered her mother's letter to Mrs Rose confirming her availability to stay over and help with the house and children while Mr Rose was in London:

Sataurday
Nov. 1st.. 11 .. 19.

Dear Mrs. Rose,

I have been talking to *Mr. Gooding.*

He is quite agreeable for me to sleep over here 3 nights you are left alone.... I shall Be Pleased to look after the children anytime you require me to do so, so you need not worry about that. I will be at your services any time. Now about the fee you will be ready to give me Per week kindly let me know this evening by note so as to get it settled for you & myself not leave it till the last moment.

My little girl will wait for an answer if you are not Busy.

Yours faithfully,
Mrs. Gooding.[61]

The letter is obliging and even reassuring, but it carries an only partially latent warning ('not leave it till the last moment'). The follow-up later the same day, after Mrs Rose had given her answer, was not deferential:

Sataurday
Nov. 1st.. 11 .. 19.

Dear Mrs. Rose,

In answer to your note do you think 3/- a day will hurt you for 7 days a week to keep your place in order also to sleep here 3 nights a week & looke after the little ones any time you should want me to.

Mr. Gooding thinks it is a very fair Price to ask as People are giving 4/- Per day & there food so I myself do not think it will Hurt you.

Remember I shall work the 5 days off first what I owe you. Let me know if this is satisfaction to you & Mr. Rose....

Yours faithfully,
Mrs. Gooding.[62]

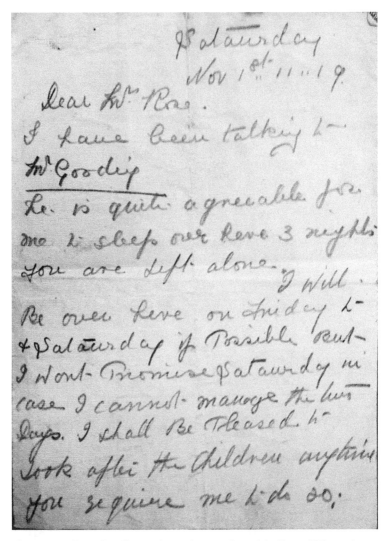

Figure 5.3. Rose Gooding writes to her employer Mrs Rose. HO 144/2452, National Archives

Here a common working-class deviation from 'Standard English', the use of 'what' as a relative pronoun instead of 'that', sits alongside the schoolbook formalities of 'satisfaction', 'Yours faithfully', the indented date.

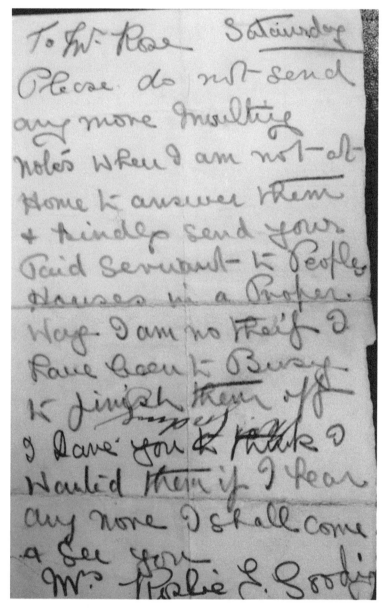

Figure 5.4. Rose Gooding writes to her former employer George F. Rose. HO 144/2452, National Archives

The second exchange—after Rose Gooding had been sacked—was, understandably, shorter and sharper. George Rose sent a servant to the Goodings' house bearing a note demanding '*all* the things you have [been] altering or repairing. It does not matter whether they are finished or not but I want them now and *will have them*.'[63] Unintimidated by this demand from a well-off former employer, Rose Gooding wrote a wonderfully affronted reply on the back of his letter:

Sataurday.

To M[r.] Rose.

Please do not send any more Insulting notes when I am not at Home to answer them & kindly send your Paid Servant to Peoples Houses in a Proper Way I am no theif I have been to Busy to finish them off I Dare you to think I wanted them if I hear any more I shall come & see you.

M[rs.] Rosie E. Gooding.[64]

The punctuation falls out of the heated sentences; the flourishes in the handwriting are bigger than usual, the initial capitals even more insistent. She did not 'hear any more' from her former employer. Rose Gooding was not the well-read autodidact valued by the late-Victorian champions of working-class literacy.[65] But she had, in her way, taken possession of the written word.

6

Circumstances Grave
and Unusual

Sir Archibald Bodkin was acutely conscious of how strange the situation was. 'In this case', the Director of Public Prosecutions said in the searching brief he dictated for the barrister who would represent the state when the Court of Criminal Appeal reconsidered Rose Gooding's case, 'Counsel is instructed... under circumstances which are as grave as it is hoped they are unusual.' When the DPP and Home Office referred Gooding's convictions back to the appeals court, Edith Swan was asked whether she would continue to stand by the prosecutions she had brought. She said no, either out of concern that they would not stand, or, at least as likely, because her family could not afford more legal bills. Responsibility therefore passed to the Director of Public Prosecutions, who had led the way in calling the convictions into question. Armed with Inspector Nicholls's findings and Bodkin's glosses on them, the barrister representing the Crown at the appeal would be a prosecutor who disowned the prosecutions. Not for nothing did Bodkin say that counsel would find 'what attitude he will adopt at the hearing of the appeal... a somewhat embarrassing question to decide'.[1]

And then there was the strangeness of the events in Littlehampton that had led to this point. Rose Gooding was in prison because it was easier to accept the 'inferential' case against her than to believe that Swan could have written humiliating letters to and about herself. ('I cannot think that Miss Swan would write to persons that employed her with a chance of losing her work', said Superintendent Peel of Arundel.)[2] Bodkin saw this not only as 'a grave miscarriage of justice' but also as a failure of judgement—on the part of the local police especially.

'[T]he country police', he reflected, 'are perhaps not so alive to the mysterious occurrences which may be met with if a woman becomes malicious towards another woman.' Bodkin's experience as a busy metropolitan barrister had alerted him to psychopathologies unknown to the West Sussex police. When he was at the bar, Bodkin 'happened to have appeared in the notorious Tugwell case', which uncannily anticipated the Littlehampton libels. It was the memory of the Tugwell case that had made Bodkin suspect early on that Edith Swan might have been perpetrator rather than victim.[3]

The Tugwell case unfolded over the course of 1909 and 1910 in Sutton, a suburban Surrey town in London's gravitational field (and within the Metropolitan Police district). The social setting was very different from that of the Littlehampton case. The principal players employed servants and lived in houses with names ('Deepdene', 'Wentworth'). 'The trouble, such as it is, appears to have had its origin in the gossips and jealousies of a number of women connected with the local Catholic Church', wrote a detective, with a combination of pithiness and trivialization.[4] Annie Tugwell, the wife of the local regis-trar of births and deaths, was a Catholic convert. So was her friend Louisa Wesley. Together they showered attention on their priest, Henry Cafferata. 'Mrs. Tugwell and Mrs. Wesley were continually hanging about the Canon's House causing him annoyance.' Canon Cafferata's housekeeper, Annie Dewey, was caught in the middle, and at some point Tugwell turned on her. Tugwell managed to obtain a sample of Dewey's writing from a fellow servant. She then imitated the house-keeper's hand in the abusive letters and postcards she began writing to herself. Tugwell also wrote to Father Warwick, who succeeded Cafferata at the Sutton Catholic church when Cafferata moved on to another parish. The letters to Warwick denounced Wesley and Tugwell herself as prostitutes. Tugwell accused Dewey of writing them. After consult-ing a solicitor, Arthur Dagg, she and Wesley brought a private prosecu-tion for criminal libel.[5] Dewey was committed for trial at the Guildford Assizes in June 1909. When the court convened, in a draughty building that was used as a theatre and cinema between assizes, the judge made Tugwell and Wesley withdraw the prosecution and pay Dewey's costs. The defence counsel 'openly stated he was of the opinion that Mrs Tugwell was the writer of the letters herself'.[6]

Cafferata believed his housekeeper when she denied any responsi-bility for the libels. He pledged to cover Dewey's legal bills. After the assizes, Cafferata began to receive mail calculated to offend a Catholic priest, including a box containing a pessary. Tugwell submitted an anonymous notice to the *Daily Express* announcing the canon's marriage to his housekeeper. The newspaper published it. Meanwhile, Tugwell continued to mail accusatory postcards to herself. Her husband, who seems to have had no inkling of what was going on, went to the police. Mr Tugwell suggested that the letters were being written by a boy from a family with whom Annie Tugwell had quarrelled, and that Dewey was putting the boy up to it. (As in the Littlehampton case, there was an attempt to throw suspicion on children as the instruments of mischievous adults.) Detective Inspector Ward dismissed this explanation. He also said that the libels were of a private character and it would be inappropriate for the police to get involved. Ward advised Mr Tugwell to take the matter up with the General Post Office, which he did. The GPO's Confidential Inquiry Branch informed him that it would not take action unless the items posted were obscene. Three days later obscene postcards started circulating. When the GPO's investigators were informed of this development, they announced an investigation and said that if they identified the writer severe punishment would follow. Again, after this information reached the Tugwell house, the libels changed so as to align them more closely with the workings of the Confidential Inquiry Branch. Until this point the libels had been anonymous; the next crop, in the same handwriting, were signed 'A Dewey'.[7]

Cafferata heard that the Tugwells were planning to prosecute Dewey again, and sought Ward's advice. The detective suggested that Cafferata 'send Dewey right away for a week or two with a view to see if the letters were still circulated'. There was thus a parallel with the effort to give Rose Gooding an alibi. Cafferata dispatched Dewey to his brother's house in Grantham. Her host did not allow her out alone, and the nearest post office was three-quarters of a mile away. It was clear that she could not have sent the three dirty letters posted in Sutton during this time.[8]

The second prosecution of Dewey, this time by Mr Tugwell alone, went to trial in March 1910. Dewey's solicitor went to great lengths to serve Mrs Tugwell with a subpoena, but she managed to elude him. She did not attend the trial, presumably to avoid being served. Her husband said she was too sick to come to court, though she was seen that evening at the Empire Music Hall in Croydon.[9] If she had been forced to testify, the defence counsel presumably would have put to her the allegation that she had written the offending letters herself. Tugwell would have had to choose between perjuring herself and confessing. After hearing the evidence, the jury found Dewey not guilty and awarded her costs.[10] Despite the order for costs, Cafferata remained out of pocket. Ministers from several protestant congregations formed a committee to raise funds to reimburse him for what he had spent on Dewey's defence.[11]

The Metropolitan Police resolved to put those involved under surveillance if the libels started up again.[12] Sure enough, they did. The canon received one that read: 'You really must keep up your payment for your child. It is growing very much like you.'[13] Tugwell also posted a letter to Louisa Wesley. Writing in the name of the housekeeper, she made her grammar slum it: 'me and the dear Canon knows', the letter declared, that Wesley and Tugwell were 'dirty street trolls'. The letter claimed that they had been seen 'on your backs for Measures in the stable he was doing it to you both'. Wesley showed the letter to Robert Measures, who was another local priest, and he took it to Detective Inspector Ward. Later, Ward and his officers searched the Tugwells' house and found a piece of blotting paper with the imprint of the words 'Annie Dewey', 'Stable—the trolls', and 'Sixpence' (as well as an irritated reference to Tugwell's solicitor, 'Gas bag Dagg').[14]

Now Tugwell herself was indicted for criminal libel. (No charges were laid concerning her attempts to get Annie Dewey wrongly convicted.) Bodkin led the prosecution at the Guildford Assizes in July 1910. Tugwell answered his questions emphatically and argumentatively; Bodkin had ample opportunity to study her manner. He worked methodically through the welter of evidence against Tugwell and, as was his wont, avoided the histrionics common among barristers of his day.[15] Tugwell's counsel had no option but to make an impassioned appeal. The defence tried to play on the jury's reluctance to believe that a woman 'who had for 20 years lived a happy married life' could have turned into 'a woman of the foulest thoughts, the beastliest imagination, and a woman of the cruellest and most persistent malice, who had stooped to every kind of forgery in order to fix the crime upon a woman who was a total stranger'. It was far-fetched, her barrister argued, to claim that the libels were 'the product of a woman's hand': but 'if they were the work of a woman, they could not be the work of a woman who had lived a life such as this woman had lived'.[16]

Unconvinced, the jury returned with a guilty verdict after quarter of an hour. The judge sentenced Tugwell to twelve months' imprisonment. Although the defence's argument about the implausibility of a happily married woman being capable of filth and conspiracy failed to overcome the evidence against Tugwell, her counsel was on to something. As a newspaper editorial reflected: 'The psychological interest of the case is great, and it was the inherent improbability of the guilt of the woman which made her conviction so difficult.'[17] For Bodkin the Sutton case was not only an education in the unexpected consequences of malice between women, but also a lesson that less worldly men would struggle to comprehend that a respectable-looking woman could behave in such a way.

The barrister who took on Bodkin's brief for Rose Gooding's appeal was also familiar with the Tugwell case. Travers Humphreys had sat through the trial at the Guildford Assizes holding a watching brief for Louisa Wesley, since Wesley definitely had a stake in the case even though she was not on trial.[18] Humphreys and Bodkin went back three decades. They had been junior barristers in the same chambers and worked together on many cases, including the once-famous 'bodies in the bath' murders. Humphreys was best man at Bodkin's wedding.[19]

Humphreys was born into an upper-middle-class family, the youngest of four sons. His brothers were all educated at Uppingham, 'where they had distinguished themselves at boxing and games generally, but, so my father said, in nothing else, and he was anxious to try a change in my case'. Travers boarded at Shrewsbury and went on to Cambridge, where the family pattern looked to repeat itself: Travers enjoyed a better reputation as a rower rather than as a scholar. However, his college was known for its lawyers as well as its oarsmen, and Humphreys went on to become one of the many establishment lawyers among Trinity Hall's alumni. (Shortly after being called to the bar, Humphreys was reproached by a fellow alumnus, Henry Dickens, for the solecism of addressing him as Mr Dickens. 'Barristers don't call each other "Mister". Did not someone tell me you are a Hall man? . . . Then you ought to be doubly ashamed of yourself.')[20] Humphreys was methodical in and out of the courtroom. He was a chartered accountant as well as a barrister, and his ability to process figures made him very effective in fraud cases.[21] By the time he was briefed in Rose Gooding's case, he was senior Treasury Counsel—the frontline prosecutor at the Central

Criminal Court. As such he appeared in most of the high-profile English criminal trials of the 1920s. His views on crime and punishment, one of his biographers remarks, were strict but 'without traditional sadism'.[22]

Humphreys was a traditionalist with quirks. Staunchly fogeyish on some matters, such as the evils of the motor car, he was also receptive to modern psychology, which many of his generation regarded as pernicious nonsense.[23] He retained some regard for, or indulgence of, one of his earliest clients, Oscar Wilde, an abomination to many authority figures. In 1895, Humphreys had been junior counsel in the greatest of all criminal libel trials, *Wilde v. Queensberry*. When the Marquess of Queensberry left a card at Wilde's club accusing him of being a sodomite, Wilde sought a warrant for criminal libel. The marquess was represented by Edward Carson, a contemporary of Wilde's at Trinity College Dublin ('No doubt he will perform his task with all the added bitterness of an old friend', was Wilde's mordant response to the news.)[24] The defence called young men to testify that they had had sex with Wilde. After their testimony, the defence handed the dossier on Wilde's sex life to the Director of Public Prosecutions, whereupon Wilde was charged with 'gross indecency' and his destruction was set in train. Wilde's solicitor was Travers Humphreys' father, Charles, which was the reason for Travers' presence in Wilde's legal team.[25] He played only a small role in support of Clarke and Wilde's other counsel, Charles Mathews: Humphreys appeared to ask for bail, and handled the cross-examination of some minor witnesses. But he was there for all three of the trials involving Wilde.[26] He also appeared for Wilde before the receiving officer when his creditors, led by Queensberry, succeeded in getting Wilde adjudged bankrupt.[27]

Humphreys presented his case, or non-case, in the matter of Rose Gooding, on 25 July 1921 in the Portland-stone grandeur of the Royal Courts of Justice on the Strand. A full bench of the Court of Criminal Appeal had convened: the Lord Chief Justice, Alfred Lawrence; Mr Justice Sankey; and Mr Justice Branson. Rose Gooding, brought up from Portsmouth prison, stood in the dock. She was represented once more by Eustace Fulton, who needed do little more than nod as Humphreys explained why the Director of Public Prosecutions did not support either of Gooding's convictions. Humphreys stated that the Home Office agreed with this course of action and added—'if I am not exceeding my rights as Counsel'—that he himself had looked carefully into the matter and come to the same conclusion.[28] It is a sign of the oddity of the situation that the punctilious court reporter for *The Times* described Humphreys as representing Rose Gooding and Eustace Fulton the Crown.[29]

Humphreys had come up with an answer to the embarrassing question of how to conduct himself at the hearing. No amount of references to learned judges and the deepest respect could disguise Bodkin's belief that Roche and Avory had handled Rose Gooding's trials badly. But it would have been unwise to press that line in court. Humphreys assured the appeals court that he saw no 'misdirection or impropriety' in either judge's directions to the jurors. He based his argument, instead, on new evidence that could not have been presented at the assize trials. While Gooding was in prison, he said, the West Sussex police 'brought some matters to the attention of the Director of Public Prosecutions', and in consequence the DPP 'obtained the services of an experienced and perfectly impartial person from Scotland Yard, Inspector Nicholls, who was the officer deputed to make enquiries in the interests of justice and not of any party at all. As a result of the report made by that Inspector, and in consequence of certain facts which were not known, and could not be known at either of those two trials, it is now established to the satisfaction of those instructing me, that the Appellant Rose Emma Gooding, was not the person who committed the offence of which she was convicted on the 3rd of March this year.' And, since the handwriting in the libels in the second case was identical to that in the exhibits from the first case, it followed that if the second conviction was wrong the first one was too.[30]

'That', submitted Humphreys, 'is the view taken by those instructing me, and it follows therefore that they could not support either of these convictions.... I would also like to say to the Court', Humphreys added, 'that I think the Appellant is entitled to have it said that in the view of the Authorities she is not a person in regard to whom there may be some doubt of her innocence, but that she is in fact innocent of both the offences of which she has been convicted.'[31]

Humphreys finished by repeating ('I am not sure if I have made it clear') that more libels had surfaced in the recent past while Rose Gooding was locked up. The implication was that a new defendant might in time be charged over the Littlehampton libels. Hence the cagey vagueness of Humphreys' account of Nicholls investigation and the 'certain facts' hanging over the proceedings. The Lord Chief Justice agreed: 'the position is somewhat unusual, because as Mr Travers Humphreys has stated, facts have come to light which require investigation. . . . In view of those new circumstances, and the opinion formed upon them by the Authorities dealing with criminal matters, it seems to this Court right...that this case should not be proceeded with in open Court.'[32] The judges quashed both of Rose Gooding's convictions.[33] She was free. An officer of the court went out to tell the witnesses waiting to give evidence that they would not be needed after all.[34] Edith Swan was one of those waiting to be called. Another was the photographer Charles Haslett.[35] If Haslett had testified, it would have been to confirm that the objectionable letter he received at the beginning of January was indeed the same letter whose address was imprinted on the blotting paper taken from the Swans' house. The way the case played out at the Royal Courts of Justice that day, nothing was said that pointed to Swan.

The Home Office quickly took the first steps towards compensating Rose Gooding. Sir Ernley Blackwell pulled the files on previous miscarriages of justice. His staff made notes on them, extracting the numbers with which to assemble a ratio of time wrongly spent in prison to money paid out.[36] At the top of the list was the most infamous failure of the criminal justice system in recent British history, the case of Adolf Beck. In 1877, a man named John Smith, who posed as an aristocrat named Lord Willoughby, was convicted of swindling London prostitutes and served five years' imprisonment with hard labour. In 1895, another group of women were tricked out of their valuables by a con man with much the same modus operandi, right down to the pseudonym. 'Lord Winton de Willoughby' gave members of the 'better class of gay women' (as the Director of Public Prosecutions described them) fraudulent cheques, made bogus offers of employment, and asked to borrow their jewellery so that he could find out their size. They never got the jewellery back, of course. The police closed in on Adolf Beck, a Norwegian businessman living in London. The officer who arrested John Smith two decades earlier was certain that Smith and Beck were the same person. The victims insisted that the Norwegian was the man who had deceived them, and Beck was committed for trial. (Horace Avory was the prosecuting counsel.) Despite evidence that Beck had been in Peru in 1877 when Smith committed his crimes, Beck went to prison. Three years after his release, another string of identical crimes led to his second apprehension, trial, and

conviction. It was at this point that he finally caught a break. While
Beck was in Brixton prison awaiting sentencing, a man calling himself
Captain Weis was arrested for con tricks from the same playbook. It
became undeniable that Weis aka William Thomas, and not Adolf Beck,
was John Smith. Beck was granted a royal pardon. The case became a
cause célèbre for the way it rattled racial thinking as well as undermin-
ing confidence in British justice. Smith was Jewish and Beck was not.
How, the popular press asked, could the authorities have confused a
Jew with a gentile?[37]

The outcry over the Adolf Beck saga precipitated the founding of
the Court of Criminal Appeal in 1907. The whole affair might have
been prevented if Beck's lawyers had been able to appeal the first trial
judge's decision to exclude evidence that would have proved that this
was a case of mistaken identity.[38] In the past, defenders of the status
quo had insisted that the criminal justice system worked well enough.
The findings of the committee of inquiry into the Beck case dealt a
heavy blow to this argument, exposing the inadequacies of the Home
Office's procedures for reviewing prisoners' petitions.[39] The Beck case
was, among other things, an indignity for the Home Office, a lesson
Blackwell cannot have forgotten.

The Home Office offered Beck £2000 in compensation. This he
refused; eventually the government paid him £5000.[40] Rose Gooding's
suffering was not in same league. Blackwell thought the most relevant
precedent was that of Mary Johnson.[41] Her case made a useful com-
parison because Johnson had been wrongly accused of writing
objectionable letters—though the crimes Johnson was convicted of
pertained to threats and sending indecent material through the post
rather than libel.[42] Johnson's first trial took place in 1912 in the same
cinema-cum-courtroom as the Sutton libel trials. Johnson's neighbours in Redhill, a couple named Woodman, accused her of sending
them obscene letters and death threats. A jury convicted Johnson and
she spent six months in prison. After she got out, the letters started
again and there was a repeat prosecution. This time the case was tried
in a more satisfactory building in Kingston. The jury found Johnson
guilty, and after some legal to-ing and fro-ing, she was sentenced to a
year in prison. She served the full term. The wheel turned again and
Ellen Woodman lobbied the police to prosecute a third time. They did,
charging Johnson's husband as well. This time the magistrates had
reservations about the evidence and refused to commit the Johnsons

for trial. A trap was set for Ellen Woodman. She was caught, and sent away for eighteen months for perjury. Counsel for the prosecution was none other than Travers Humphreys.[43] All up, Blackwell recorded in his notes, Johnson 'served 15 [months] actual imp[risonmen]ᵗ & 86 days awaiting trial'. The Home Office recommended paying her £1000 in compensation 'but the Treas[ur]y wd only give her £500'.[44]

Blackwell ascertained that the Treasury would probably agree to £250 in Rose Gooding's case. He wrote on the Home Secretary's behalf to the Secretary of the Treasury three days after the Court of Criminal Appeal hearing. Blackwell recapitulated the facts of the case, and 'placed' Rose and her family. 'Mrs Gooding is the wife of William Henry Gooding, a labourer earning £2-18-0 a week and sometimes employed as cook on coasting vessels.' They lived 'in a small cottage in Western Road, Littlehampton'. Rose Gooding had been in custody for over eight months, counting time spent awaiting trial. The time in prison was not all she had suffered. 'Mrs Gooding is a woman of good character', Blackwell declared, 'and for a long time she has borne the stigma of having committed offences of a particularly disgraceful kind, many of the letters she was supposed to have sent being of a filthy and abominable character. She . . . has in no way contributed by her own conduct to the misfortune which has overtaken her.'[45]

The Treasury did not move as quickly as the Home Office, and Blackwell and his officials had to fend off entreaties from Rose Gooding's supporters. Her solicitors, Wannop & Falconer, wrote to request that she receive compensation, though they did not suggest a figure. They noted that 'in addition to her financial losses Mrs Gooding has suffered in health'.[46] The *Daily Mirror* weighed in and did not miss the opportunity to link Rose Gooding's predicament to the 'Anti-Waste' campaign its proprietor was running against the Lloyd George government's taxing and spending.[47] 'Surely a Government which are spending millions on wild schemes could afford a solatium of £1000 to a British woman who has been twice deeply wronged.' The *Mirror* reported that Bill Gooding had spent all his money on his wife's defence, and that he had no work at the moment, the shipyard being closed. The newspaper led its story off with a statement from a Home Office official that no decision about compensation had been taken yet.[48] Civil servants at the Home Office were doubtless not pleased that theirs was the government department held responsible for the delay. The day after the *Mirror* item, Blackwell succeeded in getting confirmation that Treasury would pay the £250, as an 'act of grace'—that is, without admitting any liability.[49] 'Send notice to Press', Blackwell minuted.[50]

When the news was published, at least some people thought the compensation was 'miserably inadequate'. The Harlesden Brotherhood and Sisterhood, a Baptist group, appealed to the Home Secretary 'to take immediate steps, less cold-blooded and more humane, to secure an innocent woman something like reasonable compensation' for the 'mental and physical torture inflicted during her imprisonment on an entirely false charge'. Like the *Daily Mirror*, the Harlesden Baptists were quick to interpret the officials' actions in the light of the turbulent politics of the years immediately after the Great War: 'in these days of social unrest', it was important not to 'undermine the public respect for the governing powers' any further.[51] Further letters from north London followed. 'The Brothers & Sisters are very persistent', wrote a civil servant with the air of one who knew.[52]

All the same, £250 was a substantial sum. It was enough to keep the Gooding–Russell household above the poverty line for a year and a half.[53] Even after Bill Gooding repaid Maurice Blackman and paid the further legal fees associated with the appeal, there would be a good deal of money left. Rose Gooding's own reaction to the payout was not recorded. She had returned to Littlehampton the same day the Court of Criminal Appeal quashed her convictions.[54] In all likelihood her accuser made the same journey back, changing trains at Ford Junction before arriving at the house next door.[55]

7

Keeping Observation

The ruin of her case against Rose Gooding left Edith Swan neither subdued nor resigned. A week after the hearing at the Royal Courts of Justice, she wrote defiantly to Henry Thomas of the Littlehampton police: 'It is a most unsatisfactory ending for me. I do not intend to let it remain where it is.' Swan reported that her neighbour was bragging that she was going to receive a thousand pounds in compensation. Rose Gooding allegedly joked 'that she would not mind going to Prison again for that amount of money'. 'If I had been the victim of a grave miscarriage of justice', Swan declared, using the phrase of Sir Archibald Bodkin's that had settled itself into newspaper discussions of the case, 'no money would compensate me. I would not take one penny but I would not rest until I had brought the guilty person to book.'[1]

Edith renewed her accusations. She claimed to have eavesdropped on an incriminating conversation between Rose and her sister the day after Rose's return to Western Road. Edith promptly wrote a 'memorandum' of the conversation, which she summarized for Inspector Thomas:

I overheard Miss Russell tell Mrs Gooding, that, while she was in prison, she came across a few of Mrs Gooding's choice books, while she was cleaning out her bedroom. Miss Russell said she shewed them to Mr Gooding, and he talked it over with somebody (no names mentioned) and they decided not to destroy them but to set them about so that they should get into certain people's hands. Miss Russell added that 'We sent two up to the Police Station to old Thomas'.... It would be interesting to know what books they were and what they contained, if you really did receive them.[2]

Swan did not spell it out, but she was offering Thomas an explanation of the provenance of the two notebooks 'found in Selbourne Road'.

Her story provided support for the implausible theory that Rose had built up a stockpile of offensive writings that her family disseminated while she was locked up.[3] Swan then veered away from specifics into teasing intrigue: 'I have heard a lot since Mrs Gooding has been home, and could tell you a lot, more than I have done but I prefer to wait a little longer.'[4]

Swan cast herself as a freelance investigator in a letter to the press several days later. 'I am following up certain clues, and am in communication with the police. I am as anxious as anyone to get to the bottom of all this.'[5] She sent this letter to *John Bull*, a weekly paper that did a roaring trade exposing fraud and malpractice. At least, it exposed the frauds and malpractice of people other than its larger-than-life editor, Horatio Bottomley. Some of Bottomley's detractors conceded that he performed a public service as a muckraker and whistle-blower, but viewed from another angle *John Bull*'s exposés of cruel employers or corner-cutting manufacturers were shakedowns. The paper would run with allegations about a business, its directors would pay compensation and take out expensive advertising in *John Bull*, and the paper would publish a follow-up article reporting the happy news that the problem was solved. After their first brush with *John Bull*, some victims paid Bottomley an annual sum of protection money to keep their companies' names out of the paper.[6] Bottomley had a good war at the helm of his newspaper and in the House of Commons as the independent MP for South Hackney. He was much in demand as a patriotic speaker. '[A] nation in a false system acting in a false spirit will quite rightly choose him', D. H. Lawrence told Bertrand Russell in 1915. 'But a nation striving for the truth and the establishment of truth and right will forget him in a second.'[7] Bottomley had a hammy and sentimental style whose appeal did not long survive the war. His luck ran out at more or less the same time. After surviving a number of bankruptcies and prosecutions—he enjoyed representing himself in court—he finally went to prison in 1922 when the extent of the swindle that was his 'Victory Bonds Club' was laid bare in a protracted trial at the Old Bailey. Leading the prosecution, Travers Humphreys combed methodically through the club's finances, the detail at once numbing and scandalous.[8]

At the time of the Littlehampton libels, *John Bull* was crusading against misconduct in the Metropolitan Police and the criminal justice system as a whole. The Littlehampton case presented the paper with plenty of material. With customary exaggeration, it declared: 'Not since the "free pardon" awarded by the Crown to Adolf Beck, who served a sentence of penal servitude for a crime he never committed, has the public mind been so agitated as by the case of Mrs. Rose Emma Gooding, the Littlehampton woman who, through the action of the Court of Criminal Appeal, has been relieved of the odium of a vile and baseless charge.'[9] Bottomley, or more likely one of the journalistic henchmen who knew his mind well, dismissed the notion that Mr Justice Avory had conducted the second trial properly as 'stuff and nonsense': the evidence against Gooding was so flimsy that only a former prosecutor like Avory could find it convincing.[10] (While he was at the bar, Avory had prosecuted Bottomley, after which *John Bull* traduced him on a more or less weekly basis.)[11] *John Bull* also complained that the case was 'shrouded in secrecy. All we are permitted to know is that, while Mrs. Gooding was in gaol, Inspector Nicholls, of Scotland Yard, pursued certain inquiries at Littlehampton, the Public Prosecutor decided that Mrs. Gooding had been wrongfully convicted. All else is silence.' *John Bull* offered a reward of £100 for information exposing the real author of the libels. Swan's letter, the paper admitted, threw 'little fresh light upon the deepening mystery', but it enabled *John Bull* to claim Swan's endorsement of its effort to uncover the truth. A newspaper committed to making enemies made a show of indignantly supporting both Edith Swan and Rose Gooding.[12]

Swan made comments about her neighbour in the letters she wrote to *John Bull* and the police, and in conversations with other people living on Western Road, but the two women appear to have had no direct contact with each other. The Goodings and Russells, it was noticed, were 'keeping strictly to themselves'.[13] They announced that they would quit the cottage in Western Road, though they did not follow through for a long time.[14] For at least several months after her return, Rose said nothing to her neighbours.[15] 'Mrs. Gooding seldom or ever goes anywhere alone.'[16] If she went to the drying ground at the end of the street to hang out washing, Ruth would accompany her. Rose and Bill often stepped out together. Each afternoon they would go to meet the children from school.[17]

Bill was now unemployed. His spell at Osborne's had been brief, and he returned to Harvey's. Then the owner died and the shipyard remained shuttered for some time, leaving ninety men out of work.[18] Rose stayed home during the days, though she was no longer looking after her nephew. She and Ruth had argued about it, and Ruth now took Albert out during the day. Ruth was back working as a daily servant at Groombridge School, and her employers evidently did not object to her bringing the toddler along.[19] Rose spent her time taking strenuous care of the house ('she is always scrubbing and cleaning').[20] If the occupants of the police cottage at number 49 washed down the yard, Rose would come out afterwards and wash it again.[21]

The couple in the police cottage were new to the street. Alfred Russell retired from the West Sussex Constabulary in February 1921, not long after Rose Gooding's second trial. He had twenty-five years' service and could begin drawing a police pension. He and his wife and son left Littlehampton for Worthing.[22] The new tenants, Violet and George May, took over the cottage in June, but they did not really move in until the second week of July, when George came back from a three-month assignment in Wales. (He probably went as part of a detachment to police industrial unrest. The government took control of Britain's coal mines during the war and finally withdrew from the industry on the last day of March 1921. Free to negotiate new conditions, the South Wales mine owners proposed wage cuts of as much as 45 per cent, and miners went on strike.[23] It is not certain that the West Sussex Constabulary lent men to the affected areas in 1921, but it had sent ninety-four men to Glamorgan during a miners' strike the year before and dispatched officers again, to South Wales and Derbyshire, during the 1926 General Strike.)[24] Violet slept at her mother's house until George returned.[25] The Mays were in their twenties and did not have any children. Violet was pretty and dressed stylishly.[26] She had met Edith Swan four years earlier during her wartime stint working for Snewin's, the building firm. Violet and Edith were not close. According to Violet, Edith 'did not associate with any of the other girls' redecorating The Hillyers; she 'rarely spoke'.[27] Now that they were neighbours, however, Swan did everything she could 'to ingratiate herself with the Mays'.[28]

'Soon after I had taken up residence at 49, Western Road', Violet May recalled, 'Miss Swan offered me the use of her clothesline, the poles and prop on the drying ground. I accepted her offer and have since been on friendly terms with her and her mother, they have brought in bones for my dog and taken an interest in a kitten I have.' Edith would say hello to the dog, Bob, and one dinner time he charmed old Mrs Swan: Violet arrived home with Bob trotting beside her

carrying the shopping basket in his jaws. 'You have got a useful help',
said Mrs Swan.[29] Before long, the friendship between Violet and Edith
crossed the threshold of the Swans' cottage. Edith would invite Violet
in to speak privately.

Many of these conversations were about the plague of libellous
notes. Edith bonded with Violet May not only through friendly ges-
tures, but also by drawing her into the drama of the libels—into scenarios
where Edith could play the several roles of victim, sympathetic listener,
and problem-solver. In June of 1921, while Rose Gooding was still
in Portsmouth prison, Violet visited the vacant police cottage at 49
Western Road daily to get it ready for her and her husband to move
into. One Monday morning, she cleaned the toilet in the back garden,
scrubbing the seat and whitening the floor. She went back to her
parents' house for dinner before returning to Western Road with her
mother. Around four o'clock, her mother needed to use the toilet, and
Violet showed her where it was. 'I opened the door and went into the
W.C., and on the seat I saw a piece of paper folded with writing on it.
I picked it up and found it to be written in filthy language and mentioning Miss Swan's name.' It was one of the notes accusing of Edith of
having an affair with PC Russell. Later in the afternoon, May 'saw Miss
Swan coming out of her wash-house with washing in her hand'. She
showed her the paper, and Swan said, 'Fancy that.' May said that 'a stop
ought to be put to it'. Edith told her the story of how she had
prosecuted Rose Gooding. She brought out another of the letters to
show Violet.[30]

The Mays started to receive abusive letters. In several instances, it
was Edith who first saw the notes in the garden, or the drying ground,
and brought them to the couple's attention. On 7 September, Edith's
brother Ernest called out to Violet: 'Mrs May you are wanted.' She
went downstairs and found Edith waiting at the back door. Edith said,
'I have got something to show you in the passage', and pointed to a
piece of cardboard on the ground there. 'It was lying so that the words
"To the old Buggers May and there whore neybor" could be plainly
read.' Violet told Edith she would give it to her husband when he finished his shift. Edith said: 'I was going to leave it there and hide behind
the door until Mrs Gooding came back to see if she would pick it up.
If she did pick it up I was going [...to] say "That is what your sister
Ruth must have put there."' With a hint of dramatic collusion, Edith
added: 'You had better come inside Mrs May.' Edith's parents and her

brother Steve gathered round to read the note. Steve went out and returned a few minutes later with two unmarked pieces of cardboard that he had found on the garden path. Edith then 'compared the edges of the three pieces of cardboard, putting them together in different ways and said that the two pieces found by her brother looked like the other piece with the writing on'.[31]

Edith showed off her detective skills another time when she called Violet into her house to compare two pieces of physical evidence. The first was 'a piece of green linen cardboard', the torn cover of a notebook.[32] It was covered with rude comments about the Mays and Bedfords, the couple who ran the New Inn at the end of the block. An errand boy had found it one Sunday as he left the Swans their weekly newspapers.[33] He read it and laughed until Mrs Swan took it off him.[34] The second item was a notebook whose pages were interleaved with pink blotting paper. On the front page were the names of some of the Gooding and Russell children, and three pages in there was this:

Margerie Spicer
is a silly
little fool
and so is
Gertie
Russell[35]

Edith said to Violet: 'Look at this and that'; 'Is'nt the writing alike?' Edith then 'measured the piece of green cardboard with the book and said "that looks like the outer cover of it".'[36]

Once more, Edith was insinuating that inhabitants of 45 Western Road—Rose, Ruth, the children—were responsible for the abusive letters. The libels the Mays received were anonymous, but the wording unmistakably implied they were written by someone from number 45. They regularly lumped George and Violet May together with their old (or 'whole') 'whore neybor' Edith Swan. Once a pair of notes turned up, one addressed 'Swan' and the other 'May' (Edith 'sent hers to "John Bull" with a stamped envelope for a reply').[37] The cardboard note left in the passageway made a threat appearing to come from Rose: 'You all want burning alive. The whole whore wont laugh when she finds herself in the dock in the high court soon.'[38] The libels contained generalized abuse and responses to specific neighbourly grievances: 'You are bloody dirty or you would clean the yard sometimes.'[39] A conversation

about a bad smell on a Tuesday morning led to an obscene letter on
the Wednesday. Violet stood at her back door and called out, 'Miss
Swan can you smell a smell like a dirty drain nor a dirty lavatory?'
Edith replied from her washhouse that she could not, but then pointed
to an old fish box on the roof of the Goodings' outhouse and suggested that that was the source of the stink. Swan said she knew it was
not her drain because she had cleaned it out. Violet 'then said to Miss
Swan "I am very funny over dirty drains,"' and went back inside her
house. An hour later, Violet went out to scrub the drain at her back
door, and saw Rose Gooding doing the same. 'I heard her say something to her husband, who was inside the house but I don't remember
what it was. I do not think what she said had any reference to drains.'
The following afternoon, when she went to the drying ground to take
down her sheets, May noticed a piece of buff-coloured paper sticking
out of her peg basket. While the language in many of the libels no
longer seems as obscene as it did in 1921, the note that Violet May
found in her peg basket was timelessly offensive:

You bloody fucking flaming piss country whores go and fuck your cunt. Its
your drain that stinks not our fish box. Yo fucking dirty sods. You are as bad as
your whore neybor.[40]

Violet May doubted that Rose Gooding was the writer. 'To get to
my clothes basket Mrs Gooding would have had to go a considerable
distance past her clothes across the drying ground. I am in the habit of
leaving my peg basket on the drying ground near my clothes the
whole day when I am drying. Miss Swan knows my peg basket well
and so far as I am aware Mrs Gooding has never seen my peg basket
and does not know it.... I have only ever seen one other person use
the drying ground.... I do not know her name; she hangs her clothes
near Mrs Goodings.' May gave the note to her husband and did not
speak to Swan about it. A little later, though, she remarked to Swan
that 'it was a wonder we had not had any more pieces of paper concerning the drains. She said "It is a wonder" and started laughing.' May
regretted her 'mistake': 'I meant to say nothing about it.'[41] May had let
on that she had found the letter at the drying ground, but she did not
disclose the larger secret: that the West Sussex police were keeping tabs
on Edith Swan.

When Henry Thomas received Edith's doubling-down letter at the
beginning of August, he forwarded it to his commanding officer in

Horsham.[42] The chief constable arranged for an officer to investigate.[43] Her name was Gladys Moss. She was the daughter of a timber merchant from Gloucester and his Welsh wife. After Samuel Moss's death, his widow Fanny and some of her children, of whom there were at least six, left Gloucester. The 1911 Census records them living in Worthing, where Gladys worked as a governess.[44] She joined the West Sussex police after the First World War, when she was in her mid-thirties.[45]

Moss's background was not unusual for a female police officer. While practically every male officer came from a working-class family, many of the first recruits in the Metropolitan Police's women's squad at the end of the war were from genteel families or comfortably middle-class ones.[46] Police forces in English towns had been employing women since the 1890s, especially to deal with female prisoners. As such they discharged duties that had previously been performed by policemen's wives, especially in small towns.[47] They were also charged with bringing an appropriately feminine style to bear on situations that male officers handled reluctantly or unreliably.[48] Concerns about prostitution and women's sexuality generally drove the wartime increase in numbers of women police, and the formalization of their status as sworn constables in some forces: female officers patrolled the fringes of military encampments and munitions factories with large female workforces whose morals the authorities did not trust.[49] The idea of female police as a solution to problems of public morals caught on. Lancashire's chief constable told the 1920 committee on the employment of women on police duties about a request from the seaside resort of Morecambe, 'saying that things were a little bit fast there and they wanted women police'. The chief constable was not convinced, though he did lend Morecambe several of the 'detective girls' he had been employing in Manchester.[50]

Although communities saw a niche for women police, their numbers remained very small through the 1920s. Even a city as large as Sheffield had only two female officers, and they were 'unsworn' and did not have power of arrest.[51] Male officers usually felt uneasy or unhappy about having to work with women. The men often became skilled at passing the most tedious tasks onto their female counterparts, and women police continued to be steered into duties involving female victims and juveniles.[52] Lancashire was unusual in assigning women to criminal investigations: as well as making the CID office run, they disguised themselves and kept betting houses and cafes under surveillance, on the lookout for breaches of gaming and licensing laws.[53] Nevertheless, in other parts of the country women would be drafted into investigations when the need arose for a female observer or decoy. Moss stated that she had 'experience in keeping observation in connection with police matters' before she was assigned to Edith Swan's case.[54]

Such assignments were the exception in her time on the Worthing force, however. Moss makes few appearances in the 'occurrence books' that each division of the West Sussex police was obliged to keep. Worthing's log books include the name of the officer reporting each incident, and in the year Moss was sent to Littlehampton, her name occurs only three times. 'PW. Moss reports an accident to a child'; 'Police Woman G. Moss' reports a man riding a motorcycle with a side car on the esplanade, contrary to the town by-laws; 'Policewoman. Moss' receives a complaint about the theft of children's clothes from a shop, and makes 'enquiries during the afternoon and evening'.[55] The force did not call on her even in sensitive cases with female victims: in a case of indecent assault on a seven-year-old girl, a male inspector interviewed the victim himself.[56] Moss's surveillance work in Littlehampton was probably more responsibility than she had ever shouldered in her time with the police.

Moss's superintendent at Worthing instructed her to go to Littlehampton and 'take up observation on the Goodings and the Swans to see what was taking place'. She was not told anything further. Moss went to Littlehampton in the middle of August and found lodgings at a baker's shop on Norfolk Road. She stayed one week, 'during which time I made quiet inquiries and kept discreet observation respecting the Goodings and the Swans without learning anything of interest'. On 12 September, after the Mays started receiving insulting letters, Moss returned for another spell of observation, this time staying with Mrs Roberts of 41 Western Road. That house was 'quite close to the Goodings and the Swans on the same side of the street', but from number 41 Moss could not see or hear anything that was going on in the other houses, so after two days she got permission from the chief constable to conduct her surveillance from inside the Mays' cottage.[57]

With the Mays' cooperation, Moss stationed herself in a small room attached to their scullery. 'The window of the room looks out on to the passage between the Swans and the Goodings. The glass is frosted but there is one pane clear through which I could see. . . . I kept observation from the same place daily, varying the times, but covering part of the morning, afternoon, and evening' for a week. She got to know the various members of Gooding and Swan clans by sight. More than once she saw Edith and her mother standing in the passage 'apparently trying to hear what was going on in the Goodings'.[58]

During the same period, the back of the Swans' house and the side of the Goodings' were also under surveillance by members of the Littlehampton police. George May and no fewer than three other constables took turns watching from one of the several sheds at the edges of the garden. The shed in question was disused and boarded up, but the boards 'did not lap over, and there was a two-inch division between them', giving a good view of the yard.[59] The shed was owned by Mr Marshall, a florist on Norfolk Road. Marshall's was one of several florists' shops in the area: the hotels and apartment houses must have created demand for cut flowers. Marshall's shop backed onto the garden behind the houses on Western Road, and the officers were able to enter from the shed from the florist's without having to walk past the Swans' or Goodings' houses. Over the course of this week while Constable May was alternating between plain clothes duties and night shifts, Edith Swan badgered Violet to find out what her husband was up to. Violet 'put her off', but Inspector Thomas thought it advisable to vary the operation. He pulled Moss from the room attached to the scullery and had her replace George May and the other men keeping watch from the florist's shed.[60]

Moss took up her position around 9:15 each morning, stayed for four hours, and then left for lunch. She returned for an afternoon shift, took a half-hour break at 4:30, and then resumed observation until dusk.[61] (This was in 1921's last week of British Summer Time, which was still a novelty and had not yet been made a permanent arrangement.)[62] Moss maintained her routine uneventfully for three days. On the fourth day, 27 September, she made a breakthrough.[63]

At 11:15 that morning, Rose Gooding emerged from her house. She was dressed to go out in a long navy blue coat and 'a close fitting navy blue hat'. As usual, Rose checked that the window at the back of the house was fastened before going down the passage and out into the street, where a girl was waiting for her (Moss thought it was Dorothy but could not be sure). Just after they left, Violet May opened her back door and walked across to her dustbin, which was beyond her lavatory.

'She had a sink basket in her hand and I heard her banging the sink basket onto the dustbin.' Moss watched her head back into the house, 'looking about on the ground as was her habit to do and which I had told her to do'.[64]

Half an hour later, Edith Swan came out of her washhouse in the garden. From their different vantage points, Gladys Moss and Violet May saw different aspects of what happened next. May later stated that she spoke to Swan outside the Mays' back door. 'Hullo Bob', Edith said to the dog. Turning to Violet, she remarked that she had just seen the Goodings go out. Edith and Violet talked about the dog for a while, and then Edith said 'she must get on as she wanted to go out and see the unveiling of the War Memorial'. May remembered Edith being dressed 'in a dark skirt, light blouse and a pinafore'. Edith went back to her laundry and Violet went indoors to peel potatoes. 'Immediately afterwards I saw Miss Swan leave her washhouse with a small shovel in her hand and go up the garden out of my view. I can only just see the garden gate from my scullery window. She returned in a minute or two carrying a shovelful of cinders in her right hand, she was through the gate before I noticed her.'[65]

Moss did not witness the conversation between Violet and Edith. She saw Edith leave her washhouse and cross the garden carrying the shovel. Edith went into the one of the other sheds, where the Swans kept their rabbits. She passed out of Moss's line of sight. When she reappeared, less than a minute later, she was heading back to her house 'with what looked like cinders in the shovel. The shovel was in her right hand and when she reached the door, which was open, I saw her throw a piece of folded paper with her left hand into the corner. . . . As the paper which Miss Swan threw reached the ground it sprung open.' At the start of each shift in the shed, Moss made a point of checking that there was no paper lying about in the parts of the garden and the passage that she could see from her vantage point. 'The back of P.C. May's lavatory was well within my view and within my line of sight, I am positive that up to the time when I saw Miss Swan throw the piece of paper there was nothing on the ground at the back of P.C. May's lavatory except a little bit of brown fluff off a carpet.'[66]

Moss left the shed immediately, walking quickly through the florist's shop, down Norfolk Road and round the corner into Western Road to the Mays' house, a distance of approximately three hundred yards.[67] She let herself in the front door and found Violet in the scullery. Moss instructed her to go outside and retrieve the piece of paper.[68] Thinking quickly, Violet gave herself a pretext for going out past the lavatory: she took some potato peelings out to the dustbin and picked up the paper on her way back.[69] She brought it inside and examined it with Moss. The paper bore two penny stamps—perhaps Swan had thought to post it but changed her mind. Even before she read what was inside, Moss 'knew it was similar to other notes which had been found'.[70]

It was addressed to 'fucking old whore May, 49, Western Rd, Local'. It accused Violet and her 'fucking whore neybor', Swan, of 'throw[ing] jeers' at the ostensible author—once again, the note was written as if from the perspective of Rose Gooding or a member of her family. Like many of the preceding libels, it affixed the word 'old' to people who were in their twenties or early thirties. 'Your old bugger of a husband don't do his duty', the note continued, 'or else he would want to know what old four eyes brings home in a sack from the beach hotel. He will soon be reported by Detective Blackman.'[71] Perhaps Edith had encountered Maurice Blackman while he was helping Bill Gooding try to catch her out earlier in the year. She clearly knew that he was more than just the beach inspector. 'Old four eyes' was Edith's brother Steve, who wore very strong glasses. He had got some casual work in the kitchen of the Beach Hotel. According to Violet May, Steve would come home from work with 'bits of cabbage leaves and bread for his rabbits, and empty out the sack at the top of the garden'.[72] It does not seem like a crime the police would be very interested in. As with one of the very first libels the previous year, the note smeared one of Edith's brothers as well as Edith herself.

Moss asked Violet May to fetch Edith Swan. Violet went to her neighbours' back door and called for Edith. Her mother said she was not there. Hearing her name called, Edith emerged from her washhouse. Moss stepped out of the scullery.[73] 'I said to Miss Swan "You are Miss Swan I believe?" She said "Yes". I said, "I am a Policewoman. I must caution you that anything you say will be taken down in writing".'[74]

8

The Perfect Witness

'She was exceedingly agitated, turning white and trembling.' Gladys Moss described Edith Swan's behaviour at the moment of the confrontation as acutely as she could. The former governess dictated her statements with an assurance and fluency absent from those of the Littlehampton police. Moss had confidence in her recall of conversations and events.

I showed her the paper and said, 'Do you know anything about this?'
She said, 'I don't know anything about it.'
I said, 'I have been keeping observation and saw you throw it into the corner a few minutes ago' and I pointed to the corner.
She replied, 'I went down the garden to fetch some cinders. If it were my last word I did not put it there. I haven't any paper indoors like that.'
I said 'I shall have to report the matter to Inspector Thomas.'
Mrs. Swan then came up and said, 'What's the matter?'
Miss Swan said 'This Policewoman says she saw me throw this piece of paper.'[1]

Moss broke off the conversation and went into the Mays' house, followed by Violet, whose statement closely matches Moss's account of the exchange.[2] 'Miss Swan appeared white and upset', Violet added when she gave her statement two weeks later.[3]

Moss set off for the police station. Walking up High Street, she encountered Violet's husband, in plain clothes and off duty.[4] Moss explained what had happened, and George May headed to the station with her.[5] Inspector Thomas was away in Arundel for the morning, leaving Constable William Hutchinson in charge of the station.[6] Moss sat down in the office to wait for Thomas. After ten minutes, Edith Swan showed up. Hutchinson spoke to her outside the station. He did not know who she was, and described her as 'a young woman in black'.[7] (Moss and Violet May remembered Edith's outfit that morning as a light-coloured blouse and a dark skirt.)[8] 'I want to see the Inspector', Moss heard Swan say.[9] Hutchinson replied:

'The Inspector is out; what is your business?'
   She said 'The Police Woman is accusing me of throwing down notes.'
   I said 'You had better wait to see the Inspector then.'
   She then said 'I only picked up a piece of paper, and when I saw what it was I threw it down again.'[10]

Hutchinson said that he did not take notes but had 'a perfect recollection of what she said to me'. Edith was 'in a very excited state', he thought. She still had not seen that Moss was inside the station. Hutchinson showed Edith in and gave her a chair.[11] She and Moss sat in the office together for twenty minutes. '[N]either of us spoke', Moss recalled. 'Miss Swan was moving her mouth as if she were talking to herself the whole of the time.'[12]

   Thomas returned from Arundel shortly before one o'clock and Moss went to speak with him out of earshot of Edith Swan. Thomas then went in and took a brief statement from Edith:

I went to the garden to fetch some cinders and two cinders fell from off the shovel. I stooped down to pick them up. I saw a piece of paper lying in the corner in the garden, whether there was any writing on it I do not know. The piece of paper showed to me I do not know what was written on it as I had not my glasses and could not see without them. Its quite a mistake to say that I was seen to throw it down.[13]

Thus in the space of a few hours Edith had given three police officers (Moss, Hutchinson, and Thomas) three different stories: she did not know anything about the paper; she picked it up and threw it down again on seeing the writing on it; she did not know there was any writing on the paper.[14] (Edith's claim that she could not read the letter without her glasses is surprising. Violet May later said that Edith 'does not usually wear glasses, and I have seen her examining the pieces of paper without glasses'.)[15] Signing her statement, Edith said, 'You can keep me here if you like.' Thomas told her the matter would be reported but for the time being she was free to go.[16]

   Though Edith was agitated when she arrived at the police station, she was thinking clearly by the afternoon. At home she wrote to A. S. Williams, the chief constable of West Sussex. (Moss composed a

report to him at much the same time.)[17] 'Dear Sir', Edith wrote, 'Would
you please return to me the anonymous letters and cards found by me,
and handed to P.C. May during the past few weeks.' She understood
that the local police had forwarded them to the chief constable's office
in Horsham.'I would be glad to receive them back as I may need them
as evidence.' In a display of prudence, she enclosed a stamped, self-
addressed envelope.[18] Williams replied two days later, saying he did not
appear to have the letters and cards in question—would she provide a
fuller description of them?[19] Edith replied courteously ('I am in receipt
of your letter of September 29th'), saying that she could not describe
the letters further without sullying herself ('they are of an obscene
nature'). She said she would see Inspector Thomas and find out if he
still had the letters: it was Thomas who had told her the letters were
forwarded to Williams as they came in.'You will know by now', Edith
told Williams, 'that I have been accused by police woman Moss of
Worthing of throwing a piece of paper in the garden at the back of our
house on September 27th. I do not know the contents of the piece of
paper or who it is for. But she told me it had the same sort of stuff
written on it as there was on other papers and cards that had been
found recently.' She concluded: 'As some of them were found by me
and were intended for me, I think if I am to be prosecuted they should
be returned to me as they would help me in my defence.'[20] Williams
did not answer this second letter.[21]

The morning after Moss confronted her, Edith talked to Violet May.
Edith asked her neighbour: 'What does your husband think of the
piece of paper that Police woman accused me of ?'Violet replied: 'My
husband never discusses Police matters with me.' Swan then told Violet
a fourth story about the libel in the garden: 'she said that she went up
the garden with two shovels to fetch some cinders and put one shovel
on top of the other to keep them in, and that it was impossible for her
to throw anything into the corner.' May remained positive that Swan
had carried a single shovel.[22]

Though Edith was taking precautions, the libels against the Mays
continued. So did other mischief. For some time the Mays had been
bothered by someone taking the lid off their dustbin and leaving it on
the ground.Violet spoke to Edith about it, and Edith's father mixed up
an unpleasant solution (being a house painter, Mr Swan knew about
oils and solvents), which he instructed George to smear over the

dustbin lid and handle: 'once they get this stuff on their hands they won't get it off in a hurry'.[23] George May 'did not use this stuff but since that night my dust bin lid has not been touched'. Old Mr Swan spoke quietly, and George was sure the Goodings could not have overheard their conversation.[24] He concluded that it was one of the Swans who had been interfering with his dustbin.[25]

Two nights after the drama over the letter dropped in the garden, the Mays' dog barked suddenly. George went down to the front of the house but found nothing amiss. Bob barked again in the middle of the night; George looked around downstairs in case there was an intruder in the house. He noticed nothing wrong and went back to bed. The next morning, he found that some of his cabbage plants had been pulled up. He had a word to Mr Swan, who offered to plant some new cabbages for him, which he did several days later.[26] Mr Swan thus solved a second problem for the Mays. What was he up to? He could simply have been playing the part of the helpful busybody. It is also possible that Mr Swan was sorting out a problem of his own making.[27] Or he might have known or suspected that one of his children—Edith, maybe, or Steve—was responsible and acted to protect them. He was a vigorous, if not necessarily helpful, defender of Edith when she had fallen under suspicion earlier.

The vandalizing of the Mays' vegetable garden was another event with a written sequel. A piece of green cardboard addressed to 'P. C. May, Cabbage Leaf Villa, Western Road, Local' was allegedly left at the drying ground the following day. Edith alerted Violet:

'I did not know you had a new name for your house.'
   'A new name?'
   'Yes.... It is published up where anybody can see but I will not pick it up as I have made up my mind not to pick up any pieces of paper lying about.'[28]

Edith said that the clothesline had been pulled down and tied in knots. The culprit had also thrown a blouse of Violet's onto the grass, in Rose Gooding's patch of the drying ground. Edith handed Violet the blouse. Violet and her husband searched the drying ground but failed to turn up the postcard. 'I afterwards told Miss Swan I had not found it', Violet stated, 'and I suggested someone else must have picked it up. She then told me about her having seen the Goodings go down there.'[29] Edith thus kept up her efforts to throw suspicion on the Goodings and continued to play the detective in front of Violet.[30]

Edith behaved towards the constable's wife much as she had before Moss caught her.

At the same time, Edith continued to try to shore up her legal position. On Monday 10 October, she went to the regular sitting of the justices of the peace in the Littlehampton council chamber. Presiding was Thomas Horsman, a barrister who lived several minutes' walk and half a world away from Edith in one of the ample houses in the top half of Norfolk Road.[31] Edith applied to the magistrates to order the police to return the anonymous letters she had handed in. She had not had any success getting the letters back from Williams. Edith produced the chief constable's letter asking her to describe them more fully, which was the last communication she had received from him. Horsman asked her if she had indeed provided Williams with more detail about the letters. Edith reiterated that she could not describe them any better than she had already. Frederick Peel, the Arundel police superintendent who had taken Edith's side and could not believe that a woman with Rose Gooding's morals could be innocent, was present in the chamber and took Horsman aside. After speaking to Peel, Horsman turned to Edith and told her he could do nothing for her. As she left the room she said, 'I have still got to go about under suspicion.'[32]

Meanwhile the police operation quietly edged closer to a prosecution. Moss resumed her post in the shed and kept observation for another two weeks. Evidently the police thought that Swan had not realized how Moss had seen her drop the paper in the garden. Even if Edith had not worked it out at the time, it seems likely that one of her parents or brothers witnessed Moss leading Thomas into their garden and showing him the sight lines from the shed later on the day of the confrontation.[33] In any event, Moss saw nothing more of interest. On Saturday 8 October she travelled up to London with Thomas and Chief Constable Williams. They had an appointment with the Director of Public Prosecutions. Sir Archibald Bodkin remained fascinated by 'this remarkable case'.[34] He contacted Scotland Yard and arranged for George Nicholls to attend as well.[35] After the meeting, Bodkin told the Metropolitan Police commissioner that there were still 'a few further enquiries to be made and statements to be taken, and I cannot help thinking that it would be much more satisfactory if Inspector Nicholls could attend to these matters, rather than the local Police Inspector', who, Bodkin added discreetly, 'is perhaps not so accustomed to the taking of statements as Inspector Nicholls'.[36]

The commissioner, Sir William Horwood, assented. By the Tuesday afternoon, Nicholls was on his way to Littlehampton again. He was assisted once more by Leonard Lewis. In the four months since they first worked together, Lewis had been promoted to sergeant and transferred from his home town to Worthing.[37] Over the next two days, Nicholls interviewed Gladys Moss, Violet and George May, Henry Thomas, and William Hutchinson, taking the statements quoted earlier. Nicholls did not take the trouble to interview the Goodings or Ruth Russell. They were not suspects.

Nicholls called on Littlehampton's postmaster to discuss an inchoate investigation of two obscene notes posted the month before. One was addressed to George May and levelled the same accusation as the later note left in the garden made about May's dereliction of duty in failing to discover what 'old four eyes' was bringing home from the Beach Hotel. The other card was addressed to Edith Swan. It called her a whore and finished: 'you are a character'.[38] The Beach Town sub-post office in Norfolk Road processed both these cards on 23 September and forwarded them to the main post office in the town, where they were postmarked at 1:45 p.m. The crowded daily schedule of pickups and deliveries meant that the post office could pinpoint the time they were mailed to a two-hour period that morning. A sorting clerk noticed the obscenities on the cards and intercepted them. The postmaster submitted them to the General Post Office in London, where investigators concluded that there was not enough on which to base a full investigation under the Post Office Act.[39] The GPO did, however, notify Bodkin. He arranged to have the notes sent back to the Littlehampton post office, where they were duly passed on to Nicholls.[40]

Bodkin relished the report in which Nicholls set out his findings. He called it 'exhaustive', which was high praise coming from someone as attentive to detail as Bodkin. The report convinced him to prosecute Edith Swan. Bodkin asked to borrow Nicholls again so that he could be present 'when the warrant is executed by the local police, as it appears to me that this part of the case should receive skilful handling and possibly a search may be found of value'.[41] The DPP's office prepared the text of a warrant stating that Edith Swan had published an 'obscene libel'.[42] She had indeed used obscene words, but 'obscene libel' was the crime that publishers of pornography were charged with—'libel' in the archaic sense of an objectionable document rather than defamation.[43] Rose Gooding's convictions were for criminal libel. The clerk at Littlehampton must have gingerly raised this point: he felt 'some difficulty with regard to the form of the Information as Drawn by the Director of Public Prosecutions' and telephoned Seward Pearce in the DPP's office.[44] They agreed 'that the proceedings against Miss Swan should be on similar lines to those which were taken against Mrs. Gooding'. The Mayor of Arundel signed the new text, which used the standard formula for criminal libel informations, authorizing the arrest of Swan for 'unlawfully writing and publishing a certain false, scandalous and defamatory libel of and concerning one Violet May'.[45] There was just one count of criminal libel, the letter Gladys Moss saw Swan drop in the garden on 27 September 1921.

Nicholls and Thomas went to arrest Swan at her home at 2pm on Friday 21 October. Thomas, in plain clothes, went through the formalities of identifying himself:

'You know who I am'
   She said 'Yes'
   I said 'I have a warrant for your arrest'
   She said 'Well read it to me.'
   I then read the warrant to her and cautioned her she said 'All I can say is its quite untrue.'[46]

Swan handed Thomas the piece of green linen cardboard the paper boy had found, together with the pages of a book she claimed to have found on her scullery roof the Sunday before. She had written the dates on both items. The police then searched the house in Swan's presence and took possession of 'a quantity of memorandum books and papers'—but no blotting paper.[47] Nearly all the recent libels were written in pencil and printed in block letters. 'Miss Swan has not, of course, forgotten how her blotting paper was seized', Nicholls had observed before the arrest, 'and has probably thought a change in the character of writing necessary and that ink should be avoided.'[48]

'Miss Swan was then invited to enter a cab to go to the Police Station', Nicholls noted, 'but she stubbornly refused and proceeded on foot with Inspector Thomas'. At the station she was searched and then locked up in a holding cell. She appeared before the justices the next morning so that they could hear the evidence for the arrest.[49] They granted bail until the pre-trial hearing on 27 October.[50] Edith was able to name two sureties of £10—one was Reuben Lynn—and pledge the same sum herself.[51] She was neither friendless nor penniless, despite the considerable costs she and her family had incurred taking Rose Gooding to court. For the convenience of the justices, the magistrates' court hearing would be held at Arundel, which was part of the same petty sessional district as Littlehampton.[52]

In the days before the hearing, Nicholls followed up leads from the physical evidence. The most important items discovered in the search of the Swans' cottage were a baker's account book and 'two small memo. books each having a cover of green linen card and leaves exactly similar to those Miss Swan handed to Inspector Thomas'. The green books came from a draper's and outfitter's, Messrs McLean, Sutherland and Macrae of Brighton. Nicholls travelled to Brighton and spoke to one of the partners.[53] William McLean told Nicholls he knew the Swan family. 'We have supplied goods to Miss Swan, John Swan, Edward Swan and Steve Swan. . . . The two books now shown to me one in the name of Miss Edith Swan and the other in the name of Alf Swan were issued by my firm.' The other siblings mentioned 'were supplied with books of that description to the best of my knowledge'. McLean, Sutherland and Macrae provided every customer with an account book (the ones bound with green linen ran out in 1919 and were replaced by books with paper covers) that matched the information in the firm's ledgers. Their operation is testimony to the penetration of everyday working-class life by writing and record-keeping. It also attests to the leisureliness with which some businesses in this period called in debts. The last time the firm supplied goods to the Swans was eleven years previously, in 1910, but the most recent payment from the family dated from 1918, when Steve Swan paid off a small balance. Money was still owing on the accounts of Edith and her younger brother John, long domiciled in Australia.[54]

McLean informed Nicholls that they currently sold goods to George Spicer, the cabman and father of the 'silly little fool' Marjorie who lived near the Swans and Goodings.[55] The drapers had never supplied anything to the Goodings or Ruth Russell, though in August or September 1914 they had a single transaction with one of the previous tenants of their cottage. Nicholls thought the information from the drapers significant 'inasmuch as it appears to be in Miss Swan's mind to throw suspicion on the Gooding children, the part of the book handed to Inspector Thomas by her on arrest . . . bearing as it does what might appear to be a child's handwriting. It is clear that Miss Swan had available the material with which to make the writing found by the paper boy under her front door.' The leaves Swan claimed to have found on her scullery roof were also 'undoubtedly out of one of Messrs. McLean, Sutherland and Macrae's books'.[56]

The other book was a lesser triumph of paperwork. It came from Cocksedge's, the Littlehampton baker. (As if to satisfy the old rhyme, the baker had a brother who was a butcher.)[57] The Swans stopped using the baker's account book in April 1920, when they began paying his roundsman weekly. Francis Cocksedge's bakery was now owned by a Mr Wickham, who did not know where his predecessor bought his stationery from. Nicholls spoke to a woman in Wick who used to work at the baker's shop as book-keeper, and she was able to tell him that the books came from James Hunt, a wholesale stationer in London. Nicholls called on the stationers in Fulham, and showed Mr Hunt 'the baker's book, the paper containing the libel [dropped in the garden while Moss was watching], and also the obscene writing found in Littlehampton Post Office on the 23rd September, 1921, each consisting of two leaves'. Hunt 'stated at once that the book was four leaves short and there was no doubt in his mind that the four leaves produced were out of the book'. Hunt said that his manager, Frederick Curnow, would be available to testify in court. Curnow examined the book ('a No 2 quality pass-book') and came to the same conclusion as Hunt.[58]

Nicholls wrapped up his inquiries about the stationery on 25 October and travelled to Arundel in time for Edith Swan's appearance before the magistrates on Thursday the twenty-seventh.[59] The matter was heard in Arundel Town Hall. Now that the Littlehampton libels had become a 'sensation', the national press sent reporters and photographers. The *Daily Mirror*, which had pleaded for compensation for Rose Gooding a few months earlier, carried a photograph of Rose, Bill, and Ruth, making an excursion upriver for the hearing. Ruth is wearing a wide-brimmed hat, Rose a close-fitting one—probably the same hat Gladys Moss had seen her wearing. Bill has a service medal prominently displayed. They are all looking in different directions, perhaps unaccustomed to cameras. The *Mirror* ran head shots of Inspector Thomas and Constables May and Hutchinson, as well as a full-length portrait of Gladys Moss in uniform. There was a close-up of Violet May and a large photograph of Mrs Swan, dressed for the occasion like a Victorian matron (she may well have bought the outfit while Queen

Figure 8.1. Rose Gooding, Bill Gooding, and Ruth Russell, photographed in Arundel. *Daily Mirror*, 28 October 1921

Victoria was still on the throne), walking into the town hall with Edith—tall, saying something, casting her eyes downwards.[60] The *Daily Express* had fewer photographs but compensated with portraits in prose. Both Edith and Violet wore blue serge. Edith wore a long grey cloak over her dress. She sported a black hat 'trimmed with electric-blue ribbon' and wore a white chrysanthemum pinned to her breast. She was wearing her glasses. The *Express*'s special correspondent saw a woman 'smiling and self-possessed'.[61] The Brighton *Argus*, in contrast, described her as 'careworn and dejected'.[62]

Swan had a new solicitor, Charles Longcroft of Chichester. As it was a magistrates' court hearing rather than an assize trial, Longcroft could represent his client himself rather than instruct a barrister. Pearce, the Assistant Director of Public Prosecutions, acted for the Crown. He began by saying that 'the investigation today is quite a distinct and separate matter' from Swan's prosecutions of Rose Gooding. The present matter was confined to the events of 27 September 1921. The nub of the case, Pearce said, was that Edith Swan 'was seen to drop the libel, which was on a piece of paper torn from a book found in her house. If these facts are established the case is proved.' Pearce outlined the evidence against the defendant: the testimony of Moss, Hutchinson, and Violet May; the evidence of Frederick Curnow; and the fact that the paper dropped in the garden could be shown, by its watermarks and the place of the holes in it, to have come from the baker's book supplied

Figure 8.2. Edith Swan and her mother arriving at the magistrates' court in Arundel. *Daily Mirror*, 28 October 1921

by James Hunt. This added up to 'overwhelming evidence that Miss Swan was, if not the author, at least the publisher of the libel'.[63]

The crime of libel lay in the distribution or 'publishing' of the offending words, not the writing of them. Defending Swan, Longcroft blithely disregarded this point of law, telling the justices 'there is no evidence at all to show that [Swan] was the writer of the libel'. It was hard to believe that 'the policewoman'—that customarily nameless figure—'could have seen accurately through a slit in the shed all that took place fifteen yards away in the corner of the garden'. The evidence was all circumstantial, Longcroft said. He then tried to move the case onto the terrain of character and personal history, which had served Swan well when she was on the side of the prosecution: 'Mrs May has told us that Miss Swann has never, in conversation, used any obscene or vulgar words. Is it possible that the writer of these letters could have helped giving herself away in private conversation?'[64] Longcroft's performance was bold, but faced with such evidence for the prosecution the justices were always going to commit Swan for trial at the assizes.[65]

The trial took place at Lewes on Thursday 8 December 1921. Rose and Bill Gooding made the journey to Rose's home town and watched the proceedings from the public gallery.[66] Travers Humphreys presented the Crown's case. Although Swan had changed solicitors, she was represented in court again by the Shoreham barrister Thomas Gates. The presiding judge was Sir Clement Bailhache, another commercial lawyer with no appetite for criminal procedure. Humphreys, who had appeared before Bailhache before, remarked that the judge 'regarded the trial of a criminal case as a matter of little importance, proper to be left to Recorders, Chairmen of Quarter Sessions and such small fry, and he much disliked criminal work on Circuit'.[67] Several times in the courtroom at Lewes Bailhache made light of the proceedings. On hearing the doggerel about Gertrude Russell and Marjorie Spicer being silly little fools, Bailhache said: 'then they are both tarred with the same brush', to laughter from the gallery.[68]

Humphreys methodically examined the prosecution witnesses: Moss, Violet May, Inspector Thomas, the sorting clerk from the post office, and Frederick Curnow of the stationery firm. As at Rose Gooding's appeal at the Royal Courts of Justice, Nicholls was not on the list of witnesses. He found the witnesses and prepared them to testify by taking their statements, but in the courtroom he would simply be an observer. Insofar as newspaper reports make it possible to tell, Humphreys succeeded in getting his witnesses to recapitulate the main points of the statements they had given to Nicholls, though cross-examination by Gates and an intervention from the bench upset the prosecution's narrative somewhat. After Curnow said that the paper containing the libel had been torn from the baker's account book supplied by his firm, the judge remarked, 'I suppose this kind of book is very common', and Curnow replied, 'Yes, my lord', undercutting his testimony.[69] Gates pressed Moss to admit that it was physically possible that a third party outside her range of vision (at the back gate, say) could have thrown the piece of paper to the spot where she saw it come to rest. The barrister then flung a piece of paper across the courtroom to show that it could travel the requisite four yards before hitting the ground.[70]

Both Humphreys and Gates allowed Henry Thomas to wander off into the background to the case, such as the fact that Edith's 'sweetheart in India'—Mr Swan, too, thought his prospective son-in-law was still on the Subcontinent rather than in Iraq—had received offensive letters about her. Gates asked him whether he had received such letters himself, and Thomas replied that he had received so many that he 'placed a piece of oilcloth inside the front door to prevent things from being pushed underneath'.[71] The judge broke in: 'It seems a rather silly form of amusement. What is the object of it, officer?' Thomas said he had not the least idea. 'It may be mental trouble', Humphreys suggested.[72]

When it was time for the defence to present its case, Gates at once called Edith Swan to the stand. She identified herself as a laundress, spurning the designations commonly applied to single women in such situations, 'spinster' and 'of no profession'. Edith told the court that on the morning of 27 September she 'went down the garden to fetch some cinders' with two shovels, one in each hand. She had thus settled on the story she told Violet May the morning of the twenty-eighth, not one of the several explanations she gave Moss, Hutchinson, and Thomas.[73] Nicholls wrote a few days later: 'The defence amounted to a complete denial of the offence and insinuation throughout that the Goodings were the guilty ones.'[74] The reporter for *The Times* observed that Edith 'stoutly denied having written any of the libels, and added that at one time nearly every one in the street received them'.

Edith's reference to the earlier libels prompted Humphreys to cross-examine her about them, departing from the strategy Pearce had outlined before the magistrates when he declared that *Rex v. Swan* was strictly about the paper Swan dropped in the garden on 27 September.

Humphreys asked Swan about her two prosecutions of Rose Gooding. Bailhache had reservations about this line of questioning. Not unreasonably, he asked Humphreys why he was not prosecuting Swan for perjury if he wanted to rake over the previous trials.[75] Bailhache nevertheless let Humphreys proceed. Under cross-examination, Swan admitted that she had prosecuted Gooding 'for publishing similar libels to the one with which she herself was now charged with publishing. After these trials were over, a Scotland Yard detective came and searched her house. He found a piece of blotting paper on which was the impression of one of the libels in question.' Humphreys pressed the witness:

How do you account for that?
   Mrs. Gooding borrowed the blotting paper.
   What was the date upon it?
   January 1921.
   What did you tell the detective?
   He said to me:—'Confess to me, and say you wrote the libel.'—I said 'No, I did not write it. My father brought in some blotting paper which he found in the washhouse.'[76]

'Sensational collapse', one newspaper interjected as its report reached this point in the hearing.[77] Edith's unexpected accusation stung Nicholls; when he reported to his superiors, he felt obliged to defend himself against her 'untruthful...alleg[ation]' that he had pressured her to confess.[78] Humphreys had underestimated Swan. The experience stayed with him. In his memoir *Criminal Days*, published twenty-five years later, Humphreys wrote that he thought about the case often, because it exposed a weakness in English justice. Like most senior advocates, judges, and statesmen, he avowed that juries hardly ever convicted innocent people. But the Littlehampton libels taught him that a miscarriage of justice could occur easily if one condition was satisfied: if a respectable-looking woman was willing to perjure herself. No jury would doubt her. This was the same lesson Bodkin drew from the Tugwell case. And it was the key to Swan's success in her two prosecutions of Rose Gooding. '[S]he was the perfect witness', Humphreys reflected. 'Neat and tidy in her appearance, polite and respectful in her answers, with just that twinge of feeling to be expected in a person who knows herself to be the victim of circumstances, she would have deceived, nay she did deceive, the very

elect'—not just stout-minded English jurors, but even a criminal lawyer of Horace Avory's calibre.[79]

Bailhache too was convinced by Swan's demeanour, her self-presen-
tation as a 'victim of circumstances' trying to defend herself against
implausibly sordid accusations. There is no other explanation for his
refusal to give credence to the evidence of Moss and the others. After
letting Mr Swan give evidence—'merely to the effect that his daughter
was a thoroughly good woman'—Bailhache brought the trial to a pre-
mature end.[80] He asked Humphreys if he wished to proceed further
and announced: 'If I were on the jury, I would not convict.'[81] 'In the
face of such a statement from the Bench it was impossible to proceed
further', Humphreys recalled.[82] He told the judge: 'If that is your lordship's view, I have no doubt the jury will accept it.' 'We have heard
enough', said one of the jurors. The jury returned a verdict of not
guilty, and Swan was discharged.[83]

'A very disappointing result after Inspector Nicholls' excellent
work', wrote a Metropolitan Police lawyer whose illegible signature is
ubiquitous in case files from the 1920s.[84] Nicholls and the rest of the
police were blamed for the failure of the prosecution when *John Bull*
roused itself again. Horatio Bottomley, then in his last few months of
freedom, was no longer in charge, but his ghost and his ghost-writers
continued to guide *John Bull* under a new editor, Charles Pilley.[85]
Pilley wrote to the Metropolitan Police commissioner, Horwood,
describing himself as 'a public man' and as such duty-bound 'to give the
authorities every possible assistance towards the solution of those dif-
ficulties with which from time to time they are confronted'. The mystery of the Littlehampton libels had to be solved, and to that end Pilley
offered to lend the Metropolitan Police one of the 'trained investigators' on his staff. *John Bull* employed a stable of investigators 'recruited
from private detective agencies and retired policemen', and they had
achieved good results 'in circumstances of similar difficulty'.[86] Pilley
assured the commissioner that the offer came with no strings attached
and that any 'information which comes into their possession shall be
treated as entirely confidential, and will not be used for any journalistic
purposes'.[87] Horwood replied through his secretary that, because the
matter took place in West Sussex, the chief constable in Horsham was
the right person to approach, but he made clear his own view that 'the
employment of private individuals for the investigation of crime was
neither necessary nor conducive to the proper administration of

justice'.[88] Pilley printed the reply and fulminated about the need for 'a national police organization having its headquarters in London, and spreading a network of detective agencies throughout the land....[T]here will be no progress while a public man who seeks to elucidate a mystery which has excited the whole country is referred to Horsham!'[89]

Several months later, George Nicholls was promoted to chief inspector, becoming one of Scotland Yard's 'big four'.[90] *John Bull* gave him some advice: 'We suggest that Inspector Nicholls, before he establishes himself in his new position, should return to Littlehampton and clear up the muck and muddle he left behind him.'[91] As he had been defamed in his professional capacity, Nicholls tried to get the Home Office to sue the paper for libel. Sir Ernley Blackwell determined that the slight was too personal for the state to get involved, but Nicholls was given permission to bring a private law suit. *John Bull*'s owner, the publisher Odhams, settled out of court for 250 guineas, Nicholls's legal costs, and a muted apology on an inside page of the paper. (Nicholls's lawyers had initially demanded an apology on the front page.)[92] Pilley's experience editing a paper that constantly elicited libel writs no doubt came in useful as he wrote *Law for Journalists* (1924).[93]

Nicholls, of course, had many other claims on his attention, as did the prosecutors. Later in 1922, Humphreys appeared for the Crown in the murder trial of another woman incriminated by her letters. Edith Thompson was charged together with her boyfriend Freddy Bywaters for murdering Thompson's husband. Controversially, the prosecution used her imaginative, fantastic letters to Bywaters to argue that she was more than an accessory: that she was as guilty as the man who wielded the knife.[94] She was convicted and hanged for it. Bodkin's obsessiveness was such that he did not put old cases and missed chances out of his mind even while he shouldered far more of the day-to-day burden of public prosecutions than was necessary. The director, as he habitually referred to himself when dictating instructions, waited for another opportunity to move against Edith Swan. As his friend Humphreys put it, Bodkin 'had no intention of letting the question of who was the author of the Littlehampton libels fade into "the grey twilight of forgotten things," as my late client Oscar Wilde once wrote.'[95]

9

Bad Language

The abusive cards and letters Violet and George May received in
September and October 1921 are the only libels that survive in the
files in the National Archives. All the others were removed or simply
lost as the exhibits from successive trials passed between court clerks
and the Home Office. The originals of the libels leading up to Edith
Swan's trial at the assizes have disappeared too. What remains is a com-
pilation by a police typist, with the heading 'Indecent Writings Found'
and a brief annotation by Inspector Nicholls explaining the provenance
of two postcards.[1] To read the whole document is to come up against
the libels' nastiness and their humour, their anger and their pathos, their
surprises and their monotony.

5th September, 1921:
To old bastards Mayy. You can talk about us as much as you like you dirty
cows. You bloody fucking sods, you think you are big but we are as good as
you. You are bloody dirty or you would clean the yard sometimes you bloody
rotten buggers.

7th September, 1921:
To the two old buggers May and there whore Neybor. You bloody dirty fucking sods. You all want burning alive. The whole whore wont laugh when she
finds herself in the dock in the high court soon.

14th September 1921:—
You bloody fucking flaming piss country whores go and fuck your cunt. Its
your drain that stinks not our fish box. Yo fucking dirty sods. You are as bad as
your whore neybor.

17th September, 1921:—
(1) To the two old buggers May at 49, Western Rd, Local. You bloody fucking
piss country whores. It is your drain that stinks. Not our fish box as the old
whore said.

(2) You bloody flaming fucking piss country whores. You will get more than a stink before long. You will find yourselves in the dock the lot of you you bloody fucking buggers. We might as well be in hell as to live next door to you dirty sods.

20th September:—

Bloody fucking old bastard May and fucking old whore May and bloody fucking whore Swan. All three want boiling in tar. Go and fuck your cunts you piss country whores.

23rd September, 1921:—

(1) To fucking old bastard May, 49, Western Rd, Local. You bloody foxy ass bastard you don't do your duty or you would find out what old four eyes brings home in a sack from the Beach Hotel.

(2) To the foxy ass whore 47, Western Rd Local. you foxy ass piss country whore you are a character.[2]

27th September, 1921:—

To fucking old whore May, 49, Western Rd, Local. You and your fucking whore neybor can throw as many jeers as you like but God will punish you you foxy ass piss country whores. Your old bugger of a husband don't do his duty or else he would want to know what old four eyes brings home in a sack from the beach hotel. He will soon be reported by Detective Blackman.

7th October, 1921:—

We are not going because you want us to you poxy ass piss country whores. We shall stay all the longer now.

The complaints range from infernal torment to domestic irritation. Many of them, as we have already seen, were written as if by Rose Gooding: 'Its your drain that stinks not our fish box'; 'We are not going because you want us to.' These letters and cards threatened Swan with payment in kind, a date in court. Like Annie Tugwell in the Sutton case, trying to sound common like Canon Cafferata's housekeeper ('me and the dear Canon knows'), the Littlehampton libels could be clumsy in their attempts to ventriloquize a 'rough' housewife: 'you think you are big'; 'don't do his duty'. At other points, while still writing as Rose, Edith was careful with her syntax—'We might as well be in hell as to live next door to you'—if not refined: 'We shall stay all the longer now.' At such points, the libels of September–October 1921 recall the letter sent to the Littlehampton sanitary inspector shortly after all the trouble began, a note that combined profanity with primness: 'I don't care for your Fucking Committee.'[3] I don't care *for*, not *about*.

The libels mixed conventional curses—you want boiling in tar, living next to you is like being in hell—with decidedly strange ones. Just what is a 'foxy ass piss country whore'? The *Oxford English Dictionary* is not much help here. Nor does Eric Partridge's great *Dictionary of Slang and Unconventional English* provide any assistance in accounting for Edith's habit of joining 'piss' and 'country'—unless 'piss country' was a mis-hearing of 'piss-factory', slang for a pub, and so an imputation of drunkenness.[4] It is possible that 'piss country' was a regional expression, though as a town dweller and someone who received a board school education, Edith was less likely to know dialect words and figures of speech than an agricultural worker of her parents' generation.[5] W. D. Parish's Sussex dialect dictionary, compiled in the later nineteenth century, has nothing about 'piss' and its derivatives. Parish was a vicar and so could be expected to pass over profanities. He did, however, note the distinctive regional meaning of the verb 'fornicate': to dawdle or waste time.[6] 'A Sussex man', Parish observed, 'has a great facility for inventing words. If he has any difficulty in expressing himself, he has no hesitation about forming a word for the occasion.' '[B]esides those words in the Sussex dialect which are really valuable as having been derived from authentic sources, there are a great many which are very puzzling to the etymologist, from the fact of their having been either actually invented without any reference to the laws of language, or adapted and corrupted from other words.' These invented words were 'generally very curious indeed; and whether or not the word serves the purpose for which it was intended, it is sure to be caught up by some one else'.[7] But it is probably a stretch to think that Edith was a late exponent of this declining Sussex tradition.

'Foxy ass', at least, can be explained. (Saying 'ass' rather than 'arse' was unusual in British forms of English, but it was commonly sounded and spelled that way in some parts of southern England, though apparently not in Sussex.[8] All the documents referring to Rose Gooding's use of the word 'arsehole' spelled it the usual British way.) The note of 7 October used 'poxy', an insult of long standing, but the many instances of 'foxy' are not typing errors for 'poxy', as one of Inspector Nicholls's reports shows.[9] The appearance of the word 'foxy' in the Littlehampton libels predates its currency as a synonym for attractive or sassy. In Sussex it could be used, of the weather, to mean deceptive or uncertain ('A fisherman...remarking upon the weather, pronouncing the appearance of the sky to be very foxy').[10] Much further north, in Lincolnshire and Yorkshire, the word could also mean rank or rancid, 'having an offensive smell like a fox'.[11] The most likely meaning of the word in the context of the libels was 'denot[ing] various defects of colour and quality resulting from atmospheric conditions, improper treatment, etc'—like the 'foxing' that mars old books.[12] The *Family Dyer and Scourer* of 1818 advised how to clean silks that 'appear rusty, or what is known to the dyers by the name of copper burnt, or foxy' ('pass them through warm water in which about half a tea-spoonful of oil of vitriol has been thrown').[13] Being a laundress, Edith may well have been familiar with this sense of the word. According to Joseph Wright's monumental *English Dialect Dictionary*, compiled at the end of the nineteenth century, fabrics, flour, timber, fruit, and vegetables could all be foxy. In a variety of counties, including Worcestershire, Oxfordshire, Somerset, and Cornwall, the word meant 'Speckled, spotted with mould or mildew; having some defect in colour, uneven in shade'.[14] If this is the sense in which Edith was using the word, she was accusing her neighbours of having spotty asses.

She also called them much worse, of course. When used as an insult, 'bastard' was sometimes directed against women as well as men at this time, so referring to both the Mays as 'old bastards' was not eccentric; calling them both 'dirty cows' was, since 'cow' was almost always used against women.[15] 'Bugger' and 'sod' had long since become generalized insults and were not necessarily intended as homophobic slurs.[16] Bill Gooding had allegedly called his wife a sod and a bugger when they quarrelled.[17] In several witness statements taken in the course of Nicholls's initial investigation in June 1921, the word is spelled 'buggar', possibly reflecting the speakers' pronunciation or perhaps just the idiosyncrasy or innocence of the typist on duty. 'Bloody', 'bugger', and 'bastard' (when used solely as an insult), to say nothing of 'fuck', were all strong enough to get replaced by stars or dashes in newspapers and books. Edith also tossed around the most taboo word in the language. She used it in a very irregular construction: 'go and fuck your cunt'. There are very few documented instances of this kind of combination of 'fuck' and 'cunt' without an indirect object ('go and fuck your cunt with . . .' being slightly more common).[18] Edith's abusive language had other oddities too. She piled up adjectival forms without connecting them so that they read like lists rather than words working together: 'Bloody fucking old', 'bloody dirty fucking', 'bloody fucking piss country', 'bloody flaming fucking piss country'.

In British working-class culture, swearing was subject to codes that governed what was appropriate for men and women and what kinds of conduct belonged in and out of the home.[19] Swearing was most common, if not expected, in exclusively male workplaces: as in the armed forces, sexual humour and the persistent use of 'the sexual swear-words' were ways of demonstrating community and conformity.[20] The rules about swearing were described most fully by the social researchers Norman Dennis, Fernando Henriques, and Clifford Slaughter. Their findings can only be a rough guide to norms in Littlehampton in the 1920s, since Dennis and his colleagues did their fieldwork at a later time, the 1950s, in a very different place, the Yorkshire coal-mining town of Featherstone. In mining communities the roles—and spaces—occupied by men and women were highly segregated, much more so than in a southern English town without a dominant industry or employer and more opportunities for waged work for women. In Featherstone, swearing and 'a general attitude of toughness and near-callousness in conversation' were rituals of the pit. Dennis, Henriques, and Slaughter thought that the miners' swearing increased in intensity as the cage descended. There was less profanity in conversations above ground, though swear words still punctuated conversation in 'the club, the pub, the bookie's office, and the trade union'. All these 'places where men ... talk together ... are closed to women'. When a woman did enter a Featherstone pub one week day, a man who swore was warned that a lady was present. He only half-apologized, saying that 'she must expect to hear what comes out if she will come into the place at all'. 'This did not exonerate him, however, and he was compelled to leave.'[21] (A social anthropologist working in South Wales mining communities witnessed many fist fights that were sparked by one man swearing in front of another's wife.)[22] A man who swore vigorously down the pit moderated his language in the pub, and cleaned it up altogether at home in the presence of women and children.[23]

The 'morality of swearing', Dennis and his co-authors reflected, 'is of some significance, for it goes along with other divisions in thought and action', and above all the gender divide between work and home.[24] Women were expected not to swear, with exemptions granted for genuine crises.[25] Mothers policed their children's language. 'The two main topics about which Mums are severe are bad language and speaking about sex', wrote the social psychologist Madeleine Kerr in another of the 1950s' many 'community studies', this one about a poor quarter of Liverpool.[26] Kerr added that the prohibition on swearing was probably explained 'by the fact that these forbidden words are sexual in meaning and therefore must not be mentioned by or to children'.[27]

When George Nicholls first interviewed the people of Western Road he made a point of asking them what kind of language their neighbours used, whether they had ever heard them swearing. Their answers indicated that the ban on swearing in the home held up reasonably well. Although Ruth Russell had heard Stephen and Ernest Swan 'make use of the words "fucking and bugger" occasionally', neither she nor anyone else had ever heard Edith or Mr or Mrs Swan swear.[28] Despite the Goodings' noisy rows, many of their neighbours said that they had not heard them swear either. Mrs Swan certainly had, though she was careful to say that Rose did not swear all the time but rather when under pressure. 'She was a very foul mouthed woman when she was upset. I have heard her and her husband quarrelling, on 4 or 5 occasions during the time they have lived here. I have not heard them use bad language to the children.' Mrs Swan had, however, heard one of the children use 'filthy language'.[29]

But the prohibition on swearing at home was never watertight, and someone like Edith, who did not use profanities in conversation, was inevitably familiar with them all the same. However, because she was not a party to the banter of a masculine workplace or talk in a pub or the slanging matches of a 'rough' household, Edith was not a native speaker of four-letter words. This is why her swearing can sound childlike. A child experimenting with swear words and getting odd results—sometimes strikingly odd results—is not an initiated member of the language community where swearing is practised regularly. Edith's profanity was 'bad language' not just in the ordinary sense, but also in the allusive sense used by Greg Dening in his cultural history of the *Bounty* mutiny: a failure to master the codes of a specific social setting.[30]

In this respect Edith was the obverse of a commonly observed phenomenon in English life. Social investigators and working-class authorities explaining 'their people' to outsiders would remark on how many manual workers 'had larger vocabularies than they could pronounce'.[31] They encountered in print words that they never heard in conversation. (This is probably true of anyone who can read, but only with working-class people did it seem noteworthy.) Popular fiction as well as more daunting reading matter had this effect. Flora Thompson, whose life in Oxfordshire became the basis for her *Lark Rise* trilogy on the old rural order, told the story of a devotee of the romances and mysteries published in the hugely popular *Bow Bells* and *Family Herald* who insisted on regaling the young Laura (a proxy for Thompson) with the plot of the story she was currently reading.[32] The villain was a colonel—fictional army officers usually retired at that rank—and Mrs Braby 'pronounced it "col-on-el", as spelt', to the child's consternation. In Edith Swan's case, it was not Latinate words or the counters of melodramatic fiction that were familiar but unmastered: it was the words whose euphemistic labels—'Anglo-Saxon', 'the vernacular'— imply that they are simple and come easily.[33]

In contrast, as the letters she wrote to the chief constable of West Sussex made clear, Edith was proficient in the language of official correspondence—the 'linguistic waste of crystallized phrases' that a contemporary philologist despaired of.[34] Edith wrote far more assuredly than, say, Bill Gooding did in his communications with the Home Office. The whole dispute with the Goodings had begun when Edith wrote the National Society for the Prevention of Cruelty to Children a letter of complaint cogent enough to draw a response. Edith kept a paper trail relating to the libel case. In her first formal interview with Nicholls, Edith related the story of Rose and her mother and sister collaborating on an offensive note about Constable Russell and explained: 'I made notes of all this at the time and I copied these notes out and took them to the trial at Lewes.'[35] Searching the Swans' house after Edith's arrest, Nicholls found a collection of newspaper cuttings relating to Rose Gooding's trials as well as letters from other people mentioning the case and a copy of an outgoing letter on the same subject. Edith made what she called a memorandum of an incriminating conversation between Rose and Ruth Russell that she supposedly overheard. Edith drew from this memorandum in one of the letters she wrote to *John Bull*. She kept copies of these letters to the newspaper.[36]

Edith sometimes acted as scribe for her family, writing letters to her scattered siblings while her parents sat nearby, chipping in news or dictating passages for Edith to include. Literate children frequently wrote for their parents; in Flora Thompson's village, itinerant labourers would call at the post office and ask the postmistress to take down letters to their wives back in Ireland.[37] Edith's parents could read (her father certainly could), but Edith was probably a more proficient writer. She could also have been saving her parents from having to squint at the paper. There was a family history of short-sightedness. Steve's thick glasses have already figured in this story. Neither he nor Ernest seems to have been much of a writer. 'I never write any letters for myself', Steve told Nicholls, 'and have only posted news-papers to my brothers John and George in Australia, my sister asked me to post them.'[38]

Edith's teacher at East Street School remembered her as 'slow at school, but very clever at Essay writing, and a good penman'.[39] The inconsistency of this appraisal probably just means that Edith did poorly in parts of the curriculum that the severe Miss Boniface valued more than essay-writing. The meticulous way Edith handled official correspondence suggests pride, if not pleasure, in her writing. Describing the letters of complaint or inquiry that Soviet citizens wrote in the 1930s, the historian Sheila Fitzpatrick observes: 'Writing letters to the authorities surely was, or at least could be, as much a form of popular culture and an expression of popular creativity as the amateur theatricals and balaika playing that are usually listed under these headings.'[40] There is no indication that Edith was a scholar manquée or an active reader, let alone a participant in the formal institutions of self-improvement and adult education. Yet it seems more than possible that she shared the sense of being cheated that many representatives of the British auto-didact tradition felt, plucked prematurely from school to go to work and haunted in adulthood by lost opportunities.[41] There was an implicit assertion of superiority—in intelligence, in 'culture'—in the letter Edith wrote to the police the week after Rose Gooding returned home from prison for the second time. When she related her story of eavesdropping on Ruth Russell telling Rose that in her absence Ruth had discovered and posted several of her sister's 'choice books', Edith claimed that Rose had asked her sister whether the libellous notebooks had been sent out anonymously. Or nearly: 'Mrs Gooding asked her if they were sent out ominously (not anonymously) and she replied they were.'[42] Informing the police of a conversation she had in fact fabricated, Edith invented a malapropism to correct.

The early twentieth-century proletariat, wrote Robert Roberts, one of its most perceptive interpreters, numbered many men and women who 'possessed a much larger vocabulary than their neighbours in general. True, many of their words, having been picked up from print only, were mispronounced, but such error was a sign of intelligence struggling for self-expression. They showed impatience with the many stale saws and clichés that peppered working-class talk...'[43] Stephen

Reynolds, a middle-class political reformer who lived among Devon fishermen studying their lifeways and their politics, also detected a restlessness in many working-class people's language. 'The poor man's vocabulary, like the poet's, is quite inadequate to express his thoughts', Reynolds wrote. 'Both, in their several ways, are driven to the use of unhackneyed words and simile and metaphor; both use a language of great flexibility, for which reason we find that after the poet himself, the poor man speaks most poetically.... New words are eagerly seized; hence the malapropisms that are so frequently made fun of, without appreciation of their cause.' Reynolds gave as an example the word 'obsolete', which had passed from Navy bulletins into local working-class usage 'through sons who are bluejackets'. 'Now, when Tony wishes to sum up in one word the two facts that he is older and also less vigorous than formerly, he says, "Tony's getting obsolete, like." A soulless word, borrowed from official papers, has acquired for us a poetic wealth of meaning in which the pathos of the old ship, of declining years, and of Tony's own ageing, are present with one knows not what other suggestions beside. And when *obsolete* is fully domesticated here, the *like* will be struck off.... [E]very time Tony uses *like*, he is admitting, and explaining, that he has expressed himself as best he could, but inadequately notwithstanding. He has felt something more delicately, thought upon something more accurately, than he can possibly say.'[44]

M. E. Loane agreed that '[t]he number of words in common use among the lower classes is greatly underestimated.... A rich and picturesque vocabulary is a real pleasure to them.' Where Reynolds emphasized the dignity and creativity of working people's use of unusual words, Loane, though sympathetic, could not resist going for laughs. 'The finest word I have heard in use lately', she went on, 'came from a country groom. A lad was helping him harness a horse, and asked which of the two straps he was to buckle first. "Oh, it's quite immaterial," replied the groom. "He talks like a book" may often be truly said of the poor. They *do*; and very stiff and pompous books into the bargain. I have seen many cottage neighbours who make such remarks as: "I see your new fence is under course of construction," "My son's present habitation is in a most salubrious situation," "Our monarch would appear to be upon amicable terms with the majority of the foreign royalties."'[45] Of course, most working-class people did not use words like 'habitation' and 'salubrious' all the time. If they did, these stories would not have been worth Loane's while as a reporter on the customs of the poor. In another book, Loane remarked that people with varied vocabularies were careful about disclosing the fact: she thought that working-class people often kept their speech simple when in the company of the middle classes, lest they be thought to be putting on airs. The district nurse found that after spending a few days with a patient or family they would start 'using a far larger and more refined vocabulary than they did at first'.[46]

The Edith Swan who wrote 'ominously (not anonymously)' was not so reticent. Nor was Rose Gooding. Rose conspicuously used the word 'menagerie' one afternoon in September 1921, ten days before Gladys Moss confronted Edith. The word was so rich it nearly became a liability. A few days later, Edith called Violet May into her house and showed her an obscene note that used the same word.[47] 'Menagerie' appeared in another libel at the beginning of October.[48] This was the green notebook cover that made the paper boy laugh so. In block letters was a string of mock addresses. The joke that the Mays' house should be called 'Cabbage Leaf Villa' got another airing, and Western Road received a new name:

Old bugger May.
Cabbage leaf villa.
Old whore May
Cabbage leaf villa.
Old whore Swan zoo cottage.
Mennajearie Alley
Old whore Bedford.
Whore inn hotel.[49]

As the reference to a zoo indicates, Edith herself knew what 'menagerie' meant. Having previously impugned Rose Gooding's literacy, Edith was now using her neighbour's knowledge of a difficult word as a means of fingering her for the libels. Edith made sure that there was an independent witness to what Rose had said. 'Did you hear what they said about the menagerie?' she asked Violet May. Violet said she had. '[A] few days after Mrs. Gooding had used the word "Menagerie", Miss Swan called me into her house and showed me two pieces of paper.... The word "Menagerie" was on one of them...'[50]

The occasion for Rose's use of the magnetic word was the commotion made by a man promoting an entertainment. It was a Saturday afternoon at the end of summer, and the man made his way down

Western Road in a horse-drawn cart, ringing a bell and shouting through a megaphone about a concert party.[51] Rose and her sister heard what he was saying before they saw him. As they walked down the passage from their house out to the street, Violet May heard Rose say to Ruth, 'I wouldn't pay to go and see them I see enough pictures.'[52] Rose and Ruth came out onto Western Road. Their children joined them to watch the strangely spellbinding progress of the cart down the street. It is as if the workaday rhythm of the afternoon skipped or slowed down. The moment is almost cinematic, or like something in a modernist novel: unexpected sounds or colours disturb the urban scene, like the gaudy tins of pineapple in a shop window looming out of the grey of Henry Green's Birmingham, or the heavy sound of Big Ben becoming half-visible in Virginia Woolf's London.[53] Perhaps that is another case of literary tradition over-helpfully suggesting a way to read the documents of the past. The horse pulled its booming, clanging load away down the street. The two sisters and their children turned back in. 'We have enough of a menagerie down here', Rose said.[54]

10

It Is Not My Verdict

After Edith Swan's acquittal in late 1921 there was a lull: and then the offensive letters began circulating again. Although the lawyers and police officers who brought her to trial had no doubt that Swan wrote the libels, plenty of people who knew Edith had other ideas about who was responsible. When Caroline Johnson, a friend of Edith's living on Western Road, received a letter accusing her of being a prostitute, she decided to do something about it.

On a Saturday morning in September 1922, Rose Gooding returned home from shopping. She had just got in the door when Johnson stormed in. According to Rose, the visitor announced: 'Mrs. Gooding, I will teach you to talk about me and my friend, Miss Swan.' Without waiting for a reply, Johnson 'struck her on the face, seized her by the hair, and pushed her out of the door'. Dazed, Rose collapsed in the street. 'I reeled and remember nothing more till I was helped indoors', she explained later. It was her mother, visiting from Lewes, who assisted her back inside. Barbara Russell corroborated her daughter's story, adding that Caroline Johnson 'picked up a broom and threw it at her daughter as she lay unconscious'. Violet May 'said she did not hear much, only a lot of muttering, one smack, and a voice say, "I am old mother Johnson."' (Rose had once allegedly called Mrs Swan 'old Mother Swan'; had Caroline Johnson's letter addressed her in the same idiom?) May 'saw Mrs. Johnson going into Mrs. Gooding's house, and about three minutes later Mrs. Gooding came out in a dazed condition and fell down.' Violet helped Rose to her feet and then went to wake her husband, who was sleeping in after a shift on night duty. Caroline Johnson followed the constable's wife to the back of the Mays' house. This annoyed George, and he gave Johnson a piece of his mind. She stood her ground, telling him: 'She is not going to write anything about me, saying I walk the streets. I have not finished with her yet.'[1]

Rose responded with a private prosecution of her own. She secured the services of Thomas Gates, the same barrister who prosecuted her and defended Edith Swan. Gates obtained a summons, and Caroline Johnson had to answer a charge of assault. Johnson retained Charles Longcroft, Edith's solicitor, to defend her.[2] The offence being common assault, Johnson's case could be decided by the local justices of the peace instead of an assize judge and jury. The magistrates' court convened, as usual, on a Monday morning in the Littlehampton council chamber.

Gates related the facts of the case and noted that 'defamatory letters were being written again'.[3] Placed in the awkward situation of having to represent opposing sides at different times, Gates added: 'it may be the writer is the same person who victimised Mrs. Gooding'.[4] He called Rose, who recounted the events of that Saturday morning. Her mother also testified, as did George May. Asked whether 'libellous letters' were circulating again, May replied, 'Yes, I have had one.'[5] The defence admitted the assault, 'but urged that there were mitigating circumstances'. 'Mrs Johnson', Longcroft stated, 'had received one of these libellous letters, and it was in consequence of this that, rightly or wrongly, she went to see Mrs. Gooding about it, with the result that an assault was committed.'[6] When it was his turn to reply, Gates said that 'the defendant was obviously accusing Mrs. Gooding of publishing reports concerning her, but that was no justification for wreaking her vengeance on Mrs. Gooding in the way she did'.[7]

After deliberating in private, the justices convicted Johnson of assault and fined her £1.[8] This was a modest fine, though it was twice that imposed on another woman convicted of assault at the same hearing.[9] Magistrates' courts did not have the power to impose stiff penalties. All the same, it is remarkable that Caroline Johnson was fined a pound for entering Rose Gooding's house, hitting her, and throwing her out into the street, while writing abusive letters warranted imprisonment. The justices made no order for costs: Rose would have to pay her own legal bills.[10]

If this outcome was less satisfying than Rose might have hoped, the hearing was also the occasion for an exchange that alarmed her husband. Bill Gooding overheard Gates talking to Frederick Peel. The police superintendent at Arundel had recently been promoted to deputy chief constable of West Sussex. Peel was a regular presence at the Littlehampton magistrates' court. He was the senior police officer for the petty sessional district that encompassed both Arundel and Littlehampton. Bill heard him tell Gates 'that he is still convinced that it is my wife that writes the letters'.[11]

Frederick Peel and Caroline Johnson were not the only ones who held this view. Within two days of the assault trial, the Home Office received an anonymous note that read: 'I believe Mrs Gooding to be the leading figure assisted by others.' 'The best course', advised the writer, 'will be to send the police to caution Mrs Gooding and her relatives that should either of them be caught the person caught would receive 3 years penal servitude....Should the nuisance continue during the time the person is in prison don't let the person out.'[12] Unsurprisingly, a civil servant annotated the letter with the words 'Lay by'.[13]

The assault trial sparked a revival of national interest in the Littlehampton libels, nearly a year after Edith Swan was prosecuted. 'Special correspondents' for newspapers filed stories about the latest developments or, more often, suggested that dramatic announcements were imminent, though little detail was available. The Bognor Regis correspondent of the *Daily News* reported shortly after Caroline Johnson's conviction: 'There are likely to be surprising developments in connection with the libellous letters and offensive postcards which are being circulated anonymously at Littlehampton.' If anything, he wrote, 'the letters are being circulated in larger numbers than ever, even the inspectors, superintendent, and constables receiving them'. There was nothing new about this, of course: members of the West Sussex police were receiving obscene mail even before Rose Gooding's first trial. 'I am told', the *Daily News* correspondent concluded, 'that the police believe they are now in possession of information that will lead to the arrest of the guilty parties. Every anonymous letter now received is handed to either Inspector Thomas or Deputy Chief Constable Peel. I have reason for saying that the arrest will create a sensation in Littlehampton.'[14]

Two months later, another newspaper reported from Littlehampton that there was renewed hope that 'the mysterious writer of the hundreds of disgusting letters which have tortured the majority of the inhabitants for the past three years may be tracked down shortly'. According to the report, the libeller had switched from posting letters at the Beach post

office and now favoured a mailbox in Arundel Road. 'The search for the
criminal has been narrowed down, it is said, to the one part of the town
to which nearly all the letters referred'—again, not a great discovery.
The correspondent added that there was 'no foundation in fact for the
suggestion that a local vigilance committee is to be formed in view of
the police failure to bring the criminal to justice'.[15]

The *Daily Mail's* correspondent had the best informants. He reported
that '[i]n the last few weeks'—that is, around the time Caroline Johnson
assaulted Rose Gooding—'the letters have been more frequent, more
indecently and subtly worded, and spread over a wider area than
before. . . . Almost every variety of notepaper has been used, but the
handwriting is always similar.' The recipients included a magistrate,
court officials, solicitors, police who had testified in the several libel
cases, and the people who stood bail for both Rose and Edith. 'The
unknown author of these letters has been trying to sow suspicion
between husband and wife, girl and boy lovers, employers and employees, and friends', the *Mail's* correspondent continued. He had the
chance to examine one of the labels. It was sent to a man 'whom I will
call "Mr. X." He was surprised to find it began "Dear Mr. Y." ("Y"
being a friend of Mr. "X.") Mr X. thought it had been put in the
wrong envelope, but his eye caught the signature of a married woman
at the bottom of the letter, and also the expression: "You promised you
would come again to me, but you didn't. Why? My husband is a bigger
brute than ever." In this instance Mr. X knew his friend well enough
to have faith in him.'[16]

In despair, Bill Gooding wrote to George Nicholls in London. '[C]an
nothing be done Sir to help us clear ourselves[?]' he asked. He told
Nicholls about hearing Peel say he was still convinced that Rose
wrote the libels. 'I feel sure the police here will never do any thing
to clear my wife.' Bill then told Nicholls about a scurrilous letter he
had seen recently. He was now in charge of a yacht owned by a naval
officer (Bill signed himself 'Capt. W. H. Gooding' in consequence).
The yacht was lying at Littlehampton by the shipyard Bill where
used to work, which had since reopened under a new owner. As Bill
headed aboard one morning, the shipyard manager, Mr Adams, saw
him and called out. A letter had arrived for Mr Harvey, the late
owner of the shipyard, now dead two years or more. Adams clearly
knew something of the libels' history and showed Bill the letter.
Bill now forwarded a copy to Nicholls. He did not elaborate on the

letter's contents, but he pointed out that it had been posted in Worthing—'and I know that Mrs and Miss Swan, went to Worthing on Saturday Nov 18, do you think Sir this letter can be any think to do with them'?[17]

Nicholls informed his superintendent at the Metropolitan Police of Bill's letter, explaining that while he could not see any reference to either of the Goodings in the letter addressed to Mr Harvey, Bill's main concern was 'whether anything can be done to clear his wife of the suspicion which still rests upon her with regard to writing anonymous letters'. Whatever Nicholls thought of the West Sussex police by this time, it was their jurisdiction, not his. He suggested that Bill be advised that 'the matter is one for the Chief Constable of West Sussex at Chichester'.[18] A senior officer wrote accordingly to Bill, discreetly sending the letter in a plain envelope rather than one with Metropolitan Police livery.[19]

If Bill contacted the chief constable of West Sussex, little came of it. The sensational developments expected by the newspapers failed to eventuate. Tips continued to trickle into police stations, however. One claimed that the author of the letters was working in a Littlehampton post office.[20] The most elaborate offering came from as far away as Lac Vert, Saskatchewan. Walter D. Eastwood was a man in his late twenties living in the remote hamlet, working a family farm with his brother and probably widowed mother.[21] Somehow Eastwood managed to see a copy of the British *Daily Sketch* of 29 January 1923, which advertised a reward of £50 for a clue leading to the conviction of the culprit. It was an unlikely drama for a Saskatchewan farmer to latch onto, but in the quiet of the prairie winter Eastwood found an outlet for his imagination in the Littlehampton libels. He informed Scotland Yard:

My partner the clairvoyant describes the people concerned as follows:—

The main one is a lawyer about (5.6″) five feet six inches or slightly more in height, thick built, round featured, of fair complexion and wears dark rimmed glasses and a long peaked cap.

The second person is a woman of small build, dark complexion round featured and about forty years of age.

The third is the woman's husband he is a man who is between five feet seven and nine inches in height, slimly built, clean shaven and about forty years of age.

There seems to be some ties between the lawyer and this man and woman either by relations or close friendship.

The latter two have recently moved out of a retail store which is now vacant on the same street not far from the lawyers office on the opposite side of the street.

The lawyer started this with the idea of making money.

Eastwood drew a plan of the buildings the clairvoyant had seen. He signed off: 'Hoping for your success and a reward for ourselves.'[22]

The *Sketch's* offer of a reward, like all the press reports of rumours and investigations, treated the Littlehampton libels as a great mystery. For the Director of Public Prosecutions and the Home Office, as for Nicholls, there was no mystery. Edith Swan wrote the libels. The challenge was proving it in a way that could not be thwarted by judges' and jurors' reluctance to believe that a woman who looked and spoke like Swan could write things that were obscene, malicious, and self-destructive.

The Tugwell case that Sir Archibald Bodkin and Travers Humphreys had both taken part in before the war provided an example of a suitably objective sort of proof. Once Annie Tugwell came under suspicion following her second prosecution of Canon Cafferata's housekeeper, the police enlisted the help of the General Post Office and the newsagent from whom the Tugwells bought stamps.[23] As Bodkin explained at Annie Tugwell's trial, 'A chemical fluid was procured which had this property—that one might write with it and the writing remained invisible until a particular kind of chemical was washed over it.' The police bought a supply of halfpenny stamps, 'divided them into lots, one for each member of the Tugwell household, and marked each lot in a particular way with the invisible ink'. They then gave them to the shopkeeper to sell. One afternoon shortly afterwards, the Tugwells' servant bought six of the marked stamps.[24] Members of the Metropolitan Police then kept watch on nearby letter boxes into the evening. It was a rainy night, and the detective in charge suspected that if Tugwell posted any letters that evening, she would use the pillar box closest to her house. Twice she came out to her garden gate and carefully looked around for passers-by before returning indoors. Then she emerged again with her umbrella 'and looked up and down the road'. Seeing that it was practically deserted, 'she walked towards the letter box, turning around and looking about her twice as she was going. Upon arriving at the letter box she put something into the aperture then quickly returned indoors'. A postal official opened the box: with most people inside sheltering from the rain, and the box recently cleared, the only letters in it were the ones Tugwell had just posted. She had addressed one of them to herself. 'It is now proved beyond all doubt that Mrs Tugwell is the person who has been writing these libellous letters', the police concluded, and passed their findings on to the Director of Public Prosecutions.[25] At her trial, Tugwell's counsel tried to sow suspicions of a conspiracy. If so, Bodkin retorted, this was a conspiracy involving the police and postal officials—'If the suggestions of the defence were true, the police must have "faked" the marked stamps.'[26] The jury was not minded to dismiss the evidence of the stamps.

When the criminal justice system moved against Edith Swan for a second time, the GPO's agents played a pivotal role. '[S]ome six weeks ago', reported the *Sussex Daily News* in July 1923, 'Scotland Yard again took a hand in trying to solve the problem. They came to the conclusion that these objectionable communications were posted from certain pillar boxes in the Western-road, and at the head offices in Surrey-street. With the aid of the postal authorities, a strict watch was kept on these boxes.'[27] Other reports too suggested that the operation was a joint effort between Scotland Yard and the General Post Office. However, the Metropolitan Police files show no sign that Nicholls or anyone else from the force travelled to Littlehampton at this time. Each of Nicholls's previous assignments to Littlehampton required the permission of the commissioner or deputy commissioner to act outside the Metropolitan Police district, in the jurisdiction of another police force. Nicholls's only appearance in the case's paper trail during the months in question is an initial in a Metropolitan Police file acknowledging that he had read the newspaper clippings about the proceedings.[28] Nicholls's internal letter passing on Bill Gooding's impassioned plea may have been his last act in the Littlehampton libels case.

The GPO's investigative arm employed more than fifty detectives, as they were usually called.[29] Within the postal service, they were known portentously as 'men of secrets'; officially, being postal workers, they were designated 'clerks'.[30] Much of the Special Investigation Branch's attention was devoted to criminal activity within the postal system, such as thefts of money by letter sorters.[31] The GPO detectives were also responsible for laying the groundwork for prosecutions under the Post Office Act of 1908. A person caught mailing a letter full of swear words could be charged with an offence against the postal legislation as well as, or instead of, criminal libel. Under section 63 of the Post Office Act, a person found guilty of sending 'any indecent or obscene article'—or 'any explosive substance, any dangerous substance, any filth, any noxious or deleterious substance, any sharp instrument not properly protected, any living creature which is either noxious or likely to injure other postal packets in course of conveyance or an officer of the Post Office'—was liable for a fine of up to £10 if convicted summarily (in a magistrates' court, for instance). If tried by a judge and jury, a defendant faced imprisonment for a term not exceeding twelve months.[32] The maximum penalty was therefore comparable to that for criminal libel.

The Special Investigation Branch clerks who travelled to Littlehampton in mid-1923 were Walter Edward Bowler and Frederick Charles Cartwright. Though Cartwright was considerably older,[33] Bowler was in charge. The son of a coal porter from East London, he had moved out of the world of unskilled manual work, becoming an accounts clerk in the Post Office's telephone business before joining the Special Investigation Branch. Bowler was in his early thirties when he was despatched to Littlehampton.[34] He began to set a trap similar to the one that had caught Annie Tugwell and prepared a supply of stamps marked in invisible ink. (The technology had only improved since the Sutton case—during the First World War, the postal censorship agency established a whole 'chemistry department' to develop invisible inks and tests for them.)[35] 'To the ordinary eye', Bowler remarked, 'there was nothing to shew that the stamps had been marked.' He gave the stamps to the couple who ran the Beach Town sub-post office and news agency, Edwin and Elsie Baker. (Most small 'sub-post offices' were staffed not by government employees but by shopkeepers who provided postal services as a side-line and were paid commission by the Post Office.)[36] The Bakers emptied a drawer behind the counter and put these stamps inside, along with a label with instructions from Bowler. The stamps marked with an 'S' were to be sold only to Edith Swan. Others bore different initials, though just who else the investigators were interested in remains tantalizingly unknown.[37] It is possible that they were attempting to rule out other residents, or giving the Bakers, who of course were not professional investigators, some practice. Elsie Baker later testified that she had been selling specially marked stamps for a month before Bowler gave her six one-and-a-half-penny stamps meant for Edith Swan on 23 June.[38]

At seven o'clock that evening Edith called at the Beach post office. She purchased 13s. 9d. worth of health insurance stamps.[39] Under the National Insurance Act of 1911, lower-paid workers had to contribute to a fund that would pay them an income if they fell sick. They would buy, and keep, stamps as tokens of their contribution.[40] As with old age pension applications and payments, the post office functioned as a service point for the nascent welfare state.[41] Edith also bought two one-and-a-half-penny stamps for letters. The following day, Bowler kept the letter box at the post office under intensive surveillance from inside and from the street.[42] A special periscopic mirror was installed inside the mail drop. 'We could see without being seen', said Edwin Baker.[43] Whenever someone posted a letter, the post office staff fished it out and Bowler examined it (they had been clearing the box continually in this way for a whole month).[44] At five o'clock Bowler went out to stand with Cartwright. Nearly half an hour later, Swan approached the post office from the direction of her house.[45] 'I was on observation duty, and saw Miss Swann through the window coming towards the post-office', Edwin Baker recalled. 'Then I saw her hand in the periscopic mirror. It was raised to place something in the box. I had previously made quite certain there was nothing else in the box. I put in my hand and caught two letters as they fell.'[46] Unaware of what was going on, Edith popped into another shop to buy some chocolate before walking to Caroline Johnson's house, where she waited for her friend 'to come out with her'.[47]

As soon as Edith was gone, Bowler dashed back into the post office.[48] Once inside, he examined the two envelopes.[49] One was addressed to Edith's sister near Woking. Bowler set that letter aside. The other envelope was more promising. It was addressed to Charles Gardner, Littlehampton's new sanitary inspector. Bowler had previously secured Gardner's permission to open any suspicious mail for him.[50] This suggests that Gardner, like the last sanitary inspector, Reginald Booker, had already been pestered by anonymous letters. It is also conceivable that, since public figures in the town were being targeted, Bowler surmised it would be only a matter of time before the sanitary inspector received an obscene letter. With Edwin Baker looking on, Bowler opened the envelope and read the letter. It began with 'some improper words' and then threatened that Gardner would be sorry for calling Edith's dust boxes a nuisance.[51] The improper words were enough to make Bowler put down the letter and go out to Cartwright, who was still keeping observation. Bowler sent him off in search of Edith Swan. Cartwright found her at Johnson's house and Edith agreed to return to the post office.[52]

At the Beach post office, Bowler cautioned Edith. He then placed the two letters on the counter. 'Just stand up, Miss Swan, and watch me develop the private mark on these stamps', he said, like a conjurer on the pier.[53] It is hard to imagine George Nicholls, with his wry sobriety, indulging in such showmanship. The letter 'S' and Bowler's initials, 'W. E. B.', 'at once became visible'. Bowler informed Swan that he 'had just seen her post the two letters, and that he had the authority to open any letters'. He asked her 'if she had any explanation to offer, the letter having been found to contain obscene matter'. Choosing her words with formal precision, Edith replied: 'I have no explanation to offer other than that I am not guilty either of writing or posting any letters to the Sanitary Inspector.' She admitted purchasing two stamps the previous evening but insisted that she used them on letters to two of her sisters—the one living close to Woking and a married sister in Cranleigh in Surrey.[54] Bowler asked for Edith's written permission to search her writing desk at home, which she granted. He then appears to have gone to the Swans' cottage with the letter of consent and searched it in Mrs Swan's presence while her daughter waited at the post office with Cartwright. Bowler returned about half an hour later bearing three pieces of blotting paper, which, astonishingly, the Swans still owned despite the fact all three pieces 'had been twice previously taken by the police when they searched the house and returned to her'. Bowler had also retrieved some envelopes and stamp edging. Edith would not confess to anything, and broke off the interview to return home.[55]

It was more than a week before Edith was charged. At noon on Wednesday 4 July, Henry Thomas of the Littlehampton police station again made the trip to 47 Western Road to serve Edith with a summons to appear before the magistrates. Accompanying Thomas was Frederick Peel. 'You know me?' Peel asked, as he was supposed to. 'Yes, Superintendent Peel', Edith replied.[56] Peel cautioned her and read her the summons. She was charged under section 63 of the Post Office Act with 'attempting to send a postal packet which had thereon words of an indecent, obscene, and grossly offensive character'. She would appear before the bench at Arundel in a week's time. Edith confirmed that she understood. On the eve of the magistrates' court hearing—at four in the afternoon—Peel visited Edith again to inform her 'that he had received a telegram from London'. Bodkin's office advised that Edith 'would be further charged with libel'. 'All right', she told Peel. 'I shall have time to consult Mr. Longcroft.' In fact she did not: at the hearing the next day, the solicitor grumbled about the libel charge 'which had arisen that morning'.[57]

Once again, the committal hearing was a spectacle. 'Great public interest was taken in the case', *The Times* noted. The council chamber of Arundel's old town hall was filled with people from the Littlehampton district.[58] Many of those present were women who had come up from Littlehampton 'by train, motor-coach, and omnibus', according to the *Daily Mail* and the *News of the World*.[59] 'The Court was uncomfortably crowded for such a hot day', wrote the *Littlehampton Observer*'s reporter, 'and the atmosphere was very oppressive'.[60] (Edith arrived early, perhaps to avoid the crowd.)[61] The spectators heard Seward Pearce from the Director of Public Prosecutions' office outline the case against Swan. 'Such is the strength of the case', he declared, 'that I feel these proceedings will have the effect of putting an end to what has been for years a public nuisance in Littlehampton.'[62] 'The evidence will be direct and conclusive', he added. 'The act...was seen by at least three witnesses, and there is the additional fact that the postage stamp which was on the letter can be traced to Miss Swan.'[63]

Elsie Baker testified to selling Edith the marked stamps; Edwin Baker told of catching the two letters as they dropped through the aperture; and Bowler recounted in detail the story of the surveillance operation, his confrontation with Swan, and his search of her family's cottage. Peel and the sanitary inspector briefly gave evidence. Pearce also produced two postal workers from Surrey to contradict Edith's claim that the second letter she posted was to her sister in Cranleigh, Mrs Tomsett.[64] Mail for Cranleigh passed through the Guildford post office. A letter posted in Littlehampton on a Sunday evening would reach Guildford at eleven that night. Frederick Burchatt, a sorting clerk at Guildford, testified that at 10:40 p.m. on Sunday 24 June, he received a phone call from the postmaster at Littlehampton about the matter, 'and in consequence he searched every bag in the Post Office for a letter addressed to Mrs. Tomsett, but there was no such letter'. There were no letters for Cranleigh at all.[65]

With the prosecution's evidence concluded, Longcroft attempted to have the charges dismissed on points of law. Because the letter to the sanitary inspector had been intercepted, its contents had not been 'published'; and Gardner had not been defamed, only insulted. Longcroft also suggested that because the offensive words were on the inside of the 'packet', the relevant section of the Post Office Act did not apply. If this argument made sense in court, it was beyond the power of the *Sussex Daily News* reporter to render it convincingly. In reply, Pearce said that 'The Section clearly stated that if anything of an obscene nature was enclosed in a letter, that constituted an offence. . . . He appreciated the gallant struggle made by the defence to find a way out.'[66]

After some deliberation, the magistrates concluded that there was a case to answer, and Edith was formally charged. She pleaded not guilty. Edith stated that she would call no witnesses that day and would reserve her defence. The magistrates committed her for trial at the Lewes assizes on all the charges. Longcroft applied for bail. The chairman of the magistrates 'said the charges were serious, and they would want sureties of herself in £25, and two others in the like amount'. The solicitor replied: 'I can't find these until later in the day. The father will become one, but several hours will elapse until the other one is found.' In the meantime, Edith was taken into custody.[67]

This time the second surety was not forthcoming and Edith remained in gaol until her trial.[68] She did not have long to wait, however. Her second assize trial was fixed for 18 July 1923, a week after she faced the magistrates.[69] Like the preliminary hearing in Arundel, the trial in Lewes aroused great curiosity. '[A] large crowd, including many women', queued outside the county hall.[70] The assize trial also saw the return of people who had crossed Swan's path before. Edith would appear again before Mr Justice Avory, this time as the defendant. Travers Humphreys would prosecute her a second time.

Humphreys 'reminded the jury that they were not living in the pages of a sensational novel, but . . . were dealing with facts in real life'. He remarked that 'it had been necessary to adopt extraordinary methods' because ordinary methods had failed 'to trace the people who had been sending filthy letters through the post'.[71] Humphreys retold the story of the stamps with invisible ink and their revelation to Swan. He called the same witnesses Pearce had in the magistrates' court. They reiterated what they had said in Arundel. Only Bowler's performance was significantly different. In the witness box, he demonstrated how the invisible ink worked by developing the hidden markings on the four remaining stamps set aside for Edith Swan.[72] Under cross-examination, Bowler stated that in his search of the Swans' house he found no paper or envelopes 'to correspond with that sent to the sanitary inspector, but he found envelopes similar to those sent to the defendant's sister, Miss Swann' (the sister living near Woking).[73] The judge recalled Bowler to the stand to clarify that he found 'nothing material to the case' on the blotting paper he took from the Swans' house.[74]

After three trials with Thomas Gates as her counsel, this time Edith was represented by a barrister named Collingwood. Like Longcroft in the magistrates' court, Collingwood attempted to have the libel charge set aside because the letter to the sanitary inspector did not make a false and defamatory statement about him, 'although obviously the article was indecent to the last degree'. Avory said he thought the letter 'was capable of a defamatory meaning, but there was [also] the other question as to whether there was any evidence to go to the jury that prisoner knew the statement to be false'. Humphreys submitted that 'having regard to the extravagant statements in the libel, the statement itself was proof that the person who published it could not believe it to be true'. Faced with these abstruse considerations, Avory retreated to his original position, the conventional view that 'the question of libel or no libel was always a question for the jury'.[75]

Collingwood now had to fight the prosecution on the facts. His chief witness was Edith herself. Whether by design or by default, Edith's case again rested on her courtroom persona. At least one observer this time found her an impressive witness. The *Daily Express*'s correspondent commented: 'Miss Swann, in the witness box giving evidence in her own behalf, was a most finished witness. She gave a clear, connected narrative, answered questions quickly and well, and made no attempt at over-elaborate or too-emphatic statement. She was completely mistress of her emotions and her wits...'[76] Edith testified that she posted the letter to her sister Mrs Tomsett on the Sunday morning; when she visited the post office at 5:30 that afternoon, she mailed only one letter, to the sister near Woking. Edith told much the same story Bowler had related about the interview at the post office. However, she claimed, Bowler had omitted parts of their conversation when he gave his evidence. According to Edith, the GPO investigator crowed when he returned from searching her house: 'Mr. Bowler told her she had been properly trapped this time, and there was no loop-hole for her, so that it would be useless to deny it.' It is quite possible Edith was making this up in an attempt to win the jury's sympathy. If she was, it was a clever fabrication: this sounds like the sort of thing the man who made such a play of revealing the secret of the invisible ink might say—just as the salty remarks Edith had claimed to have overheard Rose Gooding say had an air of plausibility for listeners predisposed to believe the worst of Rose. Edith added that on arriving home from the post office 'she found her mother very ill'.[77]

Whether or not Edith cut a sympathetic figure in the courtroom at Lewes, there was a weight of evidence against her. Humphreys pursued her unremittingly. When Edith stated that 'the two 1½d. stamps she bought did not leave her possession until she put them on the letters to her sisters in the presence of her father', the barrister closed in:

> Counsel: Assuming that these were the only two stamps marked in the way they were sold to you, and one was put on the letter to the Sanitary Officer, you must have done it.
>
> Accused: I did not do it. I have never had the Sanitary Officer's letter in my hands.
>
> Further cross-examined, accused said she had written to her sister at Cranleigh asking her if she received the letter posted on the Sunday morning, and she replied that she had not received it.
>
> Counsel: So the letter has mysteriously disappeared. It had never been returned to you through the dead letter office?
>
> Accused: No. Another letter I posted to my sister was delayed for a week.
>
> Asked if she could account for the letter to the Sanitary Officer, she said it was folded and must have been hung up [in the mailbox]. She could make no suggestion as to why it should contain a stamp similar to that sold to her the previous evening.[78]

The judge then handed Edith the letter addressed to the sanitary inspector and asked her if it was in her handwriting. Again she denied it. Avory asked her if she had ever used the language that appeared in the letter. Edith was emphatic: 'Never during the whole of my life, either in writing or talking, never.' The judge asked her to read out the latter part of the note: 'I will give you ———— saying my boxes are a nuisance. You will be sorry you have made a shine over them. Do your duty.' Avory continued this cross-examination from the bench, asking Edith whether she had ever had any trouble with the sanitary inspector. No, she replied;

Gardner had 'made a complaint about an accumulation of ashes in the garden', but he had never warned the Swans about a dust box or bin.[79]

The last witness was Edward Swan, 'the grey-bearded father of the accused', as one newspaper described him. Reprising his role from the last trial, Mr Swan vouched for his daughter's character. Had he ever heard Edith use indecent language? Collingwood asked him. 'Never', Mr Swan replied. She was 'brought up quite differently. I have never heard such language from her or any others of my family of nine children.'[80] Mr Swan also offered some corroboration for Edith's story: he stated that on the evening of 23 June he saw his daughter write a letter to her sister Tomsett and put a stamp on it.[81] He did not see the letter again after Edith left the house the next morning.[82]

On the page, and from this distance in time, the defence's case looks weak. Yet Avory, at least, still found Edith a compelling witness. Humphreys accurately wrote that the judge 'summed up as favourably to the accused as was possible in the face of the evidence'.[83] The Brighton *Argus* reported the judge's concluding remarks the most fully:

In his summing up his Lordship said the charges involved the one fundamental fact that accused knew the contents of the letter. Because [the fact] that a person had posted a letter in a sealed envelope, was not of itself evidence that the person... knew the contents of the envelope. For some time past offensive libels, whether obscene or defamatory, had in fact been disseminated in Littlehampton, and the very fact that this was a matter of history obviously made it more than usually necessary that the jury should exercise the greatest possible care before coming to the conclusion that accused was guilty. If the case for the prosecution stood alone, and there was no answer to it, they would naturally have said that it was a conclusive case, but in view of what both accused and her father had sworn the jury had to ask themselves... whether there might be possibly some mistake. Was it possible that some mistake had been made either about the stamps or about the evidence of the witnesses who watched the Post Office, and was it possible that some one else may have put the letter in the letter box. Accused's demeanour in the witness box was that of a respectable, clean-mouthed woman, and the jury would have to consider whether it was conceivable that she could have written this document. There had been no evidence that the handwriting was that of the accused, and he regretted that it would be necessary for the jury to have to examine the letter which formed the subject of the case.

Although Avory apologized for the unpleasant reading the letter to the sanitary inspector would make, this time round he had not given the two female jurors an opportunity to escape.[84]

The jury did not share Avory's estimate of the relative claims of the prosecution and the defence. They took only ten minutes to find Edith Swan guilty. As the judge prepared to pass sentence, Humphreys asked him to take into account the fact that on two occasions in the past, Edith had 'given evidence against another woman, whom she accused of publishing libels'.[85] Of course, as the judge who had sentenced Rose Gooding in 1921, Avory knew this well. The press reports show no sign that Edith was permitted to speak before sentencing, but it would have been unusual for her to do so. Criminal libel and the offences under the Post Office Act were misdemeanours, and only in felony cases was it traditional for a person found guilty to address the bench before sentencing.

Avory still found it hard to credit that Edith could have written the libels. Struggling to square the guilty verdict with her manner in court, he told her: 'It is difficult to believe after listening to you in the witness box that you could be in your right mind in writing filth of this description.'[86] Avory said he 'must act upon the verdict of the jury, and in regard to the history which he now knew had been going on he must pass a severe sentence upon her'. He sentenced her to twelve months' imprisonment with hard labour.[87] Now, wrote the *Daily Express*'s correspondent, Edith's composure failed. 'The woman in the dock swayed on her heels; her pendulous lower lip quivered under the impulse of over-strained nerves; she mumbled something scarcely heard, and then controlling her voice, said, "You have sentenced an innocent woman."'[88] Avory replied: 'I can only act upon the verdict of the jury. It is not my verdict.'[89] The prison matron led Edith away and the press brought the curtain down. 'End of Littlehampton Letter Case', declared the *Argus*; 'End of Seaside Mystery', read the *Daily Mail* headline.[90]

Epilogue
Brought to Book

Rose Gooding's long ordeal was over. Though peripheral to the trial in Lewes in the summer of 1923, she was not forgotten. She travelled to her home town to observe the proceedings. A press photographer spotted Rose in the crowd and got her to pose. There she was on the front page of the *Daily Mirror*, looking straight at the camera, her arms round Willie and Dorothy.[1]

In time Rose and her family made good on their intention to leave the cottage in Western Road. They moved away from Beach Town into the centre of Littlehampton. A decade later they were living near the railway station in Howard Place, a street of terraced houses built later than the Western Road cottages and substantially bigger. Dorothy was living at the house in Howard Place when she married in 1934. She was twenty-five. The groom was two years her senior, a drapery salesman whose family ran a catering business on the high street. He and Dorothy were married at the local register office. The clerk put Bill Gooding down as her father and gave his profession as 'yacht captain'.[2] Three years later, when Willie married, Bill described himself as a master mariner, 'master' indicating that he was an employer. Willie had moved to Worthing and become a lorry driver. His bride was a young widow and the daughter of a motor engineer. Theirs too was a civil marriage.[3] Ruth Russell and her children evidently left Littlehampton, though it is not clear how long after the end of the libels that the household they shared with Rose, Bill, Dorothy, and Willie broke up. Gertrude was living in Seaford, east of Newhaven, when she married in 1935 in a parish church. The clerk drew a line through the spaces for her father's name and profession in the register.[4]

Rose and Bill were still at 4 Howard Place in the winter of 1947 when Bill died of colon cancer. He was sixty-eight.[5] Rose survived him by another two decades. She lived to the age of seventy-nine, dying of cardiac failure two days before Christmas 1968. She died at a house in East Dean, a village outside Eastbourne, though her death certificate gave her address as Dorothy's house in Farnham in Surrey. Dorothy registered her mother's death the day after it occurred, which suggests that she was with her in East Dean.[6] Perhaps they were together for the holiday. Rose Gooding's last forty-five years left only the barest public record. Aside from the occasional appearance in newspaper features on miscarriages of justice, she made no further claim on the attention of the press. Nor did she have any further dealings with the archive-generating agencies of law enforcement.

The archive tells a little more about Edith Swan following her second trial at Lewes. After her conviction she still had some legal options. Edith filed promptly for leave to appeal against both her conviction and her sentence.[7] Less than a month after the assize trial a full bench of the Court of Criminal Appeal considered the application. Edith had no legal representation at the hearing. In her letter to the court she must have mentioned the earlier history of the libels in an attempt to shift the blame, because the Lord Chief Justice, Lord Hewart, noted that 'Apparently there was some previous history of kindred matters. No evidence was given of them, but clearly both sides assumed that it was known that previous libels had circulated in Littlehampton, and the Judge had warned the jury that in these circumstances they ought to be doubly careful; and on reading the transcript of the evidence and summing up it was clear that that instruction had been carried out.' Hewart found that the facts 'were most carefully sifted and marshalled for the jury by the Judge, who put to the jury the case for the defence with every suggestion which a reasonable mind could make upon it. It was after that very careful summing up that the jury found their verdict. The Judge said that he could only act upon the verdict of the jury.' The Court of Criminal Appeal 'thought that this was essentially a case for the jury' and that there was no aspect of it 'which could usefully be explored further'. The three judges refused Edith leave to appeal.[8]

Several months later, in December of 1923, she petitioned the Home Secretary on the form the prison service supplied for the purpose. The authorities at Portsmouth described her conduct in prison as 'Good' (the other categories available were 'Bad', 'Fair', and 'Indifferent') and characterized her request variously as 'Reduction of sentence' and 'Pleads innocence and asks for her handwriting to be tested'. Edith herself told the Home Office she was 'entering this petition on the grounds of the handwriting. I had no means to provide for the services of a handwriting expert at my trial, and no evidence as to handwriting was given by the Prosecution.' Thus Edith made the same criticism of her own trial that Sir Archibald Bodkin had made of the prosecutions she had brought against Rose Gooding. Edith went on: 'Chief Detective Inspector Nicholls of New Scotland Yard, told me in July 1921, that it was absolutely impossible for any person to disguise their handwriting. He said that there were scientific means by which anybody's handwriting could be traced, however much they had disguised it.' Whether deliberately or by accident, Edith misrepresented Nicholls's part in this episode. In June 1921, *Edith* had written to Nicholls informing him: 'I read in the newspapers three or four weeks ago that there is now a scientific instrument by which anybody's handwriting can be found out, however much disguised.'[9] 'I trust it will be used in this case', she concluded then. Now, in her petition from prison, she added: 'May I, therefore, Sir, respectfully request, that a test of the handwriting, in my case, be taken so that I may have an opportunity of establishing my innocence.'[10] The response of the Home Office lawyer who received the petition was to write '?Nil.' Four days later another official annotated the file, 'Wrote [Prison] Gov'', presumably informing him that no action would be taken.[11] Edith apparently served out her sentence.

After her conviction, writers in the newspapers were freed to judge her. Edith joined the ranks of the women starring in scandalous trials in the years immediately after the First World War: Maud Allan, the dancer who prosecuted the MP who accused her of being a lesbian; Marguerite Fahmy, the French wife of an Egyptian diplomat who shot her husband dead in a corridor of the Savoy; Christabel Russell, whose divorce proceedings detailed her husband's sexual cruelty; and that other writer of striking letters, Edith Thompson.[12] In the letters she wrote her lover (who eventually stabbed her husband to death), Thompson reflected on the bestselling novels she read with love and hunger. She used their plot details to illustrate the kind of life she imagined for her and her lover with her husband out of the picture. Thompson's letters were the most articulate evidence against her. They took up ninety pages in the published trial transcript, and they were widely reprinted in newspapers during the proceedings. Thompson's absorption in fantasy and 'melodramatic novels', her critics in the press argued, compromised her reason and self-regulation: a feminine failing, and also a modern one. James Douglas, the crusading editor of the *Sunday Express*, called her 'the creature and creation of a hectic and hysterical age'.[13]

These women's experiences were very different from Edith Swan's. Her transgressions had none of the metropolitan glamour of the Savoy or Maud Allan's erotic dancing. Edith Swan's was a 'very petty sordid case' that nevertheless yielded 'a most interesting investigation', in the words of a Metropolitan Police lawyer; none of these other trials entailed detective work or sting operations as sophisticated as the Littlehampton case did.[14] Where Edith Thompson was an identifiably 'modern' woman with up-to-the-minute tastes and a successful career, Edith Swan slotted into the timeworn category of the spinster. Edith Thompson's desires articulated the zeitgeist as outraged reactionaries divined it; Edith Swan's desires did not.

Yet Swan, too, could be diagnosed like a modern patient. The *Manchester Guardian*, in its leader on the case, did not venture a specific diagnosis, but took it as read that Swan was insane. 'The case of the lady from Littlehampton who has just been sentenced to twelve months' imprisonment at the Sussex Assizes must set everyone who is jealous for English justice gravely thinking.... For three years Littlehampton has been disturbed by this scandal, which has led to three actions and twice to the conviction of the same innocent person, and there appears to be little doubt that the present prisoner has all along been the villain of the piece. For three years, that is, she has been engineering pointless obscenities, and yet the judge in summing up remarked that she gave everyone the impression of being a "respectable, clean-mouthed woman."What are we to make of an offence of this kind?'The *Guardian* thought Mr Justice Avory right to say that it was difficult to believe that Swan was in her right mind. Punishing her would not deter others, since those committing crimes for no 'intelligible reason...cannot be expected to go in fear of the consequences of their actions'. Edith Swan was 'unquestionably a subject for a mental rather than a legal specialist. But, if she is to come under a doctor, there must be a well-defined avenue in law for conducting her thither'. The newspaper cited the report of the Prison Commissioners for 1921–1922, which drew attention to the number of people certified as mentally defective while serving a term of imprisonment. Like others interested in the

reform of English prisons, the *Guardian* writer pointed to the enlightened mental health regime run by Maurice Hamblin Smith at
Birmingham prison. 'Plainly, therefore', the leader concluded, 'there is
urgent need for mobilising all our knowledge of mental disease and of
bringing it up to reinforce our law.'[15]

The *Daily Express* agreed that Swan's case 'raises in acute form the
urgent problem of insanity and crime'. Edith was a 'wretched being'
whose offence was 'obviously the product of a mental aberration. . . . Of
her guilt there can be no doubt. But also there can be no doubt that
she is morally irresponsible for her actions. The proper place for her is
an asylum, not a prison.' Prison discipline would do nothing to improve
her 'mental health', and after she served her sentence society would
'again be exposed to her morbid mania'. The *Express* floated a possible
change in the process. 'Surely it would be more humane to settle the
issue of insanity before trial instead of after it. . . . Why not avoid
the waste of time and money by differentiating in the first instance
between the sane criminal and the insane criminal?' The newspaper's
proposals drove Sir Ernley Blackwell to exclamation marks when he
scribbled over the clipping circulated within the Home Office. 'Simply
condemn them unheard to what is worse for a sane and innocent
person than imp[risonmen]ᵗ!' he wrote. Blackwell also observed that
'settling' the question of insanity before going to trial was a procedure
that 'wd have led to the certification as insane of Mʳˢ· Gooding!'[16]

The *Express* returned to the subject in its news pages the following
day, keeping the policy question alive with some approving words
about Hamblin Smith, whose article in the most recent issue in the
Lancet recommended that the courts make a full pre-trial assessment of
a defendant's mental health—the same suggestion the *Express* itself had
made the day before, the report noted.[17] This item in the *Express* combined the practical-man tone of the paper's editorial with the raciness
of its trial coverage. The reporter sought a specialist's opinion of Swan.
The doctor, unnamed but said to be famous, believed that she was
'undoubtedly suffering from a criminal impulse arising out of a sexual
disease that I have often encountered in my practice. I think that probably she could be cured completely if she were sent to an institution
and kept under the supervision of mental specialists.' The doctor
pointed to the disparity in the handling of mental health problems
among the rich and the poor: 'The deplorable factor about such cases
is that when they occur among the rich the delinquent is brought by

her relatives to a specialist for treatment and cure.' (Tellingly, the imagined patient was a woman.) 'Poor persons, on the contrary, are often allowed to give rein to their criminal impulses until they commit actions that lead to arrest, conviction, and imprisonment.'[18]

The *News of the World* too was confident that Edith Swan's psychological problems were sexual in origin. 'The medical assumption is that this letter writing forms part of an obscure but well-recognised sex mania.' The paper's judgement was heartlessly thorough: 'Miss Swann is a small, unnoticeable woman of outward respectability, unattractive in face and complexion, with weak, peering eyes and no semblance of a figure.' Slyly flattering *News of the World* readers for their cultivation, the writer commented: 'No observer would mark Miss Swann as more than a partially educated woman'—though Edith herself was a reader of the *News of the World*, or at least lived in a household that had it delivered every Sunday.[19] Despite her modest formal education, Edith proved to have 'a devilish ingenuity and...displayed a knowledge of obscenity impossible to indicate'.[20]

Travers Humphreys made much the same assessment of Edith in his memoir *Criminal Days*, which has a whole chapter on the 'Gooding-Swan tragedy'. There could be few adults, Humphreys wrote, 'who have not read something of the insistence by modern scientists and psychologists upon the importance of sex in the life of a woman. They write and speak of repressions and inhibitions, of thwarted desires perhaps unconsciously entertained, and so forth; and they seem to be agreed that there may be no outward or visible sign or any indication to the untrained observer of any abnormality on the part of the patient.' Edith Swan presented no such indication to four juries, to two of the judges she testified before, and even, it seemed, to the experienced criminal lawyer Horace Avory, who could have been expected to notice signs of abnormality. Humphreys was nonplussed that Avory and Bailache had stressed that Swan 'was never known to use bad language or indulge in indecent conversation': 'it is, I should have thought, notorious that women of the highest respectability, whose minds become affected, frequently resort to the most appalling language and make use of expressions which most women have never heard of. Given the case of a young woman, a spinster of thirty, whose mind becomes unhinged probably as the result of repressed sexual instincts, I should have thought that indecency in some form is precisely what might be expected to result.'[21]

Not every eminent lawyer of Humphreys' age and background would have given credence to modern ideas about psychology. That said, his familiarity with those ideas was clearly second- or third-hand. Humphreys assumed that repressed sexuality would erupt into indecency, whereas those versed in Freud's writings expected repression to have more indirect consequences. Hamblin Smith, a psychiatrist who embraced psychoanalysis, described another criminal case in Freudian terms: 'a woman was brought up before the courts on the charge of wilful destruction of public property; analysis proved the meaning of the act to be an attempt at expression on the part of a repressed complex which had originated in a sex experience many years before. The act was, in fact, an attempt on the part of the patient at protection against her unconscious. It is, moreover, to be noticed that sexual offences in the male, such as indecent behaviour, are, in the female, where repression of sex impulses has been more generally practised, often substituted by other offences, such as violence, attempted suicide, drunkenness, &c.'[22]

Again like the journalists, Humphreys emphasized Swan's combination of madness and cunning. Reviewing the surviving files years afterwards, courtesy of the then Director of Public Prosecutions, Humphreys identified the fearfully circular trap that Edith had set for Rose Gooding. 'What struck me as unusual in re-reading the case was the cleverness which she displayed in averting suspicion from herself and fastening it upon the unfortunate Mrs. Gooding. Her reply to the Inspector who showed her the damning evidence of her blotting paper was instantaneous and showed ingenuity which in the circumstances was positively diabolical—"Mrs. Gooding borrowed it." Impossible to refute except by the word of Mrs. Gooding. . . . But who was Mrs. Gooding? A twice convicted libeller.' Humphreys thought that Swan's attempts to throw suspicion onto the Gooding or Russell children also showed guile. 'Again one can sense the urge to write some more filthy words, but the danger of doing so while Mrs. Gooding was in prison. The ready explanation, "I expect it was Dorothy," was by no means as wild as it seems at first sight. All the libels had been written in a clumsy imitation of a child's handwriting, and Mr. Lynn had, or said he had, seen Dorothy post a letter addressed to "Swan"!' To Humphreys' mind, 'the proof of mental derangement was to be found in the indiscriminate nature of the later libels, addressed as they were to persons, some of whom . . . had no quarrel with her, such being the evidence, for instance, of the Sanitary Inspector, the intended recipient of the letter in the last case'.[23]

Yet were those later libels really indiscriminate? Edith plagued sanitary inspectors with obscene letters right from the beginning. The fateful note to Charles Gardner disputed an allegation, real or imagined, about the cleanliness and order of the Swans' yard and outbuildings. The care of her house was part of Edith's identity as an upstanding working-class woman. It belonged to the same sphere of social significance as her sexual morality. In this light, it made a certain sense for the libels to combine sexualized insults with claims about the true source of a bad smell in the yard. Edith's letters were about who she thought she was and her relationships with other people. Perhaps she was engaging in oblique fantasy when she wrote letters describing herself as a whore, or pregnant with Constable Russell's child—not necessarily wishing that for herself, but imagining herself as a different person, more like the unmistakably sexually active women she lived so close to. Though she came to disapprove fiercely of Rose Gooding, she had rushed to befriend her not so long before. Within a few months, Edith was looking after Rose Gooding's children and Rose welcomed her into her house. The pattern of quick intimacy giving way to punishment recurred with Violet May, though Edith continued to act as May's friend and confidant even as she secretly bombarded her with insulting cards.

Across this wide gap of time it is impossible to do more than guess at Edith Swan's mental state, but this behaviour suggests that she may have had a personality disorder, probably borderline personality disorder (a diagnosis not available to psychiatrists and psychologists in the 1920s).[24] Borderlines struggle to maintain a stable sense of who they are. Their self-identity is damaged, disrupted. Edith Swan was a determinedly respectable woman who turned her pen towards obscenity; someone whose response to the disappointing discovery of a friend's purported immorality was to write letters accusing herself of being immoral. The clinical term 'identity disturbance', as two contemporary experts write, does little 'to capture the severity of the emptiness, worthlessness, and aloneness' felt by people diagnosed as borderline. They make frantic attempts to avoid real or perceived abandonment, and they tend to have 'unstable and intense' relationships. They often rush into intimacy with new people, esteeming them highly, making demands on them, and volunteering very personal information to them; just as quickly they can switch to disillusionment with their new companion.[25]

One authority's survey of so-called 'discouraged' borderlines reads like a plausible description of Edith. These individuals 'have been conscientious and proper persons; they overcomply with the strictures of society, display an air of propriety, are overly respectful and deferential to authority and tend to be grim and humorless. They have learned to look to others for support and affection, but such rewards are contingent on compliance and submission.' Yet these individuals cannot be confident that they will receive that support: 'compliant and conscientious strategies have not always paid off, and the person is justly distressed and resentful. . . . The resentment and anger these borderlines feel for having been coerced into submission and then betrayed churns within them and presses hard against their usually adequate controls. Periodically, these feelings break through to the surface, erupting in an angry upsurge of fury and unbridled vituperation. This anger draws its strength not only from immediate precipitants but from a deep reservoir of animosity, filled through years of what was experienced as constraint.'[26]

Edith's constraints were those of many women of her class, living in the family home looking after her parents and brothers. But Edith was not altogether like those other women. Her teacher at East Street School had thought her different from the rest of the girls, and she had an inventive streak. An adulthood sharing a bedroom with her parents, with her promised marriage deferred indefinitely, could have seemed like an unfairly cramped life for someone of Edith's qualities. When she exploded into vituperation, it was out of proportion to the 'immediate precipitant' of the arguments she overheard that Easter. Her onslaught against Rose Gooding does seem fuelled by a deeper anger about her life.

Edith's campaign to frame Rose was also dangerous. Edith had to know that if she were caught lying to the police and under oath the consequences would be severe—all the more so since the result of her actions was a miscarriage of justice. Writing obscene letters and trying to shift the blame, to the extent of prosecuting an innocent person, involved a combination of risk-taking, self-destructiveness, and attention-seeking, all of which are common among people with borderline personality disorder. When George Nicholls interviewed Edith's former employers, he uncovered other, lesser episodes where Edith had risked criminal sanction and put herself in the spotlight. She fell off some stairs in highly suspicious circumstances and filed a successful compensation claim. As a servant in apartment houses she boldly announced that she had discovered missing jewellery or money that she had in all likelihood taken herself.

She did not simply play the victim. She also played the person who could solve a problem—in a minor way with the missing sixpence, and in elaborate fashion with the anonymous letters. Edith engineered a drama in which she was variously a woman wronged, a friend supporting others who received abusive letters, an amateur detective, and a prosecutor enforcing the king's peace when the authorities would not. Defaming herself in anonymous letters brought Edith sympathy and attention, though it also put her in a degrading situation, and one that threatened her livelihood and creditworthiness. In effect if not in intent, she was punishing herself as well as her neighbour. She provoked a crisis that prompted her fiancé to break off their engagement. Like some types of physical self-harm, her behaviour was both self-dramatizing and self-cancelling.

Many people with borderline personality disorder have experienced abuse or neglect as children; or their parents were absent or for whatever reason did not have time to give the child the emotional attention she needed (a large majority of borderlines are women).[27] During the years her activities were scrutinized by the police and the courts, Edith's parents appear to have been doting. They supported her through her trials. Her father pushed back against Inspector Nicholls and may have covered for her when the Mays' vegetable garden was vandalized. Things might have been different when she was a child. Edith was the eighth of nine children. The youngest was her brother John, who suffered from fits and 'had a mania for writing letters to himself'.[28] He probably needed a lot of his parents' time and attention. It is hard to believe that Edith's turn to writing letters to herself had no personal symbolic power.

Retrospective diagnosis is fraught at the best of times, and borderline personality disorder is protean and notoriously difficult to diagnose.[29] For all its other affinities with the detective fiction of the period, the story of Edith Swan's crimes can have no denouement where her inner mysteries are definitively explained. Whatever drove Edith to write the letters she wrote between 1920 and 1923, after that time she must have been able to manage it or channel it in ways that did not bring her within reach of the authorities. After her release from prison, Edith had no further entanglements with the law.[30]

Edith Swan did not ruffle the public record again until March 1959, when her death certificate was issued.[31] She died of a heart attack; the death certificate also recorded that she suffered from chronic bronchitis. Edith died at her last place of residence, the North View Home in Littlehampton. The building had been the town workhouse until the repeal of the Poor Law in 1929—a place with grim and shaming associations for any working-class person of Edith Swan's generation. Edith was sixty-eight. Despite her engagement to Lance Corporal Boxall in her twenties, she had never married. Lacking a husband who might help define her life for official purposes, she was described by the registrar as the daughter of the late Edward Swan, painter and decorator.

Conclusion

'Well-behaved women', Laurel Thatcher Ulrich once observed, 'seldom make history.' Ulrich's aphorism has entered popular culture, travelling a long way from its point of origin, a study of funeral elegies in colonial New England. The women in question did not preach, vote, or go to Harvard, to take three criteria for making history in early eighteenth-century New England. 'Neither, because they were virtuous women, did they question God or the magistrates.'[1] Attracting the attention of the magistrates was another way of establishing a paper trail to posterity. Edith Swan and Rose Gooding's lives after 1923, when they 'behaved well', are all but invisible to history. We are able to know more about their earlier lives than we can about most women of their time because of the records produced by the criminal justice system and a press attentive to crime.

In retrospect it is scarcely believable that insulting letters passing between obscure people in a small town should result in four assize trials and two Court of Criminal Appeal hearings, and claim the time of a distinguished Scotland Yard officer, the Director of Public Prosecutions, and the senior Treasury Counsel. That the affair went on as long as it did is not a quirk of fate but a product of social values: the instinctive judgements that the West Sussex police, judges, and jurors made about the women involved. Edith Swan personified the respectable, respectful victim of circumstances; Rose Gooding's 'roughness', illegitimate child, and heterodox family licensed people to think her capable of writing the offensive letters. These social assumptions sustained the credibility of Edith's accusations against Rose through two trials and then delivered Edith from a conviction in the face of Gladys Moss's eye-witness testimony. The Littlehampton letters case was the obverse of situations where detectives have failed to identify murderers because they came across as ordinary men, not dissimilar to the police themselves, rather than as outsized villains.[2]

Britain had a patchy record of access to justice in the early decades of the twentieth century, but with the backing of her family's savings Edith Swan was able to mobilize the full force of the criminal law against Rose Gooding in a matter involving no damage to property, life, or limb. It was a peculiarity of English law that the offence of criminal libel was capacious enough to deal with vendettas conducted through letters and postcards. Prosecutions for crimes involving words seldom raised nagging concerns about freedom of speech. Although most public figures endorsed the principle of freedom of expression, they understood it in a particular way. Freedom of speech had to be protected so that opinions could be tested and refined; speech and writing that did not contribute directly to public debate were not shielded by the law. So judges who thought of themselves as defenders of English liberties saw no objection to ordering the destruction of erotic books or imprisoning writers of obscene letters. Words could 'disturb the peace' without inciting actual violence. The way the diffuse concept of the peace was invoked in the law of libel suggested that words had a power and a slipperiness that defied simple notions of cause and effect.[3] George Nicholls, Ernley Blackwell, Travers Humphreys, and Archibald Bodkin were not given to such metaphysical thinking, but they were duly suspicious of words on paper.

Words on newsprint aroused plenty of suspicion. In the years after the First World War, the mass-market press was often held up as an example of cultural decay.[4] It also served as a platform for critics of civilization's alleged decline. Criminal cases regularly provided the press with occasions for agitated discussion of cultural values—especially what constituted proper conduct for women—and the Littlehampton libels got the full treatment.[5] The newspaper coverage briefly brought the parochial affairs of Western Road into the national culture of the press. Reporters from London and stringers from Bognor and Brighton acquainted themselves with Beach Town. The *Daily Mirror*, which placed a premium on photography, reproduced images of people from a class whose likenesses seldom survived outside the mind's eye of a relative. Even before the Littlehampton affair really became a cause célèbre—when Edith Swan appeared as a defendant for the first time—newspapers had already played a part in the case, as *John Bull* offered its help and Edith kept Bottomley's journal informed of her own investigations.

Edith's family took Sunday papers, and she kept clippings of articles documenting the drama she had set in train. Edith's triumph over Rose Gooding was undone by several sheets of blotting paper, used and re-used over many months. As well as writing on notepaper and cardboard, Edith recycled bits of tradesmen's account books in which purchases were logged meticulously. In their mundanity these items are suggestive of how far literacy had been incorporated into the routines of working-class life by the early 1920s. Letter-writing enabled working-class people to transcend a daily round that was often confined to a few streets, as it was in Edith's case—less so in Rose's, with her links back to Lewes—and keep in touch with relatives whose removal to Surrey, let alone Australia, made them remote.[6] Literacy did not simply collapse distance: notes and cards also travelled round the same local circuits as gossip. Rose and Edith both put business communications in writing even when the addressee was a few hundred yards away.

The theorist of literacy Walter J. Ong described writing as 'a technology that restructures thought'.[7] It is hard to say with certainty that literacy structured the way Rose Gooding or Edith Swan thought. But writing was undoubtedly a space where they could express themselves, even experiment with their selves. In Edith's case, writing was not the refinement of demotic speech that it was often characterized as, but an outlet for feelings or fantasies that a reputable woman like her could never voice in person. As Stephen Reynolds recognized, the 'poor man's vocabulary' was a theatre of individuality and ambition, of creative engagement with the language that enveloped the working-class person's world as well as the poet's.

In a brilliant essay several years ago, Matt Houlbrook observed that his fellow historians of popular literacy gravitated towards autodidacts, radicals, and scholarship boys and girls rather than readers of romances or crime fiction. Miners who wrote poetry or read political economy by night clearly fit the bill of the working-class intellectual: it is harder to discern the ways 'escapist' reading might entail imagination and reflection.[8] Recognizing, as Houlbrook does, that readers of romances might be active thinkers rather than passive consumers makes for a more encompassing understanding of culture. Yet it is still to focus on imaginative responses to *books*. What about the life of the word outside recognized artistic forms?[9] This book is an extended response to Houlbrook's challenge, an attempt to apprehend individuality even in bad 'bad language' and flamboyant styles of handwriting.

Cultural historians often prize behaviour that at first glance looks banal or bizarre but which, on examination, reveals people acting deliberately—or making their own history, as Marx put it.[10] Puzzling over episodes like this can also bring into relief the structures that shape people's experience. If it strains credibility that a nonviolent dispute between working-class neighbours could swell into a national spectacle, its setting was not unusual at all. The Goodings and Swans lived in a society in which employment was often precarious and working-class people used a variety of schemes to insulate the family economy from the labour market's ups and downs; where women moved back and forth between waged labour and unpaid work in the home; where reputations had economic as well as social consequences; where writing was a thoroughly domesticated aspect of working-class life; where literacy was divisive as well as empowering.[11] All these things are familiar to historians of modern Britain. But understanding the rules of the game does not make all the possible plays predictable.

This points to the larger ambition of a microhistory like this, a book that reconstructs in detail an episode in the lives of people who were sociologically unremarkable but underwent remarkable experiences. It asks the reader to see events in their context and to linger on what the context cannot explain—to notice unexpected possibility, human variety, irregular characters.[12] In their different ways both Edith and Rose were judged odd or eccentric. One was called 'wrong in her head' and the other 'not right in her head'. Each woman's story, Edith's especially but Rose's too, is a kind of English story told over and over in fiction and film but rarely in works of history: the tragicomedy of someone who could not perform the ordinariness expected of them.

Notes

INTRODUCTION

1. This book is the first detailed study of the Littlehampton libel case. There is an overview in Emily Cockayne, *Cheek by Jowl: A History of Neighbours* (London: The Bodley Head, 2012), 142–3. Dr Cockayne will discuss the case at greater length in a book she is writing about anonymous letters since the medieval period.

2. Agatha Christie, *The Moving Finger* (1943; repr., London: Collins, 1968), 104–5. On poison-pen letters in fiction and in present-day England, see John Mullan, 'The Strange Case of the Poison Pen Letters', *Guardian*, 28 June 2014.

3. Robin W. Winks (ed.), *The Historian as Detective: Essays on Evidence* (New York: Harper Colophon, 1969); Carlo Ginzburg, 'Morelli, Freud and Sherlock Holmes: Clues and Scientific Method', tr. Anna Davin, *History Workshop Journal*, no. 9 (spring 1980), 5–36, here 8–9.

4. For some historians this statement will ring alarm bells of the sort sounded in Gayatri Chakravorty Spivak, 'Can the Subaltern Speak?' in Cary Nelson and Lawrence Grossberg (eds), *Marxism and the Interpretation of Culture* (Urbana: University of Illinois Press, 1988), 271–313 or Joan Wallach Scott, 'A Statistical Representation of Work: La Statistique de l'Industrie à Paris, 1847–1848', in Scott, *Gender and the Politics of History*, rev. edn (New York: Columbia University Press, 1999), 113–38. Doubts about the possibility of moving from a representation to its referent (social reality, non-elite perspectives, and so on) have often pushed scholars away from social history towards a concern with narratives of, or by, the poor or oppressed. A terrific recent example is Mark Peel, *Miss Cutler and the Case of the Resurrected Horse: Social Work and the Story of Poverty in America, Australia, and Britain* (Chicago: University of Chicago Press, 2012). I am more interested in the textures of writing and speech than in cultural narratives. The present book is, among other things, an attempt to push my earlier exercises in intellectual or literary history 'from below' (Christopher Hilliard, *English as a Vocation: The 'Scrutiny' Movement* [Oxford: Oxford University Press, 2012], chs 4, 5; Hilliard, *To Exercise Our Talents: The Democratization of Writing in Britain* [Cambridge, MA: Harvard University Press, 2006], chs 3, 7) further, and treat vocabularies and handwriting styles as sites of individuality and ambition. Whether this kind of close reading of everyday uses of literacy

escapes the simplifications of older kinds of social and cultural history is a
question readers can decide for themselves.

5. The offence was not taken off the books until 2009: Coroners and Justice
Act 2009 (c. 25), s. 73.

6. Lord Alverstone CJ, unreported direction to a grand jury at the Somerset
assizes, 22 June 1906, quoted in Hugh Fraser, *Principles and Practice of the
Law of Libel and Slander: With Suggestions on the Conduct of a Civil Action,
Forms and Precedents, and All Statutes Bearing on the Subject*, 5th edn (London:
Butterworth, 1917), 315–16.

7. David Vincent, *Literacy and Popular Culture: England, 1750–1914* (Cambridge:
Cambridge University Press, 1989), 274–5. Contrast, for instance, Walter J.
Ong, 'Writing Is a Technology that Restructures Thought', in Gerd Baumann
(ed.), *The Written Word: Literacy in Transition* (Oxford: Clarendon Press, 1986),
23–50, here 38–9.

8. Cf. Jacques Derrida, *Of Grammatology*, tr. Gayatri Chakravorty Spivak
(1967; Baltimore: Johns Hopkins University Press, 1976), 141–268.

PROLOGUE

1. *Who's Who 1921: An Annual Biographical Dictionary with Which Is Incorporated
'Men and Women of the Time'* (London: Adam and Charles Black, n.d.), 244.

2. After the Irish nationalist Roger Casement was convicted of treason in
1916, Blackwell advised Cabinet to proceed with the execution and not
worry about alienating public opinion in America and elsewhere. Copies
of what purported to be Casement's diaries were doing the rounds. They
included detailed descriptions of a variety of sex acts with men. The wise
choice, Blackwell told Cabinet, would be 'to allow the law to take its
course, and by judicious means to use these diaries to prevent Casement
attaining martyrdom'. Ernley Blackwell, 'The Casement Case', 15 July
1916, CAB 37/151/36, National Archives, London.

3. Blackwell made a mistake here: the child in question was Rose Gooding's
nephew.

4. Edith Swan, statement, 19 June 1921, MEPO 3/380, National Archives.

5. Blackwell, untitled memo, 2 June 1921, HO 144/2452, National Archives.

6. Alfred Russell, statement, 25 June 1921; G. R. Nicholls, 'Criminal Libel',
report to Superintendent Fred Thomas, 29 June 1921, MEPO 3/380 (cited
hereafter as 'Nicholls, report of 29 June 1921').

7. Edith Swan, statement, 19 June 1921, MEPO 3/380.

8. C. Ralph to N. T. [?] Wall, 15 June 1921, HO 144/2452.

9. Blackwell, untitled memo, 2 June 1921, HO 144/2452.

10. Edith Swan, statement, 19 June 1921, MEPO 3/380.

11. Leonard Kershaw to Guy Stephenson, 25 May 1921, HO 144/2452.

12. A. H. Bodkin, '[R]e Rose Gooding', 24 May 1921; A. S. Williams to Bodkin,
1 May 1921, HO 144/2452.

13. Blackwell, untitled memo, 2 June 1921, HO 144/2452.
14. Bodkin, '[R]e Rose Gooding', 24 May 1921, HO 144/2452.
15. A. S. Williams to Bodkin, 1 May 1921, HO 144/2452.
16. F. J. Peel to Williams, 21 April 1921, HO 144/2452.
17. Williams to Bodkin, 1 May 1921, HO 144/2452.
18. Robert Jackson, *Case for the Prosecution: A Biography of Sir Archibald Bodkin, Director of Public Prosecutions, 1920–1930* (London: Arthur Barker, 1962).
19. Bodkin, '[R]e Rose Gooding', 24 May 1921, HO 144/2452.
20. Blackwell, note on minutes page of file 416617/3, 3 June 1921, HO 144/2452.
21. Ernest T. Hall to Blackwell, 1 June 1921, HO 144/2452.
22. Anon., undated (but after 15 June 1921) report quoting and summarizing letters from the chief warder and the commissioners of Portsmouth prison, HO 144/2452.
23. Blackwell to Williams, 6 June 1921; Blackwell, untitled memo, 2 June 1921, HO 144/2452.
24. Blackwell to Williams, 6 June 1921, HO 144/2452.
25. Blackwell, untitled memo, 2 June 1921, HO 144/2452.
26. Blackwell to Kershaw, 13 June 1921, HO 144/2452.
27. Peel to Williams, 8 June 1921; Blackwell to Kershaw, 13 June 1921, HO 144/2452.
28. P. J. Waller, *Town, City and Nation: England, 1850–1914* (Oxford: Clarendon Press, 1983), 268.
29. Basil Thomson, *Queer People* (London: Hodder and Stoughton, 1922), 4. Nevertheless, provincial secondments of Metropolitan Police detectives were not uncommon just after the First World War. Frederick Porter Wensley, *Detective Days: The Record of Forty-Two Years' Service in the Criminal Investigation Department* (London: Cassell, 1931), 212.
30. Bodkin to Assistant Commissioner, CID, 13 June 1921, MEPO 3/380.
31. Bodkin to Blackwell, 13 June 1921, HO 144/2452.
32. Haia Shpayer-Makov, *The Making of a Policeman: A Social History of a Labour Force in Metropolitan London, 1829–1914* (Aldershot: Ashgate, 2002), 60.
33. Examination certificate for George Robert Nicholls, warrant 84634, The Met Heritage Centre, London; report of particulars, pension number 34324, 20 February 1934, MEPO 21/69, National Archives. Thanks to Phillip Barnes-Warden of the Met Heritage Centre for supplying copies of these documents.
34. Haia Shpayer-Makov, 'Explaining the Rise and Success of Detective Memoirs in Britain', in Clive Emsley and Haia Shpayer-Makov (eds), *Police Detectives in History, 1750–1950* (Aldershot: Ashgate, 2006), 103–34, here 104; George Dilnot, *The Story of Scotland Yard* (London: Geoffrey Bles, 1926), 251–2.
35. *The Times*, 22 January 1912; *The Times*, 24 January 1912; *Evening Telegraph* (Angus), 4 July 1922.

36. *Derby Daily Telegraph*, 29 July 1929; *Evening Telegraph* (Angus), 4 July 1922.
37. G. R. Nicholls, 'Murder: Police Aid', 16 March 1921, MEPO 3/1561.
38. See Steve Adams, *Murder at the Star: Who Killed Thomas Thomas?* (Bridgend: Seren, 2015).
39. Bodkin to Blackwell, 13 June 1921, HO 144/2452; F. T. B[igham], note on minutes page of file 204/UNC/6, 14 June 1921, MEPO 3/380.
40. Nicholls, report of 29 June 1921.

CHAPTER 1

1. To be precise, 11,287. This is the total for the Littlehampton urban district, comprising Littlehampton civil parish (9814) and Wick civil parish (1473). *Census of England and Wales 1921: County of Sussex* (London: HMSO, 1923), 12 (table 5).
2. C. P. Lewis (ed.), *A History of the County of Sussex*, vol. 5, part 2, *Littlehampton and District (Arundel Rape, South-Eastern Part, Comprising Poling Hundred)*, The Victoria History of the Counties of England (London: Published for the Institute of Historical Research by Boydell & Brewer, 2009), 178–9 (hereafter referred to as '*Victoria County History*'); H. C. Brookfield, 'Three Sussex Ports, 1850–1950', *Journal of Transport History*, 2 (1955), 35–40; *The Homeland Handbooks: Littlehampton, Arundel and Amberley, with Their Surroundings*, 11th edn (London: Homeland Association, n.d. [between 1918 and 1922]), 19; *Kelly's Directory of Sussex, 1915* (London: Kelly's Directories, n.d.), 504.
3. *Kelly's Directory of Sussex, 1915*, 505.
4. *Homeland Handbook*, 19; *Kelly's Directory of Sussex, 1915*, 504.
5. Brookfield, 'Three Sussex Ports', 41.
6. Brookfield, 'Three Sussex Ports', 39–42; *Victoria County History*, 179.
7. John K. Walton, *The British Seaside: Holidays and Resorts in the Twentieth Century* (Manchester: Manchester University Press, 2000), 145.
8. *Victoria County History*, 158.
9. *Victoria County History*, 154–5.
10. John K. Walton, *The English Seaside Resort: A Social History, 1750–1914* (Leicester: Leicester University Press, 1983), 17; *A Guide to All the Watering and Sea-Bathing Places, for 1813: With a Description of the Lakes; A Sketch of a Tour in Wales; and Itineraries: Illustrated with Maps and New Views: By the Editor of the Picture of London* (London: Longman, Hurst, Rees, Orme, and Browne, n.d.), 278.
11. Ian Nairn and Nikolaus Pevsner, *The Buildings of England: Sussex* (Harmondsworth: Penguin, 1965), 262.
12. David Cannadine, *Lords and Landlords: The Aristocracy and the Towns, 1774–1967* (Leicester: Leicester University Press, 1980), 412–13.
13. *Victoria County History*, 148–9.
14. Cannadine, *Lords and Landlords*, 405.

15. *Victoria County History*, 159, 160; Allen Eyles, Frank Gray, and Alan Readman, *Cinema West Sussex: The First Hundred Years* (Chichester: Phillimore, 1996), 11. M. Dudley Clark, *Littlehampton, Sussex: With Its Surroundings* (London: Homeland Association and Frederick Warne and Co., n.d. [1915]), was, according to its title page, 'The Official Guide of the Littlehampton Urban District Council and the Littlehampton Traders' Association'.

16. Walton, *British Seaside*, 94; Violet Lily May, statement, 12 October 1921, MEPO 3/380, National Archives.

17. Rolf Zeegers, Juliet Nye, and Lucy Ashby, *Littlehampton Revisited* (Stroud: The History Press, 2007), 20, 23.

18. Walton, *British Seaside*, 94, 108.

19. Ian Friel and Rebecca Fardell (eds), *Littlehampton* (Stroud: Chalford, 1998), 97; Iris Jones and Daphne Stanford, *Littlehampton in Old Photographs* (Stroud: Alan Sutton, 1990), 117; Zeegers, Nye, and Ashby, *Littlehampton Revisited*, 21–2.

20. Eyles, Gray, and Readman, *Cinema West Sussex*, 157.

21. Walton, *British Seaside*, 97–9; Walton, *English Seaside Resort*, 42.

22. *Victoria County History*, 157; *Mr. Punch at the Seaside: As Pictured by Charles Keene, John Leech, George du Maurier, Phil May, L. Raven-Hill, J. Bernard Partridge, Gordon Browne, E. T. Reed, and Others* (London: Amalgamated Press, n.d.), 41.

23. Walton, *English Seaside Resort*, 95.

24. Littlehampton did not 'move . . . downmarket', as the usually dispassionate *Victoria County History* puts it, until 1932, when the Norfolk estate sold a tract of the green (an extension of the common) to the holiday camp magnate Billy Butlin. *Victoria County History*, 134, 159.

25. Walton, *English Seaside Resort*, ch. 2. For more context see Sandra Dawson, 'Working-Class Consumers and the Campaign for Holidays with Pay', *Twentieth Century British History*, 18 (2007), 277–305.

26. Walton, *British Seaside*, 103.

27. *Homeland Handbook*, 24; on mixing and leisure, see Ross McKibbin, *Classes and Cultures: England, 1918–1951* (Oxford: Oxford University Press, 1998), 88; Simon Gunn and Rachel Bell, *Middle Classes: Their Rise and Sprawl* (London: Phoenix, 2002), 68.

28. D. H. Lawrence to Viola Meynell, 31 July 1915, in *The Letters of D. H. Lawrence*, vol. 2, *1913–16*, ed. George T. Zytaruk and James T. Boulton (Cambridge: Cambridge University Press, 1981), 373.

29. *Homeland Handbook*, iv, xiii, xvi.

30. See the 'Commercial' listings in *Kelly's Directory of Sussex, 1915*, 507–12; and the advertisements in *Homeland Handbook*, iv, vi–xix, especially the list on p. viii, which specifies the number of bedrooms and sitting rooms at 14 establishments; *Oxford English Dictionary*, s.v. 'apartments', 2.

31. V. S. Pritchett, 'Scarborough', in Yvonne Cloud (ed.), *Beside the Seaside: Six Variations* (London: Stanley Nott, 1934), 187–226, here 213–14.

32. Of the many works that could be cited here, the ones that have influenced my understanding of this moment the most are Ross McKibbin, 'Class and Conventional Wisdom: The Conservative Party and the "Public" in Inter-war Britain', in McKibbin, *The Ideologies of Class: Social Relations in Britain, 1880–1950* (Oxford: Clarendon Press, 1990), 259–93; McKibbin, *Classes and Cultures*; Susan Pedersen, 'From National Crisis to "National Crisis": British Politics, 1914–1931', *Journal of British Studies*, 33 (1994), 322–35; Jon Lawrence, 'Forging a Peaceable Kingdom: War, Violence, and Fear of Brutalization in Post-First World War Britain', *Journal of Modern History*, 75 (2003), 557–89; Mike Savage, 'Trade Unionism, Sex Segregation, and the State: Women's Employment in "New Industries" in Inter-War Britain', *Social History*, 13 (1988), 209–30; J. B. Priestley, *English Journey: Being a Rambling but Truthful Account of What One Man Saw and Heard and Felt during a Journey through England during the Autumn of the Year 1933* (1934; repr., Harmondsworth: Penguin, 1977).

33. Jones and Stanford, *Littlehampton in Old Photographs*, 39; *Homeland Handbook*, xlvii.

34. The family's name crops up often in Littlehampton's business history—Laurence Leggett worked as an estate agent from an office next to the railway station, and an enterprising grandfather or great uncle had provided his guests in South Terrace with salt water baths in the previous century. *Kelly's Directory of Sussex, 1911* (London: Kelly's Directories, n.d.), 514; *Kelly's Directory of Sussex, 1915*, 510; *Victoria County History*, 157.

35. 1911 Census, household record for Prince of Wales Inn, [13] Western Road, Littlehampton; *Kelly's Directory of Sussex, 1915*, 511; Gwen Lansdell, *Time for a Quick One: A Brief Historical Comment on Some of Littlehampton's Inns and Pubs, Together with Words about the Brewery* (Littlehampton: Littlehampton Local History Society, 1994), 6.

36. http://pubshistory.com/SussexPubs/Littlehampton/SurreyArmsInn.shtml (accessed 8 September 2016).

37. M. J. Daunton, *House and Home in the Victorian City: Working-Class Housing, 1850–1914* (London: Edward Arnold, 1983), 92.

38. '47–51, Western Road, Littlehampton', http://www.britishlistedbuildings.co.uk/en-297522-47-51-western-road-littlehampton-west-su#.VY8XulKkrCQ; Roland B. Harris, *Littlehampton: Historic Character Assessment Report*, Sussex Extensive Urban Survey (April 2009), 27, https://www.westsussex.gov.uk/media/1734/littlehampton_eus_report_and_maps.pdf.

39. *Littlehampton Observer*, 2 November 1921.

40. *Particulars and Conditions of Sale for 15 Valuable Freehold & Leasehold Properties, to Be Sold by Auction, at the Sale Room, 21–25 High Street, Littlehampton, on Wednesday, December 4th, 1918, at 3 O'Clock Precisely* (Littlehampton: Sparks and Son, 1918), D1904, Littlehampton Museum.

41. Ross McKibbin, 'Work and Hobbies in Britain, 1880–1950', in McKibbin, *Ideologies of Class*, 139–66, here 144–5.

42. G. R. Nicholls, 'Criminal Libel', report to Superintendent Fred Thomas, 29 June 1921, MEPO 3/380 (cited hereafter as 'Nicholls, report of 29 June 1921').

43. Robert Tressell, *The Ragged Trousered Philanthropists* (London: Grant Richards, 1914). Tressell's 'Mugsborough' was modelled on Hastings.

44. Nicholls, report of 29 June 1921.

45. W. H. Gooding to Home Secretary, 9 June 1921, HO 144/2452, National Archives.

46. 1911 Census, household record for 27 Western Road, Littlehampton (the street was renumbered in early 1921, whereupon the Swans' house changed from number 27 to number 47).

47. Arnold Freeman, *Boy Life and Labour: The Manufacture of Inefficiency* (London: P. S. King and Son, 1914), 2–5, 34.

48. 1911 Census, household record for 27 Western Road; Stephen Swan, National Registration Act form, n.d., MEPO 3/380.

49. Stephen Swan, statement, 25 June 1921, MEPO 3/380. He was discharged after nine months.

50. Nicholls, report of 29 June 1921.

51. Violet May, statement, 13 October 1921, MEPO 3/380.

52. Nicholls, report of 29 June 1921.

53. Nicholls, report of 29 June 1921. There is a picture of Boniface and her charges at East Street School in Jones and Stanford, *Littlehampton in Old Photographs*, 98.

54. Nicholls, report of 29 June 1921; *Kelly's Directory of Sussex, 1915*, 509.

55. D. Robert Elleray, *Littlehampton: A Pictorial History* (Chichester: Phillimore, 1991), fig. 62 (no page numbers); [John White,] *Photographic Views of Littlehampton and Neighbourhood* ([Littlehampton:] J. White and Son, n.d.), no page numbers.

56. Nicholls, report of 29 June 1921.

57. See the table in Mike Savage and Andrew Miles, *The Remaking of the British Working Class, 1840–1940* (London: Routledge, 1994), 24.

58. Savage, 'Trade Unionism, Sex Segregation, and the State', 228–9.

59. Edward Swan, statement, 20 June 1921, MEPO 3/380; on eldest daughters' responsibilities, see Selina Todd, *Young Women, Work, and Family in England, 1918–1950* (Oxford: Oxford University Press, 2005), ch. 2; Trevor Griffiths, *The Lancashire Working Classes, c. 1880–1930* (Oxford: Oxford University Press, 2001), 230, 265.

60. Patricia E. Malcolmson, *English Laundresses: A Social History, 1850–1930* (Urbana: University of Illinois Press, 1986), ch. 1; Melanie Tebbutt, *Making Ends Meet: Pawnbroking and Working-Class Credit* (1983; repr., London: Methuen, 1984), 22.

61. See generally Paul Johnson, *Saving and Spending: The Working-Class Economy in Britain, 1870–1939* (Oxford: Oxford University Press, 1985); Griffiths, *Lancashire Working Classes*, especially 255.

62. Walton, *British Seaside*, 147–8; *George Meek, Bath Chair-Man: By Himself* (New York: E. P. Dutton and Company, 1910), 159–68 (Meek's chapter is entitled 'The Curse of Casual Employment').

63. Alice Mary Twine, statement, 22 June 1921, MEPO 3/380.

64. Kent McKeever, 'A Short History of Tontines', *Fordham Journal of Corporate and Financial Law*, 15 (2009), 491–521, here 491, 506; *Oxford English Dictionary*, s.v. 'tontine', A.3. A witness appearing before a parliamentary commission into friendly societies and building societies in 1871 said that it was curious that 'the sharing out clubs...call themselves tontines; I do not know why; of course it is a wrong name.' *Second Report of the Commissioners Appointed to Inquire into Friendly and Benefit Building Societies*, C. 514, part 2 (London: HMSO, 1872), 37–8.

65. Johnson, *Saving and Spending*, 150–1. For an example from an earlier period, see Barry Reay, 'The Context and Meaning of Popular Literacy: Some Evidence from Nineteenth-Century Rural England', *Past and Present*, no. 131 (May 1991), 89–129, here 105. For Lancashire workers and their holidays, see Madeline Kerr, *The People of Ship Street* (London: Routledge and Kegan Paul, 1958), 210.

66. Violet Lily May, statement, 22 June 1921, MEPO 3/380; Nicholls, report of 29 June 1921.

67. Medal cards for B. Boxell and Bert Boxell, WO 372/3, National Archives. Edith's fiancé's surname is consistently spelled with an A in the National Archives files on the Littlehampton libels case. I need to explain why I believe that the Lance Corporal B. Boxall to whom Edith wrote was the B. Boxell and Bert Boxell of these two medal cards, which are the source of the military service details given in the text. On a piece of blotting paper seized during the investigation into the case (in MEPO 3/380), there is the mirror image of a letter or envelope addressed by Edith to her fiancé that gives his service number (6280121). That service number corresponds to the medals card of 'B Boxell' in the East Kent Regiment who seems to have been the same man as the Bert Boxell who enlisted in the Royal Sussex Regiment. The medal cards for B. Boxell and Bert Boxell both specify the two regiments: one card relates to service in India with the Royal Sussex Regiment and the other to service in Aden in 1919 with the Buffs. The address Edith wrote includes the word 'Buffs'.

There were many Boxalls living in southern England at this time. My best guess is that this one was Albert Edwin Boxall. He appears, simply as Bert Boxall, cricket grounds keeper, in the 1911 census household record for 1 Wickersham Road, Horsham. Albert Edwin Boxall, of the same address (and working as a bricklayer's labourer), completed an army enlistment form before an officer in the Royal Sussex Regiment. The attestation form is confusing, however: it says the recruit is enlisting in a Yorkshire regiment, but then this is crossed out and nothing written in its place. If he enlisted in the Royal Sussex Regiment, his history would match the

Boxell of the medal cards. 1911 Census, household record for 1 Wickersham
Road, Horsham; Albert Edwin Boxall, short service attestation, no. 6795,
WO 363, National Archives.

68. Sir Ernley Blackwell, note on minutes page of file 416617/6, 14 June 1921,
HO 144/2452. For context see Priya Satia, 'Developing Iraq: Britain, India
and the Redemption of Empire and Technology in the First World War',
Past and Present, no. 197 (November 2007), 211–55.

69. Alfred Russell, statement, 23 June 1921, MEPO 3/380.

70. Edith Flora Russell, statement, 23 June 1921, MEPO 3/380.

71. Ben Jones, *The Working Class in Mid-Twentieth-Century England: Community,
Identity and Social Memory* (Manchester: Manchester University Press,
2012), 134; Elizabeth Roberts, *A Woman's Place: An Oral History of Working-
Class Women, 1890–1940* (Oxford: Blackwell, 1984), 188–9.

72. Nicholls, report of 29 June 1921 (punctuation as in original).

73. Edith Swan, statement, 19 June 1921, MEPO 3/380.

74. Edith Swan, statement, 19 June 1921, MEPO 3/380. Skinner lived at 45
South Terrace, where she took in paying guests: *Kelly's Directory of Sussex,
1915*, 511.

75. Leopold A. Vidler, 'The Rye River Barges', *Mariner's Mirror*, 21 (1935), 378–94.

76. Alfred Russell, statement, 23 June 1921, MEPO 3/380.

77. William Henry Gooding, statement, 18 June 1921, MEPO 3/380.

78. 1901 Census, household record for 3 Edward Street, Lewes.

79. Deborah Cohen, *Family Secrets: Living with Shame from the Victorians to the
Present Day* (London: Penguin, 2013), 124–5. See also Claire Langhamer,
The English in Love: The Intimate Story of an Emotional Revolution (Oxford:
Oxford University Press, 2013), 143–4; Ginger Frost, '"The Black Lamb of
the Black Sheep": Illegitimacy in the English Working Class, 1850–1939',
Journal of Social History, 37 (2003), 293–322, here 295–6; Ellen Ross, *Love
and Toil: Motherhood in Outcast London, 1870–1918* (New York: Oxford
University Press, 1993), 134–5. On the determination not to let children
go into the workhouse, see also Roberts, *Woman's Place*, 170–1 (in the
context of orphans rather than illegitimate children).

80. William Henry Gooding, statement, 18 June 1921, MEPO 3/380.

81. See the table in Brookfield, 'Three Sussex Ports', 40. This figure is from
1910. The gap would only have widened by 1916.

82. 1901 Census, household record for 3 Edward Street, Lewes; William Henry
Gooding, statement, 18 June 1921; Barbara Ellen Russell, statement, 25 June
1921, MEPO 3/380.

83. http://www.scotlandswar.ed.ac.uk/sites/default/files/pdf_George_
Gibson_History.pdf (accessed 12 December 2016); http://www.wrecksite.
eu/wreck.aspx?118297 (accessed 26 March 2014).

84. William Henry Gooding, statement, 18 June 1921, MEPO 3/380; Nicholls,
report of 29 June 1921.

85. Nicholls, report of 29 June 1921.

86. It was also an atypical form of 'co-residence': parents who lived with family members more commonly did so with their own parents, or single or widowed aunts and uncles. See Roberts, *Woman's Place*, 172–7.
87. William Henry Gooding, statement, 18 June 1921, MEPO 3/380.
88. Barbara Ellen Russell, statement, 25 June 1921, MEPO 3/380.
89. Nicholls, report of 29 June 1921.
90. Edith Flora Russell, statement, 23 June 1921; Edith Swan, statement, 19 June 1921, MEPO 3/380.
91. Pat Thane and Tanya Evans, *Sinners? Scroungers? Saints? Unmarried Motherhood in Twentieth-Century England* (Oxford: Oxford University Press, 2012), 6.
92. Ruth Eva Russell, statement, 25 June 1921, MEPO 3/380.
93. Nicholls, report of 29 June 1921.
94. William Henry Gooding, statement, 25 June 1921, MEPO 3/380.
95. Roberts, *Woman's Place*, 194; dating of this incident based on the interview transcript in 'Extracts from the Elizabeth Roberts Archive: Neighbours', Regional Heritage Centre, Lancaster University (http://www.lancaster.ac.uk/users/cnwrs/resources/archive.htm, accessed 29 May 2014).
96. Ross, *Love and Toil*, 84–5; Joanna Bourke, *Working-Class Cultures in Britain, 1890–1960: Gender, Class and Ethnicity* (London: Routledge, 1994), 71–4, and, especially, Jones, *Working Class in Mid-Twentieth-Century England*, 135.
97. Clive Emsley, *Hard Men: The English and Violence since 1750* (London: Hambledon and London, 2005), 60–2; Martin J. Wiener, 'Judges v. Jurors: Courtroom Tensions in Murder Trials and the Law of Criminal Responsibility in Nineteenth-Century England', *Law and History Review*, 17 (1999), 467–506, here 478, 494.
98. Nicholls, report of 29 June 1921.
99. [Maud] Pember Reeves, *Round about a Pound a Week* (London: G. Bell & Sons, 1913), 46; and see Robert Roberts, *The Classic Slum: Salford Life in the First Quarter of the Century* (1971; repr., London: Penguin, 1990), 44.
100. It is also possible that Dorothy or Gertrude, or Bill, slept on the sofa in the living room. That there was a sofa or another piece of furniture to lie down on is implied by William Gooding, statement, 18 June, 1921, MEPO 3/380.
101. Ruth Russell, statement, 18 June 1921, MEPO 3/380.
102. William Henry Gooding, statement, 18 June 1921, MEPO 3/380.
103. Barbara Ellen Russell, statement, 25 June 1921, MEPO 3/380.
104. William Henry Gooding, statement, 18 June 1921, MEPO 3/380.
105. Ernest Swan to Miss Hopkins, n.d. [*c.* 1920], MEPO 3/380; *Particulars and Conditions of Sale for 15 Valuable Freehold & Leasehold Properties*, D1904, Littlehampton Museum. According to the auction catalogue, the Swans

were paying 4s. 6d. per week to rent 47 Western Road in December 1918; Edward Swan paid the rates.

106. Ruth Eva Russell, statement, 18 June 1921, MEPO 3/380. It is unclear whether Ruth's money came from the ship's owner or from the state. The Board of Trade paid Ruth and Rose's mother £2 15s. 7d. per month and Gibson & Co. of Leith paid her compensation of £300 in monthly instalments of £3. Barbara Ellen Russell, statement, 25 June 1921, MEPO 3/380. Presumably the reason Ruth received compensation but not Rose was that as an unmarried daughter Ruth counted as her father's dependant while Rose did not.

107. Ruth Eva Russell, statement, 18 June 1921, MEPO 3/380.

108. Nicholls, report of 29 June 1921.

109. Zeegers, Nye, and Ashby, *Littlehampton Revisited*, 18; Jones and Stanford, *Littlehampton in Old Photographs*, 58; Vidler, 'Rye River Barges'.

110. Nicholls, report of 29 June 1921.

111. A. L. Bowley and Margaret H. Hogg, *Has Poverty Diminished? A Sequel to 'Livelihood and Poverty'* (London: P. S. King and Son, 1925), 36–7.

112. Alice Mary Twine, statement, 22 June 1921, MEPO 3/380.

113. Reeves, *Round about a Pound a Week*, ch. 5.

114. Kerr, *People of Ship Street*, 210.

115. Barbara Ellen Russell, statement, 25 June 1921, MEPO 3/380.

116. Violet Lily May, statement, 12 October 1921, MEPO 3/380.

117. Working Classes Cost of Living Committee, *Report*, Cd. 8980 (London: HMSO, 1918), 18.

118. Alice Mary Twine, statement, 22 June 1921, MEPO 3/380.

119. Ross, *Love and Toil*, 43.

120. See Julie-Marie Strange, 'Fatherhood, Furniture and the Inter-Personal Dynamics of Working-Class Homes, c. 1870–1914', *Urban History*, 40 (2013), 271–86; and, further back, John Tosh, *A Man's Place: Masculinity and the Middle-Class Home in Victorian England* (New Haven: Yale University Press, 1999).

121. The Great Masters Publishing Company of 18 Berners Street, London W1, is not listed in the normally undiscriminating *Writers' and Artists' Year Book* for 1921. Nor does the British Library or the Bodleian hold any books published by the firm. This could mean that the company did not provide those libraries with copies, or it could mean that its books were not subject to the legal deposit requirement—say if they were 'privately printed' reproductions of art works.

122. George Fitzhardinge Rose, statement, 2 August 1921, HO 144/2452.

123. Ruth Eva Russell, statement, 18 June 1921; *Homeland Handbook*, xxv–xxvii.

124. Nicholls, report of 29 June 1921.

125. Nicholls, report of 29 June 1921.

CHAPTER 2

1. Edith Swan, statement, 19 June 1921, MEPO 3/380, National Archives.
2. Alice Mary Twine, statement, 22 June 1921, MEPO 3/380.
3. William Henry Gooding, statement, 25 June 1921; Edith Swan, statement, 19 June 1921; Ruth Eva Russell, statement, 25 June 1921; Gertrude Russell, statement, 25 June 1921, MEPO 3/380.
4. G. R. Nicholls, 'Criminal Libel', report to Superintendent Fred Thomas, 29 June 1921, MEPO 3/380 (cited hereafter as 'Nicholls, report of 29 June 1921').
5. Ernest Swan to Miss Hopkins, n.d. [c. 1920], MEPO 3/380.
6. *Sussex Daily News*, 4 March 1921.
7. Edith Swan later said that, as relations between the families began to sour, her mother chased the Goodings' kitten out of her washhouse and Rose Gooding responded: 'Oh, you cruel old wretch, cruel old bitch, I will report you to the old age Pensions officer for taking in washing and ironing and I will get your pension taken away from you.' Edith Swan, statement, 19 June 1921, MEPO 3/380.
8. Edith Swan, statement, 19 June 1921, MEPO 3/380.
9. Edith Flora Russell, statement, 23 June 1921, MEPO 3/380.
10. Edith Flora Russell, statement, 23 June 1921, MEPO 3/380.
11. Edith Swan, statement, 19 June 1921, MEPO 3/380 (line breaks and one quotation mark and initial capital added).
12. Alfred Russell, statement, 23 June 1921, MEPO 3/380.
13. William Birkin, statement, 23 June 1921, MEPO 3/380.
14. William Henry Gooding, statement, 25 June 1921.
15. Ruth Eva Russell, statement, 25 June 1921, MEPO 3/380.
16. Nicholls, report of 29 June 1921.
17. *Argus* (Brighton), 22 September 1920.
18. Ernest Walter Swan, statement, 20 June 1921, MEPO 3/380 (line breaks added; italics added; and 'She said' and 'and Gooding said' omitted).
19. Alice Morgan, statement, 21 June 1921, MEPO 3/380.
20. Alice Morgan, statement, 21 June 1921, MEPO 3/380.
21. Mary Ann Swan, statement, 20 June 1921, MEPO 3/380.
22. Melanie Tebbutt, *Women's Talk? A Social History of 'Gossip' in Working-Class Neighbourhoods, 1880–1960* (Aldershot: Scolar Press, 1995), 141; Deborah Cohen, *Family Secrets: Living with Shame from the Victorians to the Present Day* (London: Penguin, 2013), xviii.
23. Mary Ann Swan, statement, 20 June 1921, MEPO 3/380.
24. Edith Swan, statement, 19 June 1921, MEPO 3/380.
25. *Kelly's Directory of Sussex, 1915* (London: Kelly's Directories, n.d.), 509.
26. Edith Swan, statement, 19 June 1921, MEPO 3/380.
27. Ruth Russell, statement, 25 June 1921, MEPO 3/380.

28. Mark Peel, *Miss Cutler and the Case of the Resurrected Horse: Social Work and the Story of Poverty in America, Australia, and Britain* (Chicago: University of Chicago Press, 2012), 16.
29. *Littlehampton Observer*, 19 July 1923.
30. Alice Morgan, statement, 21 June 1921, MEPO 3/380.
31. Selina Todd, *The People: The Rise and Fall of the Working Class, 1910–2010* (London: John Murray, 2014), 69–70.
32. Nicholls, report of 29 June 1921.
33. Rose Emma Gooding to Home Secretary, 6 June 1921, HO 144/2452.
34. Nicholls, report of 29 June 1921.
35. Tebbutt, *Women's Talk?*, 78.
36. Tebbutt, *Women's Talk?*, 76–80; Elizabeth Roberts, *A Woman's Place: An Oral History of Working-Class Women, 1890–1940* (Oxford: Blackwell, 1984), 193–4.
37. Ben Jones, *The Working Class in Mid-Twentieth-Century England: Community, Identity and Social Memory* (Manchester: Manchester University Press, 2012), 134; John Burnett (ed.), *Destiny Obscure: Autobiographies of Childhood, Education and Family from the 1820s to the 1920s* (London: Allen Lane, 1982), 218.
38. Jones, *Working Class in Mid-Twentieth-Century England*, 134.
39. Jones, *Working Class in Mid-Twentieth-Century England*, 134–6.
40. Ross McKibbin, *Classes and Cultures: England, 1918–1951* (Oxford: Oxford University Press, 1998), 126. See also James Vernon, *Distant Strangers: How Britain Became Modern* (Berkeley: University of California Press, 2014), 123.
41. Edith Swan, statement, 19 June 1921, MEPO 3/380.

CHAPTER 3

1. Sir Ernley Blackwell, note on minutes page of file 416617/6, 14 June 1921, HO 144/2452, National Archives; Edward Swan, statement, 20 June 1921, MEPO 3/380, National Archives.
2. Blackwell, note on minutes page of file 416617/6, 14 June 1921, HO 144/2452.
3. Kate Leggett, statement, 22 June 1921, MEPO 3/380.
4. Alice Morgan, statement, 21 June 1921, MEPO 3/380.
5. Charles Owen Haslett, statement, 20 June 1921, MEPO 3/380.
6. Asa Briggs, *Victorian Things*, rev. edn (Harmondsworth: Penguin, 1990), 362.
7. Jacques Derrida, *The Post Card: From Socrates to Freud and Beyond*, tr. Alan Bass (1980; Chicago: University of Chicago Press, 1987), 62; also 5, 27, 29, 33, 35, 53.
8. Ernest Walter Swan, statement, 20 June 1921, MEPO 3/380.

9. *Argus* (Brighton), 22 September 1920.
10. Edward Swan, statement, 20 June 1921, MEPO 3/380.
11. G. R. Nicholls, 'Criminal Libel', report to Superintendent Fred Thomas, 29 June 1921, MEPO 3/380 (cited hereafter 'Nicholls, report of 29 June 1921'). Punctuation as in original.
12. Edith Swan, statement, 19 June 1921, MEPO 3/380.
13. Mary Ann Swan, statement, 20 June 1921, MEPO 3/380.
14. Edward Swan, statement, 20 June 1921, MEPO 3/380.
15. William Henry Gooding, statement, 18 June 1921, MEPO 3/380.
16. William Henry Gooding, statement, 18 June, 1921, MEPO 3/380.
17. William Henry Gooding, statement, 18 June, 1921, MEPO 3/380.
18. Alfred Russell, statement, 23 June 1921; William Gooding, 18 June 1921, MEPO 3/380.
19. William Henry Gooding, statement, 18 June, 1921, MEPO 3/380.
20. Reuben Lynn, statement, date missing, MEPO 3/380. Nicholls, report of 29 June 1921, makes the point that Lynn meant Dorothy, not Rose.
21. William Henry Gooding, statement, 18 June 1921, MEPO 3/380.
22. 'Philis' to W. H. Gooding, postcard marked 30 August 1920, MEPO 3/380.
23. See George Orwell, 'The Art of Donald McGill' (1941), in *The Collected Essays, Journalism and Letters of George Orwell*, ed. Sonia Orwell and Ian Angus, 4 vols (Boston: Nonpareil Books, 2000), 2:155–65, here 155.
24. Edward Swan, statement, 20 June 1921, MEPO 3/380.
25. Nicholls, report of 29 June 1921; Edith Swan, statement, 19 June 1921, MEPO 3/380.
26. Reginald Edgar Booker, statement, 22 June 1921, MEPO 3/380.
27. Alfred Russell, statement, 23 June 1921, MEPO 3/380. However, Booker did not see any of their parents that day. Reginald Edgar Booker, statement, 22 June 1921, MEPO 3/380.
28. Reginald Edgar Booker, statement, 22 June 1921, MEPO 3/380.
29. F. J. Peel to A. S. Williams, 8 June 1921, HO 144/2452.
30. Edith Flora Russell, statement, 23 June 1921, MEPO 3/380.
31. Alfred Russell, statement, 23 June 1921, MEPO 3/380.
32. Travers Humphreys, *Criminal Days: Recollections and Reflections* (London: Hodder and Stoughton, 1946), 124.
33. Peel to Williams, 8 June 1921, HO 144/2452.
34. Charles Haslett, statement, 30 June 1921, MEPO 3/380.
35. Nicholls, report of 29 June 1921.
36. Alice Morgan, statement, 21 June 1921, MEPO 3/380 (about Bill Gooding going to see Haslett).
37. Alice Morgan, statement, 21 June 1921, MEPO 3/380.
38. Nicholls, report of 29 June 1921.
39. Typed copy of certificate of conviction issued by Arthur Denman, Clerk of Assize, 19 January 1921, HO 144/2452. The figure of twenty-six exhibits is derived from Nicholls, report of 29 June 1921.
40. *Kelly's Directory of Sussex, 1915* (London: Kelly's Directories, n.d.), 511.

41. Edith Swan, statement, 19 June 1921, MEPO 3/380.

42. Charles Haslett, statement, 30 June 1921; Kate Leggett, statement, 22 June 1921, MEPO 3/380.

43. Nicholls, report of 29 June 1921.

44. Nicholls, report of 29 June 1921; *Littlehampton Observer*, 29 September 1920.

45. Peter Mandler, 'Introduction: State and Society in Victorian Britain', in Mandler (ed.), *Liberty and Authority in Victorian Britain* (Oxford: Oxford University Press, 2006), 1–21, here 13–18; Martin J. Wiener, *Reconstructing the Criminal: Culture, Law, and Policy in England, 1830–1914* (Cambridge: Cambridge University Press, 1990), 7–9, 11–12, 60–1.

46. *R. v. Anon*, 33 Sol. Jo. 350 (1889), quoted in Hugh Fraser, *Principles and Practice of the Law of Libel and Slander: With Suggestions on the Conduct of a Civil Action, Forms and Precedents, and All Statutes Bearing on the Subject*, 5th edn (London: Butterworth, 1917), 315. Criminal libel was a common-law misdemeanour that was narrowed, but not redefined, by the Libel Act of 1843.

47. Lord Alverstone CJ, unreported direction to a grand jury at the Somerset assizes, 22 June 1906, quoted in Fraser, *Law of Libel and Slander*, 316. See also William Blake Odgers, *The Law of Libel and Slander: And of Actions on the Case for Words Causing Damage: With Evidence, Procedure, Practice, and Precedents of Pleadings, Both in Civil and Criminal Cases*, 5th edn (London: Stevens and Sons, 1912), 455–6.

48. H. Montgomery Hyde (ed.), *The Trials of Oscar Wilde* (London: William Hodge & Co., 1948); Lucy Bland, *Modern Women on Trial: Sexual Transgression in the Age of the Flapper* (Manchester: Manchester University Press, 2013), ch. 3; Judith R. Walkowitz, 'The "Vision of Salome": Cosmopolitanism and Erotic Dancing in Central London, 1908–1918', *American Historical Review*, 108 (2003), 337–76, here 370–6; Michael Kettle, *Salome's Last Veil: The Libel Case of the Century* (London: Hart-Davis MacGibbon, 1977).

49. See J. R. Spencer, 'Criminal Libel—A Skeleton in the Cupboard', *Criminal Law Review* (1977), part 1, 391.

50. Judges: *R. v. Doran* (1934), MEPO 3/925, National Archives; *R. v. White* (1939), CRIM 1/1097, National Archives; also Arthur Bettany's protracted effort to get the Home Office to quash his conviction for criminally libelling a judge in 1940, as detailed in HO 45/25556, National Archives. Police misconduct: *R. v. Paul and Workers Publications Ltd* (1927), CRIM 1/402, National Archives. See generally Spencer, 'Criminal Libel', part 1, 390.

51. *The Times*, 8 April 1914.

52. *R. v. Crocker* (1902), CRIM 1/70/4, National Archives (stockbroker); *R. v. Caldwell* (1909), ASSI 65/17/1, National Archives; *R. v. Brind* (1929), CRIM 1/466, National Archives; *Gurney v. Wicks* (1936), CRIM 1/812, National Archives (solicitors).

53. *R. v. Calcott* (1904), CRIM 1/90/4, National Archives (engineer); *R. v. Britton* (1904), CRIM 1/88/8, National Archives (labourer).

54. Compare J. R. Spencer, 'Criminal Libel—A Skeleton in the Cupboard', *Criminal Law Review* (1977), part 2, 465–6.

55. *Criminal Libel*, Law Commission Working Paper no. 184 (London: HMSO, 1982), 45, 192.

56. William Shepherd to Wilhelmina Flanagan, n.d., CRIM 1/593, National Archives. Shepherd himself put the phrase 'giggly ball' in quotation marks.

57. Deposition of Wilhemina Flanagan, 12 January 1932, CRIM 1/593.

58. Deposition of Samuel Linden, 12 January 1932, CRIM 1/593.

59. Shepherd to the Clerk of the Court, Central Criminal Court, n.d, CRIM 1/593. I have deleted a comma after 'law' and before 'of libel'. A similar case is *The Queen v. Adams*, 22 QBD (1889) 66.

60. A. Kensington [?] to Chief Inspector, 29 November 1935, MEPO 3/927, National Archives.

61. Charles Gray to William Browning, 19 November 1934 (copy), CRIM 1/818, National Archives.

62. John Sands to Superintendent, 20 November 1935; A. Kensington [?] to Chief Inspector, 13 January 1936; Sands to Superintendent, 14 January 1936, MEPO 3/927.

63. *R. v. Goodchild* (1942), CRIM 1/1467, National Archives. The quotation is from the deposition of Harold Greenstreet, 9 December 1942.

64. *R. v. Simner* (1938), CRIM 1/1033, National Archives (council); *R. v. Riley* (1947), CRIM 1/1880, National Archives (party branch); Georgina May Rutter to Mr Clitheroe, 15 July 1946, exhibit 3 (copy) in *R. v. Rutter*, ASSI 52/76, National Archives (WEA). An example involving a church congregation is the Sutton libel case, discussed on pp. 94–7 above.

65. [Sir Archibald Bodkin], 'Observations to Counsel', July 1921, HO 144/2452.

66. It is a small point, but the other contemporary examples of litigation between neighbours cited by Emily Cockayne in *Cheek by Jowl: A History of Neighbours* (London: The Bodley Head, 2012) involve more comfortably off households (pp. 114–15, 117–18, 120, 140–1).

67. The legal bill for Rose Gooding's second trial was at least £30 (see p. 71 above).

68. Committee on Legal Aid for the Poor, *First Report*, Cmd. 2638 (London: HMSO, 1926), 5; William Cornish, J. Stuart Anderson, Ray Cocks, Michael Lobban, Patrick Polden, and Keith Smith, *The Oxford History of the Laws of England*, vol. 13, *1820–1914: Fields of Development* (Oxford: Oxford University Press, 2010), 82–3. The scholarly literature on working-class use of the legal system is stronger on the eighteenth and nineteenth centuries than the early twentieth. See for instance Carolyn Steedman, 'A Lawyer's Letter: Everyday Uses of the Law in Early Nineteenth-Century England', *History Workshop Journal*, no. 81 (spring 2016), 62–83.

69. On the origins of the system of 'magisterial justice', see Margot C. Finn, 'The Authority of the Law', in Peter Mandler (ed.), *Liberty and Authority in Victorian Britain* (Oxford: Oxford University Press, 2006), 159−78, here 162−4, 177; and, on its workings in the interwar period, Leo Page, *Justice of the Peace* (London: Faber and Faber, 1936).

70. Nicholls, report of 29 June 1921.

71. Alice Morgan reported that the Goodings planned to retain Sharpe as their solicitor: Morgan, statement, 21 June 1921, MEPO 3/380.

72. William Herbert Smith, statement, 22 June 1921, MEPO 3/380; Roland Wild, *King's Counsel: The Life of Sir Henry Curtis-Bennett* (New York: Macmillan, 1938), 85.

73. Oswald Mosley, *My Life* (London: Nelson, 1968), 355−6. Flowers batted for three innings in 1905, with a high score of 5 and an average of 3. George Washer, comp., *A Complete Record of Sussex County Cricket, 1728 to 1957* (n.p.: Sussex County Cricket Club, 1958), 135.

74. *Argus*, 22 September 1920.

75. William Herbert Smith, statement, 22 June 1921, MEPO 3/380.

76. *Argus*, 22 September 1920.

77. *Littlehampton Observer*, 29 September 1920.

78. *Argus*, 22 September 1920.

79. Alice Morgan, statement, 21 June 1921, MEPO 3/380.

80. Edith Swan, statement, 19 June 1921, MEPO 3/380.

81. Alice Morgan, statement, 21 June 1921, MEPO 3/380.

82. Edith Swan, statement, 19 June 1921, MEPO 3/380.

83. Alice Morgan, statement, 21 June 1921, MEPO 3/380.

84. *Argus*, 22 September 1920.

85. Alice Morgan, statement, 21 June 1921, MEPO 3/380.

86. *Argus*, 22 September 1920.

87. *Argus*, 22 September 1920.

88. Cornish et al., *Fields of Development*, 82; Howard Levenson, 'Legal Aid for Mitigation', *Modern Law Review*, 40 (1977), 523−32, here 523; Committee on Legal Aid for the Poor, *First Report*, 5.

89. *Argus*, 22 September 1920.

90. Nicholls, report of 29 June 1921.

91. William Henry Gooding, statement, 18 June 1921, MEPO 3/380.

92. E. V. Lucas, *Highways and Byways in Sussex*, 2nd edn (London: Macmillan, 1904), 21.

93. William Herbert Smith, statement, 22 June 1921, MEPO 3/380.

94. Stephen Hobhouse and Fenner Brockway (eds), *English Prisons To-Day: Being the Report of the Prison System Enquiry Committee* (London: Longmans, Green & Co., 1922), 306; Committee on Insanity and Crime, *Report of the Committee Appointed to Consider What Changes, If Any, Are Desirable in the Existing Law, Practice and Procedure Relating to Criminal Trials in Which the Plea*

of Insanity as a Defence is Raised, and Whether Any and, If So, What Changes Should Be Made in the Existing Law and Practice in Respect of Cases Falling within the Provisions of Section 2 (4) of the Criminal Lunatics Act, 1884, Cmd. 2005 (London: HMSO, 1923), 10. Mindful of accusations by Irish nationalists that the British prison system drove inmates insane, governors and medical officers insisted that prisons were not mentally unhealthy. Wiener, *Reconstructing the Criminal*, 352.

95. Hobhouse and Brockway, *English Prisons To-Day*, 52–3. The quotation is from Maurice Hamblin Smith, medical officer for Birmingham prison, in his 1919–1920 report. Magistrates often refused bail to prostitutes so that they could be examined and treated by prison medical officers. Conscious of the short sentences for prostitution-related offences, some magistrates would postpone sentencing so that the remanded accused would have to submit to treatment for longer. 'Imprisonment, while retaining its penal character', Hobhouse and Brockway protested, 'has come to be looked on as an opportunity for imposing medical treatment for venereal disease—partly, perhaps, for the sufferer's own sake, but chiefly in the interests of public health.' Hobhouse and Brockway, *English Prisons To-Day*, 339. This notwithstanding the repeal of the Contagious Diseases Acts and other feminist victories. See Philippa Levine, *Prostitution, Race, and Politics: Policing Venereal Disease in the British Empire* (New York: Routledge, 2003).

96. William Herbert Smith, statement, 22 June 1921, MEPO 3/380; Ernest T. Hall to Blackwell, 1 June 1921, HO 144/2452.

97. Hall to Blackwell, 1 June 1921, HO 144/2452.

98. The case was identified as *Rex v. Gooding*, not *Swan v. Gooding*. Private prosecutors' names sometimes appeared in the case name, but often the prosecution was styled 'Rex' or 'R', in recognition of the convention that a private prosecutor was enforcing the king's peace.

99. Humphreys, *Criminal Days*, 63.

100. Ian Nairn and Nikolaus Pevsner, *The Buildings of England: Sussex* (Harmondsworth: Penguin, 1965), 555.

101. T. G. Roche and Robert Stevens, 'Roche, Alexander Adair, Baron Roche', *Oxford Dictionary of National Biography*.

102. Kershaw to Guy Stephenson, 25 May 1921, HO 144/2452.

103. Jennifer L. Mnookin, 'Scripting Expertise: The History of Handwriting Identification Evidence and the Judicial Construction of Reliability', *Virginia Law Review*, 87 (2001), 1723–845, here 1747–831; Jane Caplan, '"This or That Particular Person": Protocols of Identification in Nineteenth-Century Europe', in Jane Caplan and John Torpey (eds), *Documenting Individual Identity: The Development of State Practices in the Modern World* (Princeton: Princeton University Press, 2001), 49–66, here 56 n. 24.

104. *Pimm v. Cheeseman*, deposition of Thomas Henry Gurrin, 28 July 1903, CRIM 1/89/2, National Archives.

105. Kershaw to Stephenson, 25 May 1921, HO 144/2452.

106. See for instance Alfred Denning, *Freedom under the Law* (London: Stevens, 1949), 43; [James Caunt, comp.], *An Editor on Trial: Rex v. Caunt: Alleged Seditious Libel* (Morecambe and Heysham: Morecambe Press, n.d. [1947]), 37–9.

107. Norman S. Poser, *Lord Mansfield: Justice in the Age of Reason* (Montreal: McGill-Queen's University Press, 2013), ch. 14.

108. Libel Act, 32 Geo. III (1792), c. 60.

109. Fraser, *Law of Libel and Slander*, 345–6.

110. Nicholls, report of 29 June 1921; William Herbert Smith, statement, 22 June 1921, MEPO 3/380.

111. William Herbert Smith, statement, 22 June 1921, MEPO 3/380.

112. *Sussex Daily News*, 15 December 1920.

113. Peel to Williams, 8 June 1921; typed copy of certificate of conviction issued by Arthur Denman, Clerk of Assize, 19 January 1921, HO 144/2452.

114. *Sussex Daily News*, 15 December 1920.

CHAPTER 4

1. 'There is probably no legal phrase so imperfectly understood, or which in its application has been so embarrassing to the administration, or which has to a greater extent misled the Courts of law in assigning punishment, as the phrase "hard labour," ' wrote Sir Evelyn Ruggles-Brise, the chairman of the Prison Commission for England and Wales, in 1921. The expression 'hard labour', he wrote, gave rise to 'an impression in foreign countries that it is a very severe penalty, applied only for the greatest crimes; at home it obscures the principle that in prison all labour is hard, *i.e.*, that all prisoners are punished with an equal prescribed task, whether they be sentenced to imprisonment with or without hard labour: and in penal servitude, where the manual labour is of the hardest, the phrase has no legal existence.' At this time, male prisoners sentenced to hard labour toiled alone in their cells for the first month of their sentences before graduating to 'associated labour', that is, working alongside their fellow prisoners. Since 1909, female prisoners had proceeded straight to associated labour. The new practice of moving women straight into communal work without an initial period of cellular labour effectively erased the difference between a sentence of imprisonment with hard labour and one without. Mr Justice Roche formally sentenced Rose Gooding to imprisonment 'without hard labour', probably because the term of imprisonment was so short. Evelyn Ruggles-Brise, *The English Prison System* (London: Macmillan, 1921), 60, 114, 136–7, 140; Stephen Hobhouse and Fenner Brockway (eds), *English Prisons To-Day: Being the Report of the Prison System Enquiry Committee* (London: Longmans, Green & Co., 1922), 341; typed copy of certificate of conviction issued by Arthur Denman, Clerk of Assize, 19 January 1921, HO 144/2452, National Archives.

2. Hobhouse and Brockway, *English Prisons To-Day*, 341–2, 343, 344–5. Hobhouse and Brockway's critical investigation of the prison system was commissioned by the Labour Research Department.
3. Peel to Williams, 8 June 1921, HO 144/2452, National Archives; G. R. Nicholls, 'Criminal Libel', report to Superintendent Fred Thomas, 29 June 1921, MEPO 3/380, National Archives (cited hereafter as 'Nicholls, report of 29 June 1921').
4. Nicholls, report of 29 June 1921.
5. It was Frederick Peel, the superintendent in Arundel, who made the telephone call, not an officer from Littlehampton police station. Nicholls, report of 29 June 1921.
6. Nicholls, report of 29 June 1921.
7. William Herbert Smith, statement, 22 June 1921, MEPO 3/380.
8. William Herbert Smith, statement, 22 June 1921, MEPO 3/380; Rose Gooding, petition to Home Secretary, 6 June 1921, HO 144/2452; Ruth Russell, statement, 25 June 1921, MEPO 3/380.
9. William Gooding, statement, 18 June 1921, MEPO 3/380.
10. Barbara E. Russell, statement, 25 June 1921, MEPO 3/380.
11. Ruth Russell, statement, 25 June 1921, MEPO 3/380.
12. W. H. Gooding to Home Secretary, May 1921 (exact date unclear), MEPO 3/380. The visitor, Claude Ransome, was actually a baker himself, but he did this job for George Tidy, the baker at 4 Western Road. Claude Ransome, statement, 21 June 1921, MEPO 3/380. For Tidy, see 1911 Census, household record for 13a Western Road, Littlehampton. *Kelly's Directory of Sussex, 1915* (London: Kelly's Directories, n.d.), 511, has Tidy as a confectioner trading from the same address. Both the census record and the directory entry predate the renumbering of Western Road.
13. W. H. Gooding to Home Secretary, May 1921 (exact date unclear), MEPO 3/380.
14. Ruth Russell, statement, 25 June 1921, MEPO 3/380.
15. [Rose Gooding] to Ruth and Bill, 'Tuesday', MEPO 3/380.
16. Lynda Mugglestone, *'Talking Proper': The Rise of Accent as Social Symbol* (Oxford: Oxford University Press, 2003), 177; see also 119.
17. For a wonderful American example, see Martha Hodes, *The Sea Captain's Wife: A True Story of Love, Race, and War in the Nineteenth Century* (New York: W. W. Norton, 2006), 26–7.
18. Susan L. Cohen, 'Loane, Martha Jane', *Oxford Dictionary of National Biography*.
19. M. Loane, 'Culture among the Poor', *Contemporary Review*, 90 (August 1906), 230–40, here 232.
20. William Herbert Smith, statement, 22 June 1921, MEPO 3/380.
21. William Henry Gooding, statement, 18 June 1921, MEPO 3/380. In a letter from prison to an unnamed recipient, evidently a lawyer, Rose Gooding said that it was her husband who saw Edith Swan post this letter. Rose Gooding to Sir, 17 February 1921, MEPO 3/380.

22. Alfred Russell, statement, 23 June 1921, MEPO 3/380; Nicholls, report of 29 June 1921.
23. It was actually the evening of Thursday 6 January 1921. The train left Littlehampton at 7:10 pm.
24. Alfred Russell, statement, 23 June 1921, MEPO 3/380 (line breaks and a missing closing quotation mark added).
25. Mary Ann Swan, statement, 20 June 1921, MEPO 3/380.
26. Ruth Russell, statement, 25 June 1921, MEPO 3/380.
27. The 1911 Census has him in Horsham: household record for 48 Barttelot Road, Horsham.
28. Maurice Blackman, statement, 19 June 1921, MEPO 3/380.
29. Maurice Blackman, statement, 19 June 1921; William Henry Gooding, statement, 18 June 1921, MEPO 3/380.
30. Maurice Blackman, statement, 19 June 1921, MEPO 3/380.
31. This assumes that all the daughters recorded in the 1911 census were still alive in 1921. 1911 Census, household record for 24 Western Road, Littlehampton.
32. Maurice Blackman, statement, 19 June 1921, MEPO 3/380.
33. 'Words on Leaves of Book', typescript, n.d. (1921), MEPO 3/380.
34. Edith Swan, statement, 19 June 1921, MEPO 3/380 (one closing quotation mark and one full stop added to original). Edith actually said, 'Miss Russell's boy—Willie'. The name has been replaced with an ellipsis to avoid confusion. Edith had the boys mixed up: Willie was Rose's son.
35. Edith Swan, statement, 19 June 1921, MEPO 3/380 (one quotation mark added).
36. Edith Swan, statement, 19 June 1921, MEPO 3/380; Nicholls, report of 29 June 1921.
37. Peel to Williams, 8 June 1921, HO 144/2452.
38. Maurice Blackman, statement, 19 June 1921, MEPO 3/380; *The Times*, 2 October 1954.
39. G. R. Rubin, 'Avory, Sir Horace Edmund', *Oxford Dictionary of National Biography*.
40. *The Autobiography of Sir Patrick Hastings* (London: William Heinemann, 1948), 94–6, 121–4.
41. Humphreys, *Criminal Days*, 72–3; F. W. Ashley, *My Sixty Years in the Law* (London: John Lane The Bodley Head, 1936); Bernard O'Donnell, *The Trials of Mr. Justice Avory* (London: Rich & Cowan, 1935); Gordon Lang, *Mr. Justice Avory* (London: Herbert Jenkins, 1935).
42. It's a small world: the legal action against *The Well of Loneliness* was led by Sir Archibald Bodkin, as Director of Private Prosecutions, and the barrister representing the state was Eustace Fulton. See Alec Craig, *The Banned Books of England* (London: George Allen and Unwin, 1937), 36–9.
43. Chartres Biron, *Without Prejudice: Impressions of Life and Law* (London: Faber and Faber, 1936), 103–4.
44. At this time the previous year there had been sixteen criminal trials and two civil cases.

45. *Sussex Daily News*, 4 March 1921.

46. *Sussex Daily News*, 4 March 1921.

47. Sex Disqualification (Removal) Act, 1919 (9 & 10 Geo. 5.), s. 1(b).

48. Rubin, 'Avory'.

49. *Sussex Daily News*, 4 March 1921.

50. Charles Haslett, statement, 20 June 1921; Kate Leggett, statement, 22 June 1921, MEPO 3/380.

51. *Sussex Daily News*, 4 March 1921.

52. Rose Emma Gooding to Home Secretary, 6 June 1921, HO 144/2452; W. H. Gooding to Home Secretary, May 1921 (exact date unclear), MEPO 3/380.

53. *Sussex Daily News*, 4 March 1921.

54. *Sussex Daily News*, 4 March 1921.

55. Nicholls, report of 29 June 1921; William Henry Gooding, statement, 18 June 1921, MEPO 3/380.

56. Fred Hawkins et al. to E. P. Wannop, 17 January 1921, MEPO 3/380.

57. Nicholls, report of 29 June 1921.

58. W. J. Upton, statement, 24 June 1921, MEPO 3/380 (typos corrected and line breaks added).

59. [Sir Archibald Bodkin], 'Observations to Counsel', July 1921, HO 144/2452 (hereafter cited as 'Observations to Counsel', without archival details).

60. William Wills, *An Essay on the Principles of Circumstantial Evidence: Illustrated by Numerous Cases*, 6th edn (London: Butterworth, 1912), 143.

61. R. N. Gooderson, 'Defences in Double Harness', in P. R. Glazebrook (ed.), *Reshaping the Criminal Law: Essays in Honour of Glanville Williams* (London: Stevens, 1978), 138–53, here 138–9. Gooderson quotes the phrase 'eggs in one basket' from the New Jersey case of *State v. Petros* (1965) 214 A 2d. 2, 8 (per Francis J).

62. Bodkin, 'Observations to Counsel'.

63. Bodkin, 'Observations to Counsel'.

64. *Sussex Daily News*, 4 March 1921.

65. Spencer, 'Criminal Libel', part 1, 393.

66. *Sussex Daily News*, 4 March 1921.

67. C. Ralph, note, 15 June 1921, HO 144/2452.

68. Peel to A. S. Williams, n.d. (mid-1921), HO 144/2452. For the £30 debt: Maurice Blackman, statement, 19 June 1921, MEPO 3/380; W. H. Gooding to Home Secretary, 9 June 1921, HO 144/2452.

69. William Cornish, J. Stuart Anderson, Ray Cocks, Michael Lobban, Patrick Polden, and Keith Smith, *The Oxford History of the Laws of England*, vol. 13, *1820–1914: Fields of Development* (Oxford: Oxford University Press, 2010), 131, 134, 136–7.

70. William Herbert Smith, statement, 22 June 1921, MEPO 3/380.

71. And apparently the sentence. Gooding had appealed against her sentence as well as her conviction: Notification of Result of Applications to the Full

NOTES TO PAGES 72-77

Court, *Rex v. Rose Emma Gooding*, 18 April 1921, HO 144/2452. However, there is no sign in the admittedly incomplete record that the Court of Criminal Appeal revisited the sentence. One year's imprisonment was the maximum sentence, except where the accused knew the libel to have been false (which may not have been relevant in Rose Gooding's case), but it was not a capricious sentence for a bad case of criminal libel—and this was Gooding's second conviction, so it may be that the conviction was all that was up for consideration. On sentences for libel, see *Report of the Committee on Defamation*, Cmnd. 5909 (London: HMSO, 1975), 120.

72. Leonard Kershaw to Guy Stephenson, 25 May 1921, HO 144/2452.
73. Ernest T. Hall to Blackwell, 1 June 1921, HO 144/2452.
74. W. H. Gooding to Home Secretary, 9 June 1921, HO 144/2452.
75. Blackwell, note on minutes page of file 416617/10, 5 August 1921, HO 144/2452.

CHAPTER 5

1. G. R. Nicholls, 'Criminal Libel', report to Superintendent Fred Thomas, 29 June 1921, MEPO 3/380, National Archives (cited hereafter as 'Nicholls, report of 29 June 1921').
2. 1911 Census, household record for 2 Railway Terrace, Midhurst.
3. Nicholls, report of 29 June 1921.
4. Nicholls, report of 29 June 1921.
5. Nicholls, report of 29 June 1921.
6. Rose Emma Gooding to Home Secretary, 6 June 1921, HO 144/2452, National Archives.
7. Nicholls, report of 29 June 1921.
8. Nicholls, report of 29 June 1921.
9. Haia Shpayer-Makov, 'Explaining the Rise and Success of Detective Memoirs in Britain', in Clive Emsley and Haia Shpayer-Makov (eds), *Police Detectives in History, 1750–1950* (Aldershot: Ashgate, 2006), 103–34, here 112–13.
10. 'West Sussex Constabulary: Examination: November, 1919', Frederick Charles Peel papers, POL W/HQ15/2, West Sussex Record Office. Frederick Charles Peel was no relation of Frederick John Peel, the Arundel superintendent.
11. Committee on the Employment of Women on Police Duties, *Minutes of Evidence*, Cmd. 1133 (London: HMSO, 1921), 66.
12. Shpayer-Makov, 'Detective Memoirs', 112–13.
13. Nicholls, report of 29 June 1921. These forms were stored in the Littlehampton council building. They remain in MEPO 3/380.
14. Nicholls, report of 29 June 1921.
15. W. H. Gooding, statement, 18 June 1921, MEPO 3/380.
16. Nicholls, report of 29 June 1921.

17. A. Conan Doyle, 'The Adventure of the Missing Three-Quarter' (1904), in *The Return of Sherlock Holmes* (New York: A. Wessells Company, 1907), 291–318, here 298–9.

18. Photograph of piece of blotting paper in MEPO 3/380; *Kelly's Directory of Sussex, 1915* (London: Kelly's Directories, n.d.), 507.

19. Nicholls, report of 29 June 1921.

20. Britishers' Own 'Writing Outfit', MEPO 3/380.

21. Edith Swan, statement, 20 June 1921, MEPO 3/380; Nicholls, report of 29 June 1921.

22. Nicholls, report of 29 June 1921.

23. David Vincent, *Literacy and Popular Culture: England, 1750–1914* (Cambridge: Cambridge University Press, 1989), 3–4 and ch. 3; Alec Ellis, *Educating Our Masters: Influences on the Growth of Literacy in Victorian Working Class Children* (Aldershot: Gower, 1985).

24. Vincent, *Literacy and Popular Culture*, 3–4.

25. James C. Scott, *Seeing like a State: How Certain Schemes to Improve the Human Condition Have Failed* (New Haven: Yale University Press, 1998), especially 64–73. This judgement applies not just to the *modern* state: see M. T. Clanchy, *From Memory to Written Record: England 1066–1307* (London: Edward Arnold, 1979); Jack Goody, *The Logic of Writing and the Organization of Society* (Cambridge: Cambridge University Press, 1986), chs 3–4.

26. Jane Caplan, 'Illegibility: Reading and Insecurity in History, Law and Government', *History Workshop Journal*, no. 68 (autumn 2009), 99–121, here 101–4.

27. Patrick Joyce, *The State of Freedom: A Social History of the British State since 1800* (Cambridge: Cambridge University Press, 2013), chs 2–3.

28. See Jonathan Rose, *The Intellectual Life of the British Working Classes* (New Haven: Yale University Press, 2001).

29. Lady Bell (Mrs Hugh Bell), *At the Works: A Study of a Manufacturing Town* (London: Edward Arnold, 1907), 146–7. Bell's notes on households span pp. 146–62 of *At the Works* and provide information about 200 households.

30. John Garrett Leigh, 'What Do the Masses Read?' *Economic Review* 14 (April 1904), 166–77, here 174–6. On the what-do-the-masses-read genre, see Christopher Hilliard, 'Popular Reading and Social Investigation in Britain, 1850s–1940s', *Historical Journal*, 57 (2014), 247–71.

31. Bell, *At the Works*, 144–5; Margaret Powell, *My Mother and I* (1972; repr., London: Pan Books, 1974), 16.

32. John David Moore, statement, 13 October 1921, MEPO 3/380.

33. Edward Swan, statement, 20 June 1921, MEPO 3/380.

34. Ross McKibbin, *Classes and Cultures: England, 1918–1951* (Oxford: Oxford University Press, 1998), 527; Joseph McAleer, *Popular Reading and Publishing in Britain, 1914–1950* (Oxford: Oxford University Press, 1992).

35. Ronald F. Batty, *How to Run a Twopenny Library* (London: John Gifford, 1938), 9, 20.

36. Q. D. Leavis, *Fiction and the Reading Public* (London: Chatto and Windus, 1932), 7.
37. W. T. Mason, letter to editor, *Bookseller*, 2 March 1934, 144; James Glaisher, letter to editor, *Bookseller*, 16 March 1934, 167; 'Cigarette Coupons', *Publisher and Bookseller*, 18 November 1932, 949–55; 'Cigarette Coupons', *Publisher and Bookseller*, 25 November 1932, 985–9; 'Cigarette Coupons', *Publisher and Bookseller*, 2 December 1932, 1049–52.
38. Hilliard, 'Popular Reading and Social Investigation', 256–8.
39. Pioneer exercise book belonging to John Swan, MEPO 3/380. The lyrics appear to be copied from 1892 numbers of *All the World*; John Swan would have been born in 1891 or 1892, so they were clearly old copies.
40. Photographs of pieces of blotting paper, MEPO 3/380.
41. Nicholls, 'Blotting paper', undated handwritten notes, MEPO 3/380.
42. Joyce, *State of Freedom*, 79–80; Caplan, 'Illegibility', 107–9; *Vere Foster's New Civil Service Copy-Books: Medium Series* (London: Blackie & Son, n.d.).
43. Nicholls, report of 29 June 1921.
44. Bodkin, 'Observations to Counsel'.
45. Nicholls, report of 29 June 1921.
46. Nicholls, report of 29 June 1921.
47. Edith Swan, statement, 19 June 1921, MEPO 3/380.
48. Barbara Ellen Russell, statement, 25 June 1921, MEPO 3/380.
49. Nicholls, report of 29 June 1921.
50. Timeline of events in the Littlehampton libels case (anonymous typescript, early 1922), HO 144/2452.
51. Nicholls, report of 29 June 1921; Nicholls to Acting Superintendent, 6 July 1921, MEPO 3/380.
52. Long since lost or removed from the surviving files, alas.
53. Christmas Humphreys, rev. Mark Pottle, 'Bodkin, Sir Archibald Henry', *Oxford Dictionary of National Biography*.
54. Bodkin, 'Observations to Counsel'.
55. F. T. B[igham], note on minutes page of file 204/UNC/6, 5 July 1921, MEPO 3/380. On Bigham see George Dilnot, *Scotland Yard: The Methods and Organisation of the Metropolitan Police* (London: Percival Marshall, 1915), 17.
56. On 'proving' handwriting in court, see Jennifer L. Mnookin, 'Scripting Expertise: The History of Handwriting Identification Evidence and the Judicial Construction of Reliability', *Virginia Law Review*, 87 (2001), 1723–845, here 1760–4.
57. Humphreys and Pottle, 'Bodkin, Sir Archibald Henry'.
58. Bodkin, 'Observations to Counsel'. Comparisons of handwriting became permissible in criminal trials with the passage of the Common Law Procedure Act 1854 (17 & 18 Vict., c. 125). Mnookin, 'Scripting Expertise', 1774.
59. Bodkin, 'Observations to Counsel'. Although Bodkin could make out the shadow of a school copy book from long ago, he was adamant that the

lettering was not that of a child. When the case first crossed his desk, he thought there might be something to Superintendent Peel's suggestion that Dorothy Gooding or Gertrude Russell wrote the libels, but Bodkin was now convinced that they had not. Bodkin, 'Observations to Counsel'.

60. Bodkin, 'Observations to Counsel'.

61. Rose Gooding to Mrs Rose, 1 November 1919, HO 144/2452. Italics indicate underlining in the original.

62. Rose Gooding to Mrs Rose, 1 November 1919, HO 144/2452. The quotation omits the last sentence before the closing salutation, a mysterious reference to Alice Morgan: 'Alice shall know nothing from me, trust for that.'

63. George F. Rose to Rose Gooding, n.d. (c. 24 January 1920), HO 144/2452. Italics indicate underlining in the original.

64. Rose Gooding to George Rose, Saturday (probably 24 January 1920), HO 144/2452.

65. Geo. R. Humphery, 'The Reading of the Working Classes', *Nineteenth Century*, 33 (April 1893), 690–701; Andrew Lang and '"X", A Working Man', 'The Reading Public', *Cornhill Magazine*, n.s., 11 (December 1901), 783–95.

CHAPTER 6

1. [Sir Archibald Bodkin], 'Observations to Counsel', July 1921, HO 144/2452, National Archives (hereafter cited as 'Observations to Counsel', without archival details).

2. F. J. Peel to A. S. Williams, 8 June 1921, HO 144/2452.

3. Bodkin, 'Observations to Counsel'.

4. John Ciane to [Superintendent], 23 August 1909, MEPO 3/189, National Archives.

5. He is just 'Mr Dagg' in the paper trail of the case, but the solicitor was surely the Arthur Dagg living in Sutton two years later. 1911 Census, household record for Strawberry Lodge, Sutton, Surrey.

6. A. Ward, 'Libel: Result', 6 March 1910, MEPO 3/189. The detail about the building comes from Bechhofer Roberts, *Sir Travers Humphreys: His Career and Cases* (London: John Lane The Bodley Head, 1936), 99.

7. A. Ward, 'Libel: Result', 6 March 1910, MEPO 3/189.

8. A. Ward, 'Libel: Result', 6 March 1910, MEPO 3/189.

9. A. Ward, 'Libel: Result', 6 March 1910, MEPO 3/189.

10. *The Times*, 4 March 1910.

11. *The Times*, 8 September 1910.

12. A. Ward, 'Libel: Result', 6 March 1910, MEPO 3/189.

13. *The Times*, 29 July 1910.

14. A. Ward, 'Libel—Arrests', 22 April 1910, MEPO 3/189; 1901 Census, household record for St Mary's, Sutton (identifying Measures). Annie Tugwell left the Catholic Church, and made contact with the Protestant

Alliance, at some point during 1909 or 1910. Precisely when is not clear. On her arrest, she claimed to be the victim of 'a Catholic conspiracy'. In the witness box, she said that Father Warwick 'told her that all the influence of the Catholic Church would be brought to bear on her, and Canon Cafferata had declared he would injure her husband and not leave her a bed to lie on'. Warwick assisted Tugwell in her campaign against Cafferata's housekeeper at least as late as October 1909. *The Times*, 30 July 1910, 1 August 1910; A. Ward, 'Libel: Result', 6 March 1910, MEPO 3/189.

15. *The Times*, 1 August 1910. On Bodkin's prosecuting style, see Christmas Humphreys, rev. Mark Pottle, 'Bodkin, Sir Archibald Henry', *Oxford Dictionary of National Biography*.

16. *The Times*, 2 August 1910.

17. *Star*, 2 August 1910.

18. *The Times*, 29 July 1910, 30 July 1910, 1 August 1910, 2 August 1910. Humphreys omitted to mention his involvement in his comments on the Sutton case in his memoirs: Travers Humphreys, *Criminal Days: Recollections and Reflections* (London: Hodder and Stoughton, 1946), 134.

19. Stanley Jackson, *The Life and Cases of Mr. Justice Humphreys* (London: Odhams Press, 1952), 22.

20. Humphreys, *Criminal Days*, 14, 15, 62. On this custom see also Ernest Bowen-Rowlands, *Seventy-Two Years at the Bar: A Memoir* (London: Macmillan, 1924), 10.

21. Jackson, *Life and Cases of Mr. Justice Humphreys*, ch. 1; Julian Symons, *Horatio Bottomley: A Biography* (London: Cresset Press, 1955), 250, 251–2.

22. F. H. Cowper, rev. Alec Samuels, 'Humphreys, Sir (Richard Somers) Travers Christmas', *Oxford Dictionary of National Biography*.

23. Jackson, *Life and Cases of Mr. Justice Humphreys*, 11; Humphreys, *Criminal Days*, 123.

24. Travers Humphreys, foreword to H. Montgomery Hyde (ed.), *The Trials of Oscar Wilde* (London: William Hodge, 1948), 1–8 (quotation from p. 8); Humphreys, *Criminal Days*, 128, 226.

25. Humphreys, foreword to Hyde (ed.), *Trials of Oscar Wilde*, 1.

26. [Christopher Millard and Cecil Palmer (eds)], *Oscar Wilde: Three Times Tried* (London: Ferrestone Press, n.d. [c. 1920]), 22, 117, 149, 151, 158, 160, 167, 175, 176, 178, 181, 183, 191–2, 331, 408.

27. H. Montgomery Hyde, *Oscar Wilde: A Biography* (London: Eyre Methuen, 1976), 303. Travers Humphreys is not to be confused with his son, Travers Christmas Humphreys. The son was likewise a prominent prosecutor. He was also a Buddhist and wrote books and articles explaining Buddhism to British audiences. In this respect, at least, he was not a chip off the old block. *Both Sides of the Circle: The Autobiography of Christmas Humphreys* (London: Allen and Unwin, 1978).

28. *Rex v. Rose Emma Gooding*, Court of Criminal Appeal, 25 July 1921, shorthand notes, HO 144/2452.

29. *The Times*, 27 July 1921.
30. *Rex v. Gooding*, Court of Criminal Appeal, 25 July 1921, shorthand notes, HO 144/2452.
31. *Rex v. Gooding*, Court of Criminal Appeal, 25 July 1921, shorthand notes, HO 144/2452.
32. *Rex v. Gooding*, Court of Criminal Appeal, 25 July 1921, shorthand notes, HO 144/2452. In his memoirs, Humphreys said it was unprecedented for the court to quash convictions 'without hearing any evidence or being given any reason except that the Authorities were satisfied that the Appellant was innocent and that the publication of any details would be contrary to the interests of justice'. Humphreys, *Criminal Days*, 126.
33. Court of Criminal Appeal, Notification of Result of Final Appeal, 25 July 1921, HO 144/2452.
34. George Nicholls to Superintendent, 3 August 1921, HO 144/2452.
35. Nicholls to Acting Superintendent, 19 July 1921, MEPO 3/380.
36. 'Compensation in Criminal Cases', handwritten notes, n.d. (July 1921), HO 144/2452.
37. Deborah Cohen, 'Who Was Who? Race and Jews in Turn-of-the-Century Britain', *Journal of British Studies* 42 (2002), 460–83, here 462–9. For more detail on the facts of the case, see Committee of Inquiry into the Case of Mr. Adolf Beck, *Report from the Committee: Together with Minutes of Evidence, Appendix, and Facsimiles of Various Documents*, Cd. 2315 (London: HMSO, 1904), vi–xvii, especially vi–vii.
38. William Cornish, J. Stuart Anderson, Ray Cocks, Michael Lobban, Patrick Polden, and Keith Smith, *The Oxford History of the Laws of England*, vol. 13, *1820–1914: Fields of Development* (Oxford: Oxford University Press, 2010), 134 n. 48.
39. Cornish et al., *Fields of Development*, 134.
40. 'Compensation in Criminal Cases', handwritten notes, n.d. (July 1921), HO 144/2452.
41. Blackwell, note on minutes page of file 416617/8, 28 July 1921, HO 144/2452.
42. *The Times*, 5 January 1915.
43. Roberts, *Sir Travers Humphreys*, 99–101; Humphreys, *Criminal Days*, 135.
44. Blackwell, note on minutes page of file 416617/8, 28 July 1921, HO 144/2452.
45. Blackwell to Secretary, H. M. Treasury, 28 July 1921 (carbon copy), HO 144/2452.
46. Wannop & Falconer to Home Secretary, 3 August 1921, HO 144/2452.
47. Adrian Bingham, *Gender, Modernity, and the Popular Press in Inter-War Britain* (Oxford: Oxford University Press, 2004), 128–9. At this time the *Daily Mirror* usually followed a right-wing editorial line and catered to a middle-class readership. Its reinvention as a left-leaning paper took place in the mid-1930s. On this transformation, see Adrian Bingham, 'Representing

the People? The *Daily Mirror*, Class, and Political Culture in Inter-War Britain', in Laura Beers and Geraint Thomas (eds), *Brave New World: Imperial and Democratic Nation-building in Britain between the Wars* (London: Institute of Historical Research, 2012), 109–28.

48. *Daily Mirror*, 9 August 1921. Bodkin was fielding inquiries from journalists too: Bodkin, untitled note, n.d. (August 1921), HO 144/2452.

49. Blackwell, note on minutes page of file 416617/11, 10 August 1921; R. S. Mieklejohn to Undersecretary of State, Home Office, 10 August 1921, HO 144/2452.

50. Blackwell, note on minutes page of file 416617/11, 10 August 1921, HO 144/2452.

51. W. A. Beere and G. H. May to [Home Secretary], n.d. (received at Home Office on 17 August 1921), HO 144/2452.

52. A. L., note on minutes page of file 416617/13, 14 September 1921, HO 144/2452.

53. Using the figures from pp. 29–30 above.

54. G. R. Nicholls to Superintendent, 15 October 1921, MEPO 3/380.

55. For the trains, see M. Dudley Clark, *Littlehampton, Sussex: With Its Surroundings* (London: Homeland Association and Frederick Warne and Co., n.d. [1915]), 5.

CHAPTER 7

1. Edie Emily Swan to Sir, 2 August 1921 (copy), MEPO 3/380, National Archives.

2. Edie Emily Swan to Sir, 2 August 1921 (copy), MEPO 3/380. 'A few' is rendered 'afew'; since the police typist rather than Swan could have run the two words together, I have quietly corrected it in the text. For 'memorandum' see Nicholls to Superintendent, 4 November 1921, MEPO 3/380.

3. Thomas apparently took the hint: Henry Thomas, statement, 13 October 1921, MEPO 3/380.

4. Swan to Sir, 2 August 1921 (copy), MEPO 3/380.

5. *John Bull*, 13 August 1921.

6. Julian Symons, *Horatio Bottomley: A Biography* (London: Cresset Press, 1955), 83–6.

7. D. H. Lawrence to Bertrand Russell, 26 July 1915, in *The Letters of D. H. Lawrence*, vol. 2, *1913–16*, ed. George T. Zytaruk and James T. Boulton (Cambridge: Cambridge University Press, 1981), 371.

8. Symons, *Horatio Bottomley*, 250–3.

9. *John Bull*, 6 August 1921.

10. *John Bull*, 13 August 1921. On the henchmen, see Symons, *Horatio Bottomley*, 79–80.

11. Travers Humphreys, *Criminal Days: Recollections and Reflections* (London: Hodder and Stoughton, 1946), 80.

12. *John Bull*, 6 August 1921.

13. Gladys Moss, statement, 12 October 1921, MEPO 3/380.

14. George May, statement, 13 October 1921, MEPO 3/380.

15. Gladys Moss, statement, 12 October 1921; Violet Lily May, statement, 12 October 1921, MEPO 3/380.

16. Gladys Moss, statement, 12 October 1921, MEPO 3/380.

17. Gladys Moss, statement, 12 October 1921, MEPO 3/380.

18. Nicholls to Superintendent, 15 October 1921, MEPO 3/380.

19. Nicholls to Superintendent, 15 October 1921; George May, statement, 13 October 1921, MEPO 3/380.

20. George May, statement, 13 October 1921, MEPO 3/380.

21. George May, statement, 13 October 1921, MEPO 3/380.

22. Alfred Russell, statement, 25 June 1921, MEPO 3/380.

23. Barry Supple, *1913–1946: The Political Economy of Decline*, vol. 4 of *The History of the British Coal Industry* (Oxford: Clarendon Press, 1987), 158–61; David Gilbert, *Class, Community, and Collective Action: Social Change in Two British Coalfields, 1850–1926* (Oxford: Clarendon Press, 1992), 93–6.

24. Anon., 'An Introduction to the West Sussex Constabulary', n.d. (*c.* 1963), no page numbers, POL W/HQ15/8, West Sussex Record Office. The Police Act of 1890 'permitt[ed] local authorities to lend each other men in emergencies': P. J. Waller, *Town, City and Nation: England, 1850–1914* (Oxford: Clarendon Press, 1983), 268.

25. Violet May, statement, 22 June 1921; Violet May, statement, 12 October 1921, MEPO 3/380.

26. *Daily Express*, 23 October 1921.

27. Violet May, statement, 22 June 1921, MEPO 3/380.

28. Nicholls to Superintendent, 15 October 1921, MEPO 3/380.

29. Violet May, statement, 12 October 1921, MEPO 3/380.

30. Violet May, statement, 22 June 1921, MEPO 3/380. Swan showed May the letter that had been sent to her fiancé Bert Boxall telling him she was pregnant with Alfred Russell's child. This letter was not an exhibit in either of Rose Gooding's trials, which explains why it was still in Swan's possession.

31. Violet May, statement, 12 October 1921, MEPO 3/380.

32. Violet May, statement, 13 October 1921, MEPO 3/380.

33. John David Moore, statement, 13 October 1921, MEPO 3/380.

34. Violet May, statement, 12 October 1921, MEPO 3/380.

35. 'Words on leaves of book', undated typescript, MEPO 3/380.

36. Violet May, statement, 13 October 1921, MEPO 3/380 (punctuation as in original—or rather, in the copy made by the police typist).

37. Violet May, statement, 13 October 1921, MEPO 3/380.

38. 'Indecent Writings Found', undated typescript, libel of 7 September 1921, MEPO 3/380.

39. 'Indecent Writings Found', libel of 5 September 1921, MEPO 3/380.

40. Violet May, statement, 12 October 1921; 'Indecent Writings Found', libel of 14 September 1921, MEPO 3/380. Both May's statement and the transcription of the libels are clear that the 'You' at the start of the third sentence was written 'Yo'.
41. Violet May, statement, 12 October 1921, MEPO 3/380.
42. Henry Mark Thomas, statement, 13 October 1921, MEPO 3/380.
43. Gladys Moss, statement, 12 October 1921, MEPO 3/380.
44. 1881 Census, household record for 10 Spa Road, Gloucester; 1911 Census, household record for 44 South Street, Worthing.
45. Gladys Moss, statement, 12 October 1921, MEPO 3/380.
46. Louise A. Jackson, *Women Police: Gender, Welfare and Surveillance in the Twentieth Century* (Manchester: Manchester University Press, 2006), 108; Joan Lock, *The British Policewoman: Her Story* (London: Robert Hale, 1979), 92.
47. Lock, *British Policewoman*, 96.
48. Committee on the Employment of Women on Police Duties, *Minutes of Evidence*, Cmd. 1133 (London: HMSO, 1921); Lock, *British Policewoman*, 91, 93.
49. Clive Emsley, *The English Police: A Political and Social History*, 2nd edn (Harlow: Longman, 1996), 127; Mark Rawlings, *Policing: A Short History* (Cullompton: Willan, 2002), 197–8; Philippa Levine, ' "Walking the Streets in a Way No Decent Woman Should": Women Police in World War I', *Journal of Modern History*, 66 (1994), 34–78.
50. Committee on the Employment of Women on Police Duties, *Minutes of Evidence*, 67.
51. Committee on the Employment of Women on Police Duties, *Minutes of Evidence*, 47–8.
52. Emsley, *English Police*, 157; Lock, *British Policewoman*, 95.
53. Jackson, *Women Police*, 110.
54. Gladys Moss, statement, 12 October 1921, MEPO 3/380.
55. West Sussex Constabulary, Worthing Division, Occurrence Book, 1921–1923, POL/W/W/1/10, West Sussex Record Office, entries for 6 April 1921, 9 July 1921, and 30 October 1921.
56. West Sussex Constabulary, Worthing Division, Occurrence Book, 1919–1921, POL/W/W/1/9, West Sussex Record Office, entry for 26 January 1921.
57. Gladys Moss, statement, 12 October 1921, MEPO 3/380.
58. Gladys Moss, statement, 12 October 1921, MEPO 3/380.
59. *Argus* (Brighton), 27 October 1921.
60. Gladys Moss, statement, 12 October 1921, MEPO 3/380.
61. Gladys Moss, statement, 12 October 1921, MEPO 3/380.
62. Vanessa Ogle, *The Global Transformation of Time, 1870–1950* (Cambridge, MA: Harvard University Press, 2015), 49–52.
63. Gladys Moss, statement, 12 October 1921, MEPO 3/380.
64. Gladys Moss, statement, 12 October 1921, MEPO 3/380.

65. Violet May, statement, 12 October 1921, MEPO 3/380.
66. Gladys Moss, statement, 12 October 1921, MEPO 3/380.
67. Nicholls to Superintendent, 15 October 1921, MEPO 3/380; Gladys Moss, statement, 12 October 1921, MEPO 3/380.
68. Gladys Moss, statement, 12 October 1921, MEPO 3/380.
69. Violet May, statement, 12 October 1921, MEPO 3/380.
70. Gladys Moss, statement, 12 October 1921, MEPO 3/380.
71. 'Indecent Writings Found', libel of 27 September 1921, MEPO 3/380.
72. Violet May, statement, 13 October 1921; Nicholls to Superintendent, 15 October 1921, MEPO 3/380.
73. Violet May, statement, 12 October 1921, MEPO 3/380.
74. Gladys Moss, statement, 12 October 1921, MEPO 3/380.

CHAPTER 8

1. Gladys Moss, statement, 12 October 1921, MEPO 3/380, National Archives. Line breaks and closing quotation marks added.
2. Gladys Moss, statement, 12 October 1921, MEPO 3/380.
3. Violet May, statement, 12 October 1921, MEPO 3/380.
4. George May, statement, 13 October 1921, MEPO 3/380.
5. Gladys Moss, statement, 12 October 1921, MEPO 3/380.
6. Henry Mark Thomas, statement, 13 October 1921; William Hutchinson, statement, 12 October 1921, MEPO 3/380.
7. William Hutchinson, statement, 12 October 1921, MEPO 3/380.
8. Gladys Moss, statement, 12 October 1921; Violet May, statement, 12 October 1921, MEPO 3/380. Both also said that she was wearing an apron or pinafore, but presumably she took that off after leaving her washhouse for the police station.
9. Gladys Moss, statement, 12 October 1921, MEPO 3/380.
10. William Hutchinson, statement, 12 October 1921, MEPO 3/380 (line breaks added; 'she' at the beginning of the second sentence changed to 'She'). George May heard Edith speaking to Hutchinson 'and I overheard her say to him to the best of my recollection "I only picked it up and put it down again"'. George May, statement, 13 October 1921, MEPO 3/380.
11. William Hutchinson, statement, 12 October 1921, MEPO 3/380.
12. Gladys Moss, statement, 12 October 1921, MEPO 3/380.
13. Edith Swan, copy of statement dated 29 September 1921 (but actually 27 September); Gladys Moss, statement, 12 October 1921; Henry Mark Thomas, statement, 13 October 1921, MEPO 3/380.
14. Nicholls to Superintendent, 15 October 1921, MEPO 3/380.
15. Violet May, statement, 13 October 1921, MEPO 3/380.
16. Henry Mark Thomas, statement, 13 October 1921, MEPO 3/380.
17. Gladys Moss, statement, 12 October 1921; Moss to A. S. Williams, 27 September 1921 (copy), MEPO 3/380.

18. Edith Emily Swan to A. S. Williams, 27 September 1921, MEPO 3/380.
19. Williams to Swan, 29 September 1921 (copy), MEPO 3/380.
20. Swan to Williams, 1 October 1921 (copy), MEPO 3/380.
21. Williams to Nicholls, 13 October 1921, MEPO 3/380.
22. Violet May, statement, 12 October 1921, MEPO 3/380.
23. George May, statement, 13 October 1921, MEPO 3/380.
24. George May, statement, 13 October 1921, MEPO 3/380.
25. Nicholls to Superintendent, 15 October 1921, MEPO 3/380.
26. George May, statement, 13 October 1921, MEPO 3/380.
27. At the beginning of his investigation three months earlier, George Nicholls thought Mr Swan might have been behind the anonymous letters.
28. Violet May, statement, 12 October 1921, MEPO 3/380.
29. Violet May, statement, 12 October 1921, MEPO 3/380.
30. Violet May, statement, 12 October 1921, MEPO 3/380.
31. *Kelly's Directory of Sussex, 1915* (London: Kelly's Directories, n.d.), 505, 507; 1911 Census, household record for 48 Norfolk Road, Littlehampton.
32. Henry Mark Thomas, statement, 13 October 1921, MEPO 3/380. The main event at the hearing that morning was Harry Joseph's attempt to undercut his competitors in the town's entertainment industry. 'At the County Petty Sessions on Monday the application by Mr. Harry Joseph for the removal of the music and dancing license [*sic*] of the Casino, Pier Road, was strongly opposed by Mr. L. Casson, Secretary of the Actors' Association. Various allegations were made, and stoutly repudiated. After a prolonged and exciting hearing the Bench refused the application.' *Littlehampton Observer*, 12 October 1921.
33. Henry Mark Thomas, statement, 13 October 1921, MEPO 3/380.
34. Sir Archibald Bodkin to Commissioner, Metropolitan Police, 8 October 1921, MEPO 3/380.
35. Bodkin to F. T. Bigham, 6 October 1921, MEPO 3/380.
36. Bodkin to Commissioner, Metropolitan Police, 8 October 1921, MEPO 3/380.
37. Nicholls to Superintendent, 15 October 1921, MEPO 3/380.
38. 'Indecent Writings Found', undated typescript, libels of 23 September 1921, MEPO 3/380.
39. Nicholls to Superintendent, 15 October 1921, MEPO 3/380.
40. Bodkin to Nicholls, 11 October 1921, MEPO 3/380.
41. Bodkin to Commissioner, 18 October 1921, MEPO 3/380.
42. Typed information and complaint to be completed by a local justice of the peace, n.d., MEPO 3/380.
43. On this crime, see Colin Manchester, 'A History of the Crime of Obscene Libel', *Journal of Legal History*, 12 (1991), 36–57; Christopher Hilliard, ' "Is It a Book That You Would Even Wish Your Wife or Your Servants to Read?" Obscenity Law and the Politics of Reading in Modern England', *American Historical Review*, 118 (2013), 653–78.

44. Calling him the justices' clerk is a simplification. He was actually the justices' clerk's clerk.

45. Nicholls to Superintendent, 4 November 1921, MEPO 3/380. The mayor of Arundel was a justice of the peace *ex officio*. For administrative purposes, Littlehampton was an 'urban district', not a town, and so had no mayor. Arundel's mayor had jurisdiction because Littlehampton and Arundel were both part of the same petty sessional district.

46. Henry Mark Thomas, statement, n.d. (21 October 1921 or later), MEPO 3/380. Line breaks and initial capitals added.

47. Nicholls to Superintendent, 4 November 1921, MEPO 3/380. There is an inventory of the items seized on p. 5 of this report by Nicholls.

48. Nicholls to Superintendent, 15 October 1921, MEPO 3/380.

49. Nicholls to Superintendent, 4 November 1921, MEPO 3/380.

50. *Daily Express*, 24 October 1921; *Aberdeen Daily Journal*, 24 October 1921.

51. *Evening Telegraph* (Angus), 10 January 1923; *Daily Express*, 24 October 1921.

52. Nicholls to Superintendent, 4 November 1921, MEPO 3/380; *Kelly's Directory of Sussex, 1915*, 505.

53. Nicholls to Superintendent, 4 November 1921, MEPO 3/380.

54. William McLean, statement, 25 October 1921, MEPO 3/380.

55. William McLean, statement, 25 October 1921, MEPO 3/380.

56. Nicholls to Superintendent, 4 November 1921, MEPO 3/380.

57. *Kelly's Directory of Sussex, 1915*, 512; 1901 Census, household record for 20 High Street, Littlehampton; 1871 Census, household record for 27 Warwick Street, Brighton.

58. Nicholls to Superintendent, 4 November 1921; Frederick John Curnow, statement, 25 October 1921, MEPO 3/380.

59. Nicholls to Superintendent, 4 November 1921, MEPO 3/380.

60. *Daily Mirror*, 28 October 1921.

61. *Daily Express*, 28 October 1921.

62. *Argus* (Brighton), 27 October 1921.

63. *Daily Express*, 28 October 1921; *Littlehampton Observer*, 2 November 1921.

64. *Daily Express*, 28 October 1921.

65. Nicholls to Superintendent, 4 November 1921, MEPO 3/380.

66. *Portsmouth Evening News*, 9 December 1921.

67. Travers Humphreys, *Criminal Days: Recollections and Reflections* (London: Hodder and Stoughton, 1946), 127–8; *Who's Who 1921: An Annual Biographical Dictionary with Which is Incorporated 'Men and Women of the Time'* (London: Adam and Charles Black, n.d.), 103.

68. *The Times*, 10 December 1921.

69. *The Times*, 10 December 1921.

70. *Daily Mirror*, 10 December 1921.

71. *Daily Mirror*, 10 December 1921; Edward Swan, statement, 20 June 1921, MEPO 3/380.

72. *News of the World*, 11 December 1921.

73. *The Times*, 10 December 1921.

74. Nicholls to Superintendent, 13 December 1921, MEPO 3/380.

75. Humphreys, *Criminal Days*, 128. Ellen Woodman, who had Mary Johnson wrongly convicted of criminal libel, was ultimately charged with perjury.

76. *The Times*, 10 December 1921.

77. *Yorkshire Post and Leeds Intelligencer*, 10 December 1921.

78. Nicholls to Superintendent, 13 December 1921, MEPO 3/380.

79. Humphreys, *Criminal Days*, 120, 129, 132, 133.

80. Nicholls to Superintendent, 13 December 1921, MEPO 3/380.

81. *The Times*, 10 December 1921; *Lancashire Evening Post*, 10 December 1921; *Derby Daily Telegraph*, 10 December 1921; Nicholls to Superintendent, 13 December 1921, MEPO 3/380.

82. Humphreys, *Criminal Days*, 127.

83. *The Times*, 10 December 1921; Nicholls to Superintendent, 13 December 1921, MEPO 3/380.

84. Note on minutes page of file 204/UNC/25, 15 December 1921, MEPO 3/380.

85. Julian Symons, *Horatio Bottomley: A Biography* (London: Cresset Press, 1955), 266–7.

86. *John Bull*, 21 January 1922; Symons, *Horatio Bottomley*, 80.

87. *John Bull*, 21 January 1922.

88. Timeline appended to letter from Sir William Horwood to Sir John Anderson, 19 July 1922, HO 144/2452, National Archives; *John Bull*, 21 January 1922.

89. *John Bull*, 21 January 1922. On the lack of police coordination across regions, see P. J. Waller, *Town, City and Nation: England, 1850–1914* (Oxford: Clarendon Press, 1983), 268.

90. *John Bull*, 15 July 1922; *Derby Daily Telegraph*, 29 July 1929.

91. *John Bull*, 29 July 1922.

92. Sir Ernley Blackwell, notes on minutes pages of files 416617/16, 24 July 1922, and 416617/17, 11 October 1922; Nicholls to Superintendent, 23 October 1922; Horwood to Anderson, 10 October 1922, HO 144/2452; *John Bull*, 23 September 1922.

93. Charles Pilley, *Law for Journalists* (London: Sir Isaac Pitman and Sons, 1924). Pilley was also a barrister.

94. See Filson Young (ed.), *Trial of Frederick Bywaters and Edith Thompson* (Glasgow: William Hodge and Company, 1923) (Edith Thompson's letters are reproduced on pp. 161–250); Matt Houlbrook, ' "A Pin to See the Peepshow": Culture, Fiction and Selfhood in Edith Thompson's Letters, 1921–1922', *Past and Present*, no. 207 (May 2010), 215–49; Lucy Bland, 'The Trials and Tribulations of Edith Thompson: The Capital Crime of Sexual Incitement in 1920s England', *Journal of British Studies*, 47 (2008), 624–48; Lucy Bland, *Modern Women on Trial: Sexual Transgression in the Age of the Flapper* (Manchester: Manchester University Press, 2013), ch. 3; and Jill Dawson's novel *Fred and Edie* (London: Sceptre, 2000).

95. Humphreys, *Criminal Days*, 128. Humphreys must have been thinking of a passage near the beginning of *De Profundis*: 'the light that creeps down through the thickly-muffled glass of the small iron-barred window beneath which one sits is grey and niggard. It is always twilight in one's cell, as it is always twilight in one's heart. And in the sphere of thought, no less than in the sphere of time, motion is no more. The thing that you personally have long ago forgotten, or can easily forget, is happening to me now, and will happen to me again to-morrow.' Oscar Wilde, *De Profundis*, in *The Complete Works of Oscar Wilde*, ed. Ian Small, vol. 2 (Oxford: Oxford University Press, 2005), 159.

CHAPTER 9

1. 'Indecent Writings Found', undated typescript, MEPO 3/380, National Archives.
2. In the margin beside the text of the two libels of 23 September 1921, Nicholls wrote: 'Stopped in the Post'. These were the two postcards intercepted by a sorting clerk, submitted to the GPO's Special Investigative Branch, and then returned to the Littlehampton post office. Bodkin to Nicholls, 11 October 1921, MEPO 3/380. See p. 122 above.
3. Reginald Edgar Booker, statement, 22 June 1921, MEPO 3/380.
4. Eric Partridge, *A Dictionary of Slang and Unconventional English: Slang— Including the Language of the Underworld, Colloquialisms and Catch-phrases, Solecisms and Catachreses, Nicknames, Vulgarisms and Such Americanisms as Have Been Naturalized* (London: George Routledge, 1937), s.v. 'piss-factory'; also John S. Farmer and W. E. Henley (eds), *Slang and its Analogues Past and Present: A Dictionary, Historical and Comparative, of the Heterodox Speech of All Classes of Society for More Than Three Hundred Years: With Synonyms in English, French, German, Italian, etc.*, 7 vols (London, 1890–1904), s.v. 'piss'.
5. For more nuance, see P. J. Waller, 'Democracy and Dialect, Speech and Class', in P. J. Waller (ed.), *Politics and Social Change in Modern Britain: Essays Presented to A. F. Thompson* (Brighton: Harvester Press, 1987), 1–33, here 9–15. There is an impressionistic sampling of Sussex dialect in E. V. Lucas, *Highways and Byways in Sussex*, 2nd edn (London: Macmillan, 1904), ch. 41.
6. W. D. Parish, *A Dictionary of the Sussex Dialect and Collection of Provincialisms in Use in the County of Sussex*, 2nd edn (Lewes: Farncombe and Co., 1875), 45.
7. Parish, *Dictionary of the Sussex Dialect*, 5–6.
8. Joseph Wright (ed.), *The English Dialect Dictionary: Being the Complete Vocabulary of All Dialect Words Still in Use, or Known to Have Been in Use during the Last Two Hundred Years*, 6 vols (London: Henry Frowde, 1898–1905), s.v. 'arse', sb.
9. On 'poxy' see Geoffrey Hughes, *Swearing: A Social History of Foul Language, Oaths and Profanity in English* (Oxford: Blackwell, 1991), 226–7.

10. Wright (ed.), *English Dialect Dictionary*, s.v. 'foxy', adj. and sb., 1.
11. Wright (ed.), *English Dialect Dictionary*, s.v. 'foxy', adj. and sb., 5.
12. *Oxford English Dictionary*, s.v. 'foxy', 3.
13. William Tucker, *The Family Dyer and Scourer: Being a Complete Treatise on the Arts of Dying and Cleaning Every Article of Dress, Bed and Window Furniture, Silks, Bonnets, Feathers, &c., Whether Made of Flax, Silk, Cotton, Wool, or Hair: Also, Carpets, Counterpanes, and Hearth-rugs: Ensuring a Saving of Eighty Per Cent*, 2nd edn (London: Sherwood, Neely, and Jones, 1818), 78.
14. Wright (ed.), *English Dialect Dictionary*, s.v. 'foxy', adj. and sb., 3.
15. See the table in Hughes, *Swearing*, 208, and Madeline Kerr, *The People of Ship Street* (London: Routledge and Kegan Paul, 1958), 62.
16. See Hughes, *Swearing*, 230–1.
17. Edith Flora Russell, statement, 23 June 1921, MEPO 3/380. For another example, see Margaret Powell, *My Mother and I* (1972; repr., London: Pan Books, 1974), 36.
18. The British National Corpus of contemporary written and spoken British English includes no instances of 'fuck your cunt' (www.natcorp.ox.ac.uk, accessed 18 February 2015). Even a Google search for the phrase retrieves only a few, nearly all of them taking the form 'fuck your cunt with...'. No similar expression appears in the many varied uses of 'fuck' as a verb catalogued in Jesse Sheidlower (ed.), *The F-Word* (New York: Oxford University Press, 2009), 83–103.
19. And not just in Britain. See for instance S. A. Smith, 'The Social Meanings of Swearing: Workers and Bad Language in Late Imperial and Early Soviet Russia', *Past and Present*, no. 160 (August 1998), 167–202, here 176–7.
20. Ross McKibbin, *Classes and Cultures: England, 1918–1951* (Oxford: Oxford University Press, 1998), 130; Norman Dennis, Fernando Henriques, and Clifford Slaughter, *Coal Is Our Life: An Analysis of a Yorkshire Mining Community* (London: Tavistock, 1956), 214.
21. Dennis, Henriques, and Slaughter, *Coal Is Our Life*, 212–15.
22. Robert Frankenberg, *Communities in Britain: Social Life in Town and Country*, rev. edn (Harmondsworth: Penguin, 1969), 127.
23. Dennis, Henriques, and Slaughter, *Coal Is Our Life*, 214. Robert Roberts observed of the Salford of his early-twentieth-century youth: 'Men had one language for the mine, mill or factory, another for home and a third for social occasions.' Robert Roberts, *The Classic Slum: Salford Life in the First Quarter of the Century* (1971; repr., London: Penguin, 1990), 57. See also Waller, 'Democracy and Dialect', 15–16.
24. Dennis, Henriques, and Slaughter, *Coal Is Our Life*, 214.
25. McKibbin, *Classes and Cultures*, 166.
26. Kerr, *People of Ship Street*, 165. On the community study, see Mike Savage, *Identities and Social Change in Britain since 1940: The Politics of Method* (Oxford: Oxford University Press, 2010), chs 6–7.
27. Kerr, *People of Ship Street*, 165; McKibbin, *Classes and Cultures*, 167.

28. Ruth Eva Russell, statement, 25 June 1921, MEPO 3/380.

29. Mary Ann Swan, statement, 20 June 1921, MEPO 3/380.

30. Greg Dening, *Mr Bligh's Bad Language: Passion, Power and Theatre on the Bounty* (1992; repr., Cambridge: Canto, 1994), 55–80, 379 (quotation from 379).

31. Brian Jackson and Dennis Marsden, *Education and the Working Class: Some General Themes Raised by a Study of 88 Working-Class Children in a Northern Industrial City*, rev. edn. (Harmondsworth: Penguin, 1966), 65; Roberts, *Classic Slum*, 177.

32. On these papers and their readership, see Richard D. Altick, *The English Common Reader: A Social History of the Mass Reading Public, 1800–1900* (1957; repr., Columbus: Ohio State University Press, 1998), 360–1; Christopher Hilliard, 'Popular Reading and Social Investigation in Britain, 1850s–1940s', *Historical Journal*, 57 (2014), 247–71, here 250–8.

33. 'Anglo-Saxon' is a misnomer: 'shit', 'arse', and 'fart' have Anglo-Saxon origins, but none of the other common English swear words do. Hughes, *Swearing*, 24–5.

34. Henry Cecil Wyld, *The Historical Study of the Mother Tongue: An Introduction to Philological Method* (London: John Murray, 1906), 349.

35. Edith Swan, statement, 19 June 1921, MEPO 3/380.

36. Nicholls to Superintendent, 4 November 1921, MEPO 3/380.

37. Flora Thompson, *Lark Rise to Candleford: A Trilogy* (1939–1943; Harmondsworth: Penguin, 1973), 471–2; David Vincent, *Literacy and Popular Culture: England, 1750–1914* (Cambridge: Cambridge University Press, 1989), 50.

38. Stephen Swan, statement, 25 June 1921, MEPO 3/380.

39. G. R. Nicholls, 'Criminal Libel', report to Superintendent Fred Thomas, 29 June 1921, MEPO 3/380.

40. Sheila Fitzpatrick, *Tear Off the Masks! Identity and Imposture in Twentieth-Century Russia* (Princeton: Princeton University Press, 2005), 168.

41. Jackson and Marsden, *Education and the Working Class*, 73–4, 129; Willy Goldman, *East End My Cradle* (London: Faber and Faber, 1940), especially 75; Jonathan Rose, *The Intellectual Life of the British Working Classes* (New Haven: Yale University Press, 2001), chs 12–13.

42. Edith Swan to [Henry Thomas], 2 August 1921, MEPO 3/380.

43. Roberts, *Classic Slum*, 177. The people Roberts had in mind were not autodidacts—self-consciously self-improving and often regarded by their fellows as 'different' or 'queer'—but 'integral part[s] of the working community'.

44. Stephen Reynolds, *A Poor Man's House*, 2nd edn (London: John Lane The Bodley Head, 1909), 85–7.

45. M. Loane, *From Their Point of View* (London: Edward Arnold, 1908), 80, 82, 83.

46. M. Loane, *The Next Street but One* (London: Edward Arnold, 1907), 14. See also Julie-Marie Strange, 'Reading Language as a Historical Source', in Simon Gunn and Lucy Faire (eds), *Research Methods for History* (Edinburgh: Edinburgh University Press, 2012), 167–83, here 175–7.

47. Nicholls to Superintendent, 15 October 1921, MEPO 3/380.

48. After Moss's confrontation with Edith but before her arrest.

49. 'Contents of green linen card and leaves of book handed to Inspector Thomas by Miss Swan on arrest', '2nd. Oct.' (1921), MEPO 3/380.

50. Violet Lily May, statements, 12 and 13 October 1921, MEPO 3/380.

51. Nicholls to Superintendent, 15 October 1921; Violet Lily May, statement, 12 October 1921, MEPO 3/380.

52. Violet Lily May, statement, 12 October 1921, MEPO 3/380.

53. Henry Green, *Living* (1929) in *Living, Loving, Party Going* (New York: Penguin, 1993), 290; Virginia Woolf, *Mrs Dalloway* (1925; repr., London: Grafton, 1976), 44 and elsewhere.

54. Nicholls to Superintendent, 15 October 1921, MEPO 3/380.

CHAPTER 10

1. *Littlehampton Observer*, 11 October 1922; *Sussex Daily News*, 10 October 1922; *Evening News*, 9 October 1922; *Daily Express*, 18 October 1922.

2. *Daily Chronicle*, 10 October 1922.

3. *The Times*, 10 October 1922.

4. *Evening News*, 9 October 1922.

5. *Evening News*, 9 October 1922.

6. *The Times*, 10 October 1922; *Evening News*, 9 October 1922.

7. *The Times*, 10 October 1922.

8. *Portsmouth Evening News*, 9 October 1922.

9. Arundel Division Summons Book, 1916–1933, POL/W/A/3/2, West Sussex Record Office, entry for summons 94, served 30 September 1922.

10. *Portsmouth Evening News*, 9 October 1922.

11. W. H. Gooding to George Nicholls, 22 November 1922, MEPO 3/380, National Archives.

12. Anonymous letter, date stamped 11 October 1922 by the Home Office, HO 144/2452, National Archives. The letter itself has no addressee and the envelope has not been preserved in the Home Office file.

13. 'H. B. S.', note on minutes page of file 416617/18, 11 October 1922, HO 144/2452.

14. *Daily News*, 12 October 1922.

15. *Evening News*, 7 December 1922.

16. *Daily Mail*, 16 October 1922 (extraneous full stop deleted).

17. W. H. Gooding to Nicholls, 22 November 1922, MEPO 3/380.

18. Nicholls to Superintendent, 23 November 1922, MEPO 3/380. The headquarters of the West Sussex Constabulary shifted from Horsham to Chichester in 1922: anon., 'An Introduction to the West Sussex Constabulary', undated (c. 1963) typescript, no page numbers, POL W/ HQ15/8, West Sussex Record Office.

19. 'N. K.' to W. H. Gooding (copy), 27 November 1922, MEPO 3/380.

20. 'J. N.' to 'Chief of Police, Scotland Yard', 11 December 1922; A. Mitchell to Superintendent, 8 February 1923 (enclosing an anonymous letter), MEPO 3/380.

21. Sixth Census of Canada, 1921, Saskatchewan, district no. 216, sub-district 58, p. 9.

22. Walter D. Eastwood to Chief Inspector, Scotland Yard, 5 March 1923, MEPO 3/380.

23. A. Ward, 'Libel', 18 April 1910, MEPO 3/189.

24. The Times, 29 July 1910.

25. A. Ward, 'Libel', 18 April 1910, MEPO 3/189.

26. The Times, 2 August 1910.

27. Sussex Daily News, 12 July 1923.

28. Nicholls, note on minutes page of file 204/UNC/54, MEPO 3/380. These minutes cover the period from April 1923 until after the resolution of the Littlehampton letters case in July 1923, so no relevant part of the file is missing.

29. Christopher Browne, Getting the Message: The Story of the British Post Office (Stroud: Alan Sutton, 1993), 156.

30. Browne, Getting the Message, 156; Sussex Daily News, 19 July 1923; London Gazette, 2 July 1920, 7144 (concerning Walter Edward Bowler, one of the Special Investigation Branch officers in the Littlehampton case).

31. Browne, Getting the Message, 156.

32. Post Office Act 1908 (8 Edw. 7, ch. 48), s. 63.

33. 1901 Census, household record for 10 Worlingham Road, Camberwell. Cartwright's occupation in 1901 was 'Messenger at G.P.O.'

34. This is my interpretation of the description of him in the 1911 Census. The entry in the 'Personal Occupation' column reads: 'Clerk—Accountants business'. The 'Industry or Service with which worker is connected' column reads: 'Telephone industry'. 1911 Census, household record for 12 Reeves Road, Bow, E.

35. Kristie Macrakis, Prisoners, Lovers, and Spies: The Story of Invisible Ink from Herodotus to al-Qaeda (New Haven: Yale University Press, 2014), 143–6.

36. M. J. Daunton, Royal Mail: The Post Office since 1840 (London: Athlone Press, 1985), 280.

37. Sussex Daily News, 19 July 1923.

38. Sussex Daily News, 19 July 1923.

39. Sussex Daily News, 19 July 1923.

40. See the photographs in E. P. Hennock, *The Origin of the Welfare State in England and Germany, 1850–1914: Social Policies Compared* (Cambridge: Cambridge University Press, 2007), 269.

41. Martin Pugh, 'Working-Class Experience and State Social Welfare, 1909–1914: Old Age Pensions Reconsidered', *Historical Journal*, 45 (2002), 775–96, here 780–1; Daunton, *Royal Mail*, 111.

42. *Sussex Daily News*, 19 July 1923.

43. *News of the World*, 22 July 1923.

44. *News of the World*, 15 July 1923; *Sussex Daily News*, 19 July 1923.

45. *Daily Mirror*, 19 July 1923; *Sussex Daily News*, 19 July 1923.

46. *News of the World*, 22 July 1923.

47. *Argus* (Brighton), 19 July 1923.

48. *Sussex Daily News*, 12 July 1923.

49. *Sussex Daily News*, 19 July 1923.

50. *Sussex Daily News*, 12 July 1923.

51. *News of the World*, 22 July 1923.

52. *Sussex Daily News*, 12 July 1923; *Argus*, 19 July 1923.

53. *Sussex Daily News*, 12 July 1923.

54. *Sussex Daily News*, 19 July 1923; *Argus*, 19 July 1923.

55. *Argus*, 19 July 1923.

56. Edith could have been unaware of Peel's promotion or knew that he should still be addressed as Superintendent Peel. Deputy Chief Constable was a role but not an honorific. See Arundel Division Summons Book, 1916–1933, POL/W/A/3/2, West Sussex Record Office, entry for summons 108, 4 July 1923 (the summons served on Swan), which refers to him as Superintendent Peel, Deputy Chief Constable.

57. *Sussex Daily News*, 12 July 1923.

58. *The Times*, 12 July 1923.

59. *Daily Mail*, 12 July 1923; *News of the World*, 15 July 1923; *Sussex Daily News*, 12 July 1923.

60. *Littlehampton Observer*, 18 July 1923.

61. *Daily Mirror*, 12 July 1923.

62. *Daily Express*, 12 July 1923.

63. *Daily Mirror*, 12 July 1923. The report spells Swan's name 'Swann': I have corrected it rather than imply that Pearce himself got the name wrong.

64. Press reports variously spelled the name 'Tomsett', 'Thomsett', 'Thompset', and 'Thompsett'. I have settled on 'Tomsett'.

65. *Sussex Daily News*, 12 July 1923; *The Times*, 12 July 1923.

66. *Sussex Daily News*, 12 July 1923.

67. *Sussex Daily News*, 12 July 1923; *The Times*, 12 July 1923.

68. Arundel Division Summons Book, 1916–1933, POL/W/A/3/2, West Sussex Record Office, entry for summons 108, 4 July 1923; *Daily Mirror*, 12 July 1923.

69. *The Times*, 17 July 1913.

70. *Argus*, 19 July 1923.
71. *Argus*, 19 July 1923.
72. *Sussex Daily News*, 19 July 1923.
73. *The Times*, 19 July 1923.
74. *Argus*, 19 July 1923.
75. *Argus*, 19 July 1923.
76. *Daily Express*, 20 July 1923.
77. *Argus*, 19 July 1923; *Daily Express*, 20 July 1923.
78. *Argus*, 19 July 1923.
79. *Argus*, 19 July 1923; *The Times*, 20 July 1923; text of the letter from *Daily Mirror*, 19 July 1923.
80. *Argus*, 19 July 1923; *The Times*, 20 July 1923.
81. *The Times*, 20 July 1923.
82. *Argus*, 19 July 1923.
83. Humphreys, *Criminal Days*, 129; *Littlehampton Observer*, 25 July 1923.
84. *Argus*, 19 July 1923.
85. *Argus*, 19 July 1923.
86. *News of the World*, 22 July 1923.
87. *Argus*, 19 July 1923; Arundel Division Summons Book, 1916–1933, POL/ W/A/3/2, West Sussex Record Office, entry for summons 108, served 4 July 1923. The newspaper reports do not specify what proportion of the sentence was for libel and what for the charges under the Post Office Act. The police notes in the summons book similarly suggest that the twelve-month sentence covered both offences.
88. *Daily Express*, 20 July 1923; *The Times*, 20 July 1923; *Daily Mail*, 20 July 1923.
89. *Argus*, 19 July 1923.
90. *Argus*, 19 July 1923; *Daily Mail*, 20 July 1923. There are photographs of the matron leading Edith away in the *Daily Mirror*, 20 July 1923, and *News of the World*, 22 July 1923.

EPILOGUE

1. *Daily Mirror*, 20 July 1923. 'Mrs. Gooding with her children', read the caption. 'Her innocence was established after five months.'
2. Marriage solemnized at the register office in East Preston, County of Sussex, 27 June 1934. Certified Copy of an Entry of Marriage, 11 May 2015.
3. Marriage solemnized at the register office in the district of Worthing, County of Sussex, 19 June 1937. Certified Copy of an Entry of Marriage, 11 May 2015.
4. Marriage solemnized at the parish church of East Blatchington, County of Sussex. 12 January 1935. Certified Copy of an Entry of Marriage, 11 May 2015.

5. Death registered 10 December 1947, Littlehampton sub-district, Worthing registration district, County of West Sussex. Certified Copy of an Entry of Death, 11 May 2015.

6. Death registered 24 December 1968, Hailsham sub-district, Hailsham registration district, County of East Sussex. Certified Copy of an Entry of Death, 6 December 2013.

7. Court of Criminal Appeal, Notification of Result of Applications to the Full Court, *Rex v. Edith Emily Swan*, 13 August 1923, HO 144/2452. The notification was signed by Sir Leonard Kershaw, the court's registrar.

8. *The Times*, 4 August 1923.

9. G. R. Nicholls, 'Criminal Libel', report to Superintendent Fred Thomas, 29 June 1921, MEPO 3/380 (cited hereafter as 'Nicholls, report of 29 June 1921').

10. Edith Emily Swan, petition to Home Secretary, 17 December 1923, HO 144/2452.

11. L. S. B[rass] and 'H. B. S.', notes on minutes page of file 416617/23, 24 and 28 December 1923, HO 144/2452.

12. Lucy Bland, *Modern Women on Trial: Sexual Transgression in the Age of the Flapper* (Manchester: Manchester University Press, 2013). See also Laura Doan, *Fashioning Sapphism: The Origins of a Modern English Lesbian Culture* (New York: Columbia University Press, 2001).

13. Matt Houlbrook, '"A Pin to See the Peepshow": Culture, Fiction and Selfhood in Edith Thompson's Letters, 1921–1922', *Past and Present*, no. 207 (May 2010), 215–49, here 217, 248; Bland, *Modern Women on Trial*, ch. 3; Filson Young (ed.), *Trial of Frederick Bywaters and Edith Thompson* (Glasgow: William Hodge and Company, 1923), 161–250.

14. This was the Metropolitan Police lawyer with the distinctive but illegible signature (see p. 131 above). Note on minutes page of file 204/UNC/25, 7 November 1921, MEPO 3/380.

15. *Manchester Guardian*, 21 July 1923. On Hamblin Smith, see Paul Bowden, 'Pioneers in Forensic Psychiatry: Maurice Hamblin Smith: The Psychoanalytic Panacea', *Journal of Forensic Psychiatry* 1 (1990), 103–13; and, for more context, Claire Valiér, 'Psychoanalysis and Crime in Britain during the Inter-War Years', in *The British Criminology Conferences: Selected Proceedings*, vol. 1, *Emerging Themes in Criminology: Papers from the British Criminology Conference, Loughborough University, 18–21 July 1995*, ed. Jon Vagg and Tim Newburn (1998), www.britsoccrim.org/volume1/012.pdf (accessed 6 December 2015).

16. *Daily Express*, 20 July 1923, and Sir Ernley Blackwell's annotations in the copy in HO 144/2452.

17. M. Hamblin Smith and G. W. Pailthorpe, 'Mental Tests for Delinquents, and Mental Conflict as a Cause of Delinquency', *Lancet*, 202, no. 5212 (21 July 1923), 112–14, here 114.

18. *Daily Express*, 21 July 1923.

19. John David Moore, statement, 13 October 1921, MEPO 3/380.

20. *News of the World*, 22 July 1923.

21. Travers Humphreys, *Criminal Days: Recollections and Reflections* (London: Hodder and Stoughton, 1946), 131, 123, 129–30.
22. Hamblin Smith and Pailthorpe, 'Mental Tests for Delinquents', 113–14. For Hamblin Smith's reading of Freud, see M. Hamblin Smith, *The Psychology of the Criminal* (London: Methuen, 1922), esp. ch. 3.
23. Humphreys, *Criminal Days*, 124, 130.
24. There is nothing in Edith's prison records—such as they are—to suggest that Dr MacGregor, Portsmouth prison's medical officer, classified her as needing to be handled differently from other prisoners.
25. American Psychiatric Association, *Diagnostic and Statistical Manual of Mental Disorders*, 5th edn. (*DSM-5*) (Arlington, VA: American Psychiatric Association, 2013), 663–4; Francis Mark Mondimore and Patrick Kelly, *Borderline Personality Disorder: New Reasons for Hope* (Baltimore: Johns Hopkins University Press, 2011), 10 ('emptiness, worthlessness, and aloneness'); also John G. Gunderson and Paul S. Links, *Borderline Personality Disorder: A Clinical Guide*, 2nd edn (Arlington, VA: American Psychiatric Publishing, 2008).
26. Theodore Millon et al., *Disorders of Personality: DSM-IV and Beyond*, 2nd edn (New York: John Wiley and Sons, 1996), 668.
27. Mondimore and Kelly, *Borderline Personality Disorder*, 33.
28. Nicholls, report of 29 June 1921.
29. Mondimore and Kelly, *Borderline Personality Disorder*, 18.
30. Swan's experience contrasts with that of Annie Tugwell, who faced a further trial several years after getting out of prison—this time for breaching the Post Office Protection Act by posting indecent letters to her sister-in-law and two solicitors. Tugwell was separated from her husband ('I am almost a widow—worse than one, in fact', she said) and living in central London, working for a dressmaker with a view to starting a business of her own. She was convicted a second time and, Travers Humphreys heard, ended her days in an asylum. A. Ward, 'Libel', 30 August 1913, MEPO 3/189, National Archives; *The Times*, 2 September 1913, 9 September 1913 (the source of the quotation), 18 October 1913, 20 October 1913; Humphreys, *Criminal Days*, 134.
31. Death registered 16 March 1959, Littlehampton sub-district, Worthing registration district, County of West Sussex. Certified Copy of an Entry of Death, 13 December 2013.

CONCLUSION

1. Laurel Thatcher Ulrich, 'Vertuous Women Found: New England Ministerial Literature, 1668–1735', *American Quarterly*, 28 (1976), 20–40, here 20. On the afterlife of Ulrich's dictum, see Laurel Thatcher Ulrich, *Well-Behaved Women Seldom Make History* (New York: Vintage Books, 2007), xiii–xxix.

2. Joan Smith, 'There's Only One Yorkshire Ripper', in Smith, *Misogynies* (London: Faber and Faber, 1989), 117–51, esp. 123–4.

3. For an elaboration of this argument (and evidence for it), see Christopher Hilliard, 'Words That Disturb the State: Hate Speech and the Lessons of Fascism in Britain, 1930s–1960s', *Journal of Modern History*, 88 (2016), 764–96.

4. Which is not to say that the popular press was universally condemned, or that there were not more constructive forms of engagement with it. See Adrian Bingham, *Gender, Modernity, and the Popular Press in Inter-war Britain* (Oxford: Clarendon Press, 2004); and, on the longer history of debate on the press, Mark Hampton, *Visions of the Press in Britain, 1850–1950* (Urbana: University of Illinois Press, 2004).

5. Lucy Bland, *Modern Women on Trial: Sexual Transgression in the Age of the Flapper* (Manchester: Manchester University Press, 2013); John Carter Wood, *The Most Remarkable Woman in England: Poison, Celebrity, and the Trials of Beatrice Pace* (Manchester: Manchester University Press, 2012). The genealogy of these books on the 1920s includes Anna Clark, 'Queen Caroline and the Sexual Politics of Popular Culture in London, 1820', *Representations*, no. 31 (summer 1990), 47–68; Judith R. Walkowitz, *City of Dreadful Delight: Narratives of Sexual Danger in Late-Victorian London* (Chicago: University of Chicago Press, 1992); Sarah Maza, *Private Lives and Public Affairs: The Causes Célèbres of Prerevolutionary France* (Berkeley: University of California Press, 1993); Sarah Maza, 'Stories in History: Cultural Narratives in Recent Works in European History', *American Historical Review*, 101 (1996), 1493–515.

6. James Vernon, *Distant Strangers: How Britain Became Modern* (Berkeley: University of California Press, 2014), 47.

7. Walter J. Ong, 'Writing Is a Technology that Restructures Thought', in Gerd Baumann (ed.), *The Written Word: Literacy in Transition* (Oxford: Clarendon Press, 1986), 23–50; Walter J. Ong, *Orality and Literacy: The Technologizing of the Word* (London: Methuen, 1982), ch. 4.

8. Matt Houlbrook, '"A Pin to See the Peepshow": Culture, Fiction and Selfhood in Edith Thompson's Letters, 1921–1922', *Past and Present*, no. 207 (May 2010), 215–49, here 248.

9. This reproach applies not only to Houlbrook but also to Christopher Hilliard, *To Exercise Our Talents: The Democratization of Writing in Britain* (Cambridge, MA: Harvard University Press, 2006).

10. The *loci classici* are E. P. Thompson, 'The Moral Economy of the English Crowd in the Eighteenth Century', *Past and Present*, no. 50 (February 1971), 76–136; Robert Darnton, *The Great Cat Massacre and Other Episodes in French Cultural History* (New York: Basic Books, 1984), 75–104. The Marx quotation is from *The Eighteenth Brumaire of Louis Napoleon* (1852), in Robert C. Tucker (ed.), *The Marx–Engels Reader*, 2nd edn (New York: W. W. Norton, 1978), 595.

11. Melanie Tebbutt, *Women's Talk? A Social History of 'Gossip' in Working-Class Neighbourhoods, 1880–1960* (Aldershot: Scolar Press, 1995); Elizabeth Roberts, *A Woman's Place: An Oral History of Working-Class Women, 1890–1940* (Oxford: Blackwell, 1984); Paul Johnson, *Saving and Spending: The Working-Class Economy in Britain, 1870–1939* (Oxford: Oxford University Press, 1985); Ross McKibbin, *Classes and Cultures: England, 1918–1951* (Oxford: Oxford University Press, 1998); Ben Jones, *The Working Class in Mid-Twentieth-Century England: Community, Identity and Social Memory* (Manchester: Manchester University Press, 2012); David Vincent, *Literacy and Popular Culture: England, 1750–1914* (Cambridge: Cambridge University Press, 1989).

12. This book is thus much more in the Anglophone—especially American—tradition of microhistory than the Italian mode of *microstoria* and its French interlocutors. The Italian and French varieties of microhistory have been concerned above all with social structures and the use of anomalous cases to revise general narratives about structures and processes. American microhistory, in contrast, places a premium on agency and on narrative forms of exposition, as Francesca Trivellato points out in a perceptive essay. She elaborates: 'Agency is more than a catch-all word. In our discipline it stands for an emphasis on the individual's ability to resist and shape the larger forces of history and is, almost inevitably, intertwined with a narrative writing style. A narrative style—as opposed to a social scientific type of analysis—is prized not only for its accessibility to a larger audience but also for its suitability to recover the subjectivity, and even the interiority, of individual protagonists.' Francesca Trivellato, 'Microstoria/Microhistoire/Microhistory', *French Politics, Culture and Society*, 33 (2015), 122–34, here 127. For France and Italy see Jacques Revel, 'Micro-analyse et construction du social,' in Revel (ed.), *Jeux d'échelles: la micro-analyse à l'expérience* (Paris: Gallimard/Seuil, 1996), 15–36.

References

The key sources for this book are the Home Office and Metropolitan Police files on the Littlehampton libel case: HO 144/2452 and MEPO 3/380, both held at the National Archives, London. The files on other criminal cases are also held by the National Archives, mostly in the MEPO and CRIM (Central Criminal Court) series, with others in the ASSI (Justices of Assize) series. The notes also refer to ephemera held by the Littlehampton Museum and police records held by the West Sussex Record Office in Chichester, chiefly the 'occurrence books' for the Littlehampton and Worthing police stations and the Arundel Division summons book. The main other unpublished sources, which are not itemized in the following list, are census and birth, death, and marriage records, sourced from the General Register Office, Ancestry.com, and UK Census Online.

A. PRIMARY SOURCES

I. Manuscripts and archives

Littlehampton Museum, Littlehampton
Document Collection
Photographic Collection
The Met Heritage Centre, London
Examination certificate for George Robert Nicholls
The National Archives, London
Cabinet (CAB)
Home Office (HO)
Justices of Assize (ASSI)
Metropolitan Police (MEPO)
War Office (WO)
West Sussex Record Office, Chichester
West Sussex Constabulary Records

II. Official publications

Census of England and Wales 1921: County of Sussex (London: HMSO, 1923).
Committee of Inquiry into the Case of Mr Adolf Beck, *Report from the Committee: Together with Minutes of Evidence, Appendix, and Facsimiles of Various Documents*, Cd. 2315 (London: HMSO, 1904).

Committee on Defamation, *Report of the Committee on Defamation*, Cmnd. 5909 (London: HMSO, 1975).

Committee on Insanity and Crime, *Report of the Committee Appointed to Consider What Changes, If Any, Are Desirable in the Existing Law, Practice and Procedure Relating to Criminal Trials in Which the Plea of Insanity as a Defence is Raised, and Whether Any and, If So, What Changes Should Be Made in the Existing Law and Practice in Respect of Cases Falling within the Provisions of Section 2 (4) of the Criminal Lunatics Act, 1884*, Cmd. 2005 (London: HMSO, 1923).

Committee on Legal Aid for the Poor, *First Report*, Cmd. 2638 (London: HMSO, 1926).

Committee on the Employment of Women on Police Duties, *Minutes of Evidence*, Cmd. 1133 (London: HMSO, 1921).

Law Commission, *Criminal Libel*, Law Commission Working Paper no. 184 (London: HMSO, 1982).

Second Report of the Commissioners Appointed to Inquire into Friendly and Benefit Building Societies, C. 514, part 2 (London: HMSO, 1872).

Working Classes Cost of Living Committee, *Report*, Cd. 8980 (London: HMSO, 1918).

III. Newspapers

Aberdeen Daily Journal
Argus (Brighton)
Daily Chronicle
Daily Express
Daily Mail
Daily Mirror
Daily News
Daily Telegraph
Derby Daily Telegraph
Evening News
Evening Telegraph (Angus)
John Bull
Lancashire Evening Post
Littlehampton Observer
News of the World
Portsmouth Evening News
Southern Weekly News
Sussex Daily News
Sussex Weekly News
The Times
Yorkshire Post and Leeds Intelligencer

IV. Books and articles

Anon., *A Guide to All the Watering and Sea-Bathing Places, for 1813: With a Description of the Lakes; A Sketch of a Tour in Wales; and Itineraries: Illustrated with Maps and New Views: By the Editor of the Picture of London* (London: Longman, Hurst, Rees, Orme, and Browne, n.d.).

Anon., *Mr. Punch at the Seaside: As Pictured by Charles Keene, John Leech, George du Maurier, Phil May, L. Raven-Hill, J. Bernard Partridge, Gordon Browne, E. T. Reed, and Others* (London: Amalgamated Press, n.d.).

Anon., *Vere Foster's New Civil Service Copy-Books: Medium Series* (London: Blackie & Son, n.d.).

Ashley, F. W., *My Sixty Years in the Law* (London: John Lane The Bodley Head, 1936).

Batty, Ronald F., *How to Run a Twopenny Library* (London: John Gifford, 1938).

Bell, Lady (Mrs Hugh Bell), *At the Works: A Study of a Manufacturing Town* (London: Edward Arnold, 1907).

Biron, Chartres, *Without Prejudice: Impressions of Life and Law* (London: Faber and Faber, 1936).

Bowen-Rowlands, Ernest, *Seventy-Two Years at the Bar: A Memoir* (London: Macmillan, 1924).

Bowley, A. L. and Margaret H. Hogg, *Has Poverty Diminished? A Sequel to 'Livelihood and Poverty'* (London: P. S. King and Son, 1925).

Burnett, John (ed.), *Destiny Obscure: Autobiographies of Childhood, Education and Family from the 1820s to the 1920s* (London: Allen Lane, 1982).

[Caunt, James, comp.], *An Editor on Trial: Rex v. Caunt: Alleged Seditious Libel* (Morecambe and Heysham: Morecambe Press, n.d. [1947]).

Christie, Agatha, *The Moving Finger* (1943; repr., London: Collins, 1968).

Clark, M. Dudley, *Littlehampton, Sussex: With Its Surroundings* (London: Homeland Association and Frederick Warne and Co., n.d. [1915]).

Cloud, Yvonne (ed.), *Beside the Seaside: Six Variations* (London: Stanley Nott, 1934).

Dawson, Jill, *Fred and Edie* (London: Sceptre, 2000).

Denning, Alfred, *Freedom under the Law* (London: Stevens, 1949).

Dennis, Norman, Fernando Henriques, and Clifford Slaughter, *Coal Is Our Life: An Analysis of a Yorkshire Mining Community* (London: Tavistock, 1956).

Doyle, A. Conan, 'The Adventure of the Missing Three-Quarter' (1904), in *The Return of Sherlock Holmes* (New York: A. Wessells Company, 1907), 291–318.

Fraser, Hugh, *Principles and Practice of the Law of Libel and Slander: With Suggestions on the Conduct of a Civil Action, Forms and Precedents, and All Statutes Bearing on the Subject*, 5th edn (London: Butterworth, 1917).

Freeman, Arnold, *Boy Life and Labour: The Manufacture of Inefficiency* (London: P. S. King and Son, 1914).

Goldman, Willy, *East End My Cradle* (London: Faber and Faber, 1940).

Green, Henry, *Living* (1929) in *Living, Loving, Party Going* (New York: Penguin, 1993).

Hamblin Smith, M., *The Psychology of the Criminal* (London: Methuen, 1922).

Hamblin Smith, M. and G. W. Pailthorpe, 'Mental Tests for Delinquents, and Mental Conflict as a Cause of Delinquency', *Lancet*, 202, no. 5212 (21 July 1923), 112–14.

Hastings, Patrick, *The Autobiography of Sir Patrick Hastings* (London: William Heinemann, 1948).

Hobhouse, Stephen and Fenner Brockway (eds), *English Prisons To-Day: Being the Report of the Prison System Enquiry Committee* (London: Longmans, Green & Co., 1922).

The Homeland Handbooks: Littlehampton, Arundel and Amberley, with Their Surroundings, 11th edn (London: Homeland Association, n.d. [between 1918 and 1922]).

Humphery, Geo. R., 'The Reading of the Working Classes', *Nineteenth Century*, 33 (April 1893), 690–701.

Humphreys, Christmas, *Both Sides of the Circle: The Autobiography of Christmas Humphreys* (London: Allen and Unwin, 1978).

Humphreys, Travers, *Criminal Days: Recollections and Reflections* (London: Hodder and Stoughton, 1946).

Humphreys, Travers, foreword to H. Montgomery Hyde (ed.), *The Trials of Oscar Wilde* (London: William Hodge, 1948), 1–8.

Hyde, H. Montgomery (ed.), *The Trials of Oscar Wilde* (London: William Hodge & Co., 1948).

Jackson, Brian and Dennis Marsden, *Education and the Working Class: Some General Themes Raised by a Study of 88 Working-Class Children in a Northern Industrial City*, rev. edn (Harmondsworth: Penguin, 1966).

Kelly's Directory of Sussex, 1911 (London: Kelly's Directories, n.d.).

Kelly's Directory of Sussex, 1915 (London: Kelly's Directories, n.d.).

Kelly's Directory: Sussex, 1922 (London: Kelly's Directories, n.d.).

Kerr, Madeline, *The People of Ship Street* (London: Routledge and Kegan Paul, 1958).

Lang, Andrew, and '"X", A Working Man', 'The Reading Public', *Cornhill Magazine*, n.s., 11 (December 1901), 783–95.

Lawrence, D. H., *The Letters of D. H. Lawrence*, vol. 2, *1913–16*, ed. George T. Zytaruk and James T. Boulton (Cambridge: Cambridge University Press, 1981).

Leavis, Q. D., *Fiction and the Reading Public* (London: Chatto and Windus, 1932).

Leigh, John Garrett, 'What Do the Masses Read?' *Economic Review*, 14 (April 1904), 166–77.

Loane, M., 'Culture among the Poor', *Contemporary Review*, 90 (August 1906), 230–40.

Loane, M., *The Next Street but One* (London: Edward Arnold, 1907).

Loane, M., *From Their Point of View* (London: Edward Arnold, 1908).

Lucas, E. V., *Highways and Byways in Sussex*, 2nd edn (London: Macmillan, 1904).

Meek, George, *George Meek, Bath Chair-Man: By Himself* (New York: E. P. Dutton and Company, 1910).

[Millard, Christopher, and Cecil Palmer (eds),] *Oscar Wilde: Three Times Tried* (London: Ferrestone Press, n.d. [c. 1920]).

Mitton, G. E. (ed.), *The Writers' and Artists' Year Book 1921: A Directory for Writers, Artists and Photographers* (London: A. & C. Black, n.d.).

Mosley, Oswald, *My Life* (London: Nelson, 1968).

Odgers, William Blake, *The Law of Libel and Slander: And of Actions on the Case for Words Causing Damage: With Evidence, Procedure, Practice, and Precedents of Pleadings, Both in Civil and Criminal Cases*, 5th edn (London: Stevens and Sons, 1912).

Orwell, George, 'The Art of Donald McGill' (1941), in *The Collected Essays, Journalism and Letters of George Orwell*, ed. Sonia Orwell and Ian Angus, 4 vols (Boston: Nonpareil Books, 2000), 2: 155–65.

Page, Leo, *Justice of the Peace* (London: Faber and Faber, 1936).

Parish, W. D., *A Dictionary of the Sussex Dialect and Collection of Provincialisms in Use in the County of Sussex*, 2nd edn (Lewes: Farncombe and Co., 1875).

Pilley, Charles, *Law for Journalists* (London: Sir Isaac Pitman & Sons, 1924).

Powell, Margaret, *My Mother and I* (1972; repr., London: Pan Books, 1974).

Priestley, J. B., *English Journey: Being a Rambling but Truthful Account of What One Man Saw and Heard and Felt during a Journey through England during the Autumn of the Year 1933* (1934; repr., Harmondsworth: Penguin, 1977).

Reeves, Mrs [Maud] Pember, *Round about a Pound a Week* (London: G. Bell & Sons, 1913).

Reynolds, Stephen, *A Poor Man's House*, 2nd edn (London: John Lane The Bodley Head, 1909).

Roberts, Robert, *The Classic Slum: Salford Life in the First Quarter of the Century* (1971; repr., London: Penguin, 1990).

Ruggles-Brise, Evelyn, *The English Prison System* (London: Macmillan, 1921).

Thompson, Flora, *Lark Rise to Candleford: A Trilogy* (1939–1943; Harmondsworth: Penguin, 1973).

Thomson, Basil, *Queer People* (London: Hodder and Stoughton, 1922).

Tressell, Robert, *The Ragged Trousered Philanthropists* (London: Grant Richards, 1914).

Tucker, Robert C. (ed.), *The Marx-Engels Reader*, 2nd edn (New York: W. W. Norton, 1978).

Tucker, William, *The Family Dyer and Scourer: Being a Complete Treatise on the Arts of Dying and Cleaning Every Article of Dress, Bed and Window Furniture, Silks, Bonnets, Feathers, &c., Whether Made of Flax, Silk, Cotton, Wool, or Hair: Also, Carpets, Counterpanes, and Hearth-rugs: Ensuring a Saving of Eighty Per Cent*, 2nd edn (London: Sherwood, Neely, and Jones, 1818).

Wensley, Frederick Porter, *Detective Days: The Record of Forty-Two Years' Service in the Criminal Investigation Department* (London: Cassell, 1931).

[White, John], *Photographic Views of Littlehampton and Neighbourhood* ([Littlehampton:] J. White and Son, n.d.).

Who's Who 1921: An Annual Biographical Dictionary with Which Is Incorporated 'Men and Women of the Time' (London: Adam and Charles Black, n.d.).

Wilde, Oscar, *De Profundis*, in *The Complete Works of Oscar Wilde*, ed. Ian Small, vol. 2 (Oxford: Oxford University Press, 2005).

Wills, William, *An Essay on the Principles of Circumstantial Evidence: Illustrated by Numerous Cases*, 6th edn (London: Butterworth, 1912).

Woolf, Virginia, *Mrs Dalloway* (1925; repr., London: Grafton, 1976).

Wyld, Henry Cecil, *The Historical Study of the Mother Tongue: An Introduction to Philological Method* (London: John Murray, 1906).

Young, Filson (ed.), *Trial of Frederick Bywaters and Edith Thompson* (Glasgow: William Hodge and Company, 1923).

B. SECONDARY SOURCES

I. Books and articles

Adams, Steve, *Murder at the Star: Who Killed Thomas Thomas?* (Bridgend: Seren, 2015).

Altick, Richard D., *The English Common Reader: A Social History of the Mass Reading Public, 1800–1900* (1957; repr., Columbus: Ohio State University Press, 1998).

American Psychiatric Association, *Diagnostic and Statistical Manual of Mental Disorders*, 5th edn (*DSM-5*) (Arlington, VA: American Psychiatric Association, 2013).

Berenson, Edward, *The Trial of Madame Caillaux* (Berkeley: University of California Press, 1992).

Bingham, Adrian, *Gender, Modernity, and the Popular Press in Inter-War Britain* (Oxford: Oxford University Press, 2004).

Bingham, Adrian, 'Representing the People? The *Daily Mirror*, Class, and Political Culture in Inter-War Britain', in Laura Beers and Geraint Thomas (eds), *Brave New World: Imperial and Democratic Nation-building in Britain between the Wars* (London: Institute of Historical Research, 2012), 109–28.

Bland, Lucy, 'The Trials and Tribulations of Edith Thompson: The Capital Crime of Sexual Incitement in 1920s England', *Journal of British Studies*, 47 (2008), 624–48.

Bland, Lucy, *Modern Women on Trial: Sexual Transgression in the Age of the Flapper* (Manchester: Manchester University Press, 2013).

Bourke, Joanna, *Working-Class Cultures in Britain, 1890–1960: Gender, Class and Ethnicity* (London: Routledge, 1994).

Bowden, Paul, 'Pioneers in Forensic Psychiatry: Maurice Hamblin Smith: The Psychoanalytic Panacea', *Journal of Forensic Psychiatry*, 1 (1990), 103–13.

Briggs, Asa, *Victorian Things*, rev. edn (Harmondsworth: Penguin, 1990).

Brookfield, H. C., 'Three Sussex Ports, 1850-1950', *Journal of Transport History*, 2 (1955), 35–40.

Browne, Christopher, *Getting the Message: The Story of the British Post Office* (Stroud: Alan Sutton, 1993).

Cannadine, David, *Lords and Landlords: The Aristocracy and the Towns, 1774–1967* (Leicester: Leicester University Press, 1980).

Caplan, Jane, '"This or That Particular Person": Protocols of Identification in Nineteenth-Century Europe', in Jane Caplan and John Torpey (eds), *Documenting Individual Identity: The Development of State Practices in the Modern World* (Princeton: Princeton University Press, 2001), 49–66.

Caplan, Jane, 'Illegibility: Reading and Insecurity in History, Law and Government', *History Workshop Journal*, no. 68 (autumn 2009), 99–121.

Clanchy, M. T., *From Memory to Written Record: England 1066–1307* (London: Edward Arnold, 1979).

Clark, Anna, 'Queen Caroline and the Sexual Politics of Popular Culture in London, 1820', *Representations*, no. 31 (summer 1990), 47–68.

Cockayne, Emily, *Cheek by Jowl: A History of Neighbours* (London: The Bodley Head, 2012).

Cohen, Deborah, 'Who Was Who? Race and Jews in Turn-of-the-Century Britain', *Journal of British Studies*, 42 (2002), 460–83.

Cohen, Deborah, *Family Secrets: Living with Shame from the Victorians to the Present Day* (London: Penguin, 2013).

Cornish, William, J. Stuart Anderson, Ray Cocks, Michael Lobban, Patrick Polden, and Keith Smith, *The Oxford History of the Laws of England*, vol. 13, *1820–1914: Fields of Development* (Oxford: Oxford University Press, 2010).

Craig, Alec, *The Banned Books of England* (London: George Allen and Unwin, 1937).

Darnton, Robert, *The Great Cat Massacre and Other Episodes in French Cultural History* (New York: Basic Books, 1984).

Daunton, M. J., *House and Home in the Victorian City: Working-Class Housing, 1850–1914* (London: Edward Arnold, 1983).

Daunton, M. J., *Royal Mail: The Post Office since 1840* (London: Athlone Press, 1985).

Dawson, Sandra, 'Working-Class Consumers and the Campaign for Holidays with Pay', *Twentieth Century British History*, 18 (2007), 277–305.

Dening, Greg, *Mr Bligh's Bad Language: Passion, Power and Theatre on the Bounty* (1992; repr., Cambridge: Canto, 1994).

Derrida, Jacques, *Of Grammatology*, tr. Gayatri Chakravorty Spivak (1967; Baltimore: Johns Hopkins University Press, 1976).

Derrida, Jacques, *The Post Card: From Socrates to Freud and Beyond*, tr. Alan Bass (1980; Chicago: University of Chicago Press, 1987).

Dilnot, George, *Scotland Yard: The Methods and Organisation of the Metropolitan Police* (London: Percival Marshall, 1915).

Dilnot, George, *The Story of Scotland Yard* (London: Geoffrey Bles, 1926).

Doan, Laura, *Fashioning Sapphism: The Origins of a Modern English Lesbian Culture* (New York: Columbia University Press, 2001).

Elleray, D. Robert, *Littlehampton: A Pictorial History* (Chichester: Phillimore, 1991).

Ellis, Alec, *Educating Our Masters: Influences on the Growth of Literacy in Victorian Working Class Children* (Aldershot: Gower, 1985).

Emsley, Clive, *The English Police: A Political and Social History*, 2nd edn (Harlow: Longman, 1996).

Emsley, Clive, *Hard Men: The English and Violence since 1750* (London: Hambledon and London, 2005).

Eyles, Allen, Frank Gray, and Alan Readman, *Cinema West Sussex: The First Hundred Years* (Chichester: Phillimore, 1996).

Farmer, John S., and W. E. Henley (eds), *Slang and its Analogues Past and Present: A Dictionary, Historical and Comparative, of the Heterodox Speech of All Classes of Society for More Than Three Hundred Years: With Synonyms in English, French, German, Italian, etc.*, 7 vols (London: published for subscribers only, 1890–1904).

Fitzpatrick, Sheila, *Tear Off the Masks! Identity and Imposture in Twentieth-Century Russia* (Princeton: Princeton University Press, 2005).

Frankenberg, Robert, *Communities in Britain: Social Life in Town and Country*, rev. edn (Harmondsworth: Penguin, 1969).

Freeman, Arthur, Mark H. Stone, and Donna Martin (eds), *Borderline Personality Disorder: A Practitioner's Guide to Comparative Treatments* (New York: Springer, 2005).

Friel, Ian, and Rebecca Fardell (eds), *Littlehampton* (Stroud: Chalford, 1998).

Frost, Ginger, '"The Black Lamb of the Black Sheep": Illegitimacy in the English Working Class, 1850–1939', *Journal of Social History*, 37 (2003), 293–322.

Gilbert, David, *Class, Community, and Collective Action: Social Change in Two British Coalfields, 1850–1926* (Oxford: Clarendon Press, 1992).

Ginzburg, Carlo, 'Morelli, Freud and Sherlock Holmes: Clues and Scientific Method', tr. Anna Davin, *History Workshop Journal*, no. 9 (spring 1980), 5–36.

Gooderson, R. N., 'Defences in Double Harness', in P. R. Glazebrook (ed.), *Reshaping the Criminal Law: Essays in Honour of Glanville Williams* (London: Stevens, 1978), 138–53.

Goody, Jack, *The Logic of Writing and the Organization of Society* (Cambridge: Cambridge University Press, 1986).

Griffiths, Trevor, *The Lancashire Working Classes, c. 1880–1930* (Oxford: Oxford University Press, 2001).

Gunderson, John G., Paul S. Links, *Borderline Personality Disorder: A Clinical Guide*, 2nd edn (Arlington, VA: American Psychiatric Publishing, 2008).

Gunn, Simon, and Rachel Bell, *Middle Classes: Their Rise and Sprawl* (London: Phoenix, 2002).

Hampton, Mark, *Visions of the Press in Britain, 1850–1950* (Urbana: University of Illinois Press, 2004).

Hennock, E. P., *The Origin of the Welfare State in England and Germany, 1850–1914: Social Policies Compared* (Cambridge: Cambridge University Press, 2007).

Hilliard, Christopher, *To Exercise Our Talents: The Democratization of Writing in Britain* (Cambridge, MA: Harvard University Press, 2006).

Hilliard, Christopher, *English as a Vocation: The 'Scrutiny' Movement* (Oxford: Oxford University Press, 2012).

Hilliard, Christopher, ' "Is It a Book That You Would Even Wish Your Wife or Your Servants to Read?" Obscenity Law and the Politics of Reading in Modern England', *American Historical Review*, 118 (2013), 653–78.

Hilliard, Christopher, 'Popular Reading and Social Investigation in Britain, 1850s–1940s', *Historical Journal*, 57 (2014), 247–71.

Hilliard, Christopher, 'Words That Disturb the State: Hate Speech and the Lessons of Fascism in Britain, 1930s–1960s', *Journal of Modern History*, 88 (2016), 764–96.

Hodes, Martha, *The Sea Captain's Wife: A True Story of Love, Race, and War in the Nineteenth Century* (New York: W. W. Norton, 2006).

Houlbrook, Matt, ' "A Pin to See the Peepshow": Culture, Fiction and Selfhood in Edith Thompson's Letters, 1921–1922', *Past and Present*, no. 207 (May 2010), 215–49.

Hughes, Geoffrey, *Swearing: A Social History of Foul Language, Oaths and Profanity in English* (Oxford: Blackwell, 1991).

Hyde, H. Montgomery, *Oscar Wilde: A Biography* (London: Eyre Methuen, 1976).

Jackson, Louise A., *Women Police: Gender, Welfare and Surveillance in the Twentieth Century* (Manchester: Manchester University Press, 2006).

Jackson, Robert, *Case for the Prosecution: A Biography of Sir Archibald Bodkin, Director of Public Prosecutions, 1920–1930* (London: Arthur Barker, 1962).

Jackson, Stanley, *The Life and Cases of Mr. Justice Humphreys* (London: Odhams Press, 1952).

Johnson, Paul, *Saving and Spending: The Working-Class Economy in Britain, 1870–1939* (Oxford: Oxford University Press, 1985).

Jones, Ben, *The Working Class in Mid-Twentieth-Century England: Community, Identity and Social Memory* (Manchester: Manchester University Press, 2012).

Jones, Iris and Daphne Stanford, *Littlehampton in Old Photographs* (Stroud: Alan Sutton, 1990).

Joyce, Patrick, *The State of Freedom: A Social History of the British State since 1800* (Cambridge: Cambridge University Press, 2013).

Kettle, Michael, *Salome's Last Veil: The Libel Case of the Century* (London: Hart-Davis MacGibbon, 1977).

Lang, Gordon, *Mr. Justice Avory* (London: Herbert Jenkins, 1935).

Langhamer, Claire, *The English in Love: The Intimate Story of an Emotional Revolution* (Oxford: Oxford University Press, 2013).

Lansdell, Gwen, *Time for a Quick One: A Brief Historical Comment on Some of Littlehampton's Inns and Pubs, Together with Words about the Brewery*, Littlehampton Monograph no. 2 (Littlehampton: Littlehampton Local History Society, 1994).

Lawrence, Jon, 'Forging a Peaceable Kingdom: War, Violence, and Fear of Brutalization in Post-First World War Britain', *Journal of Modern History*, 75 (2003), 557–89.

Levenson, Howard, 'Legal Aid for Mitigation', *Modern Law Review*, 40 (1977), 523–32.

Levine, Philippa, ' "Walking the Streets in a Way No Decent Woman Should": Women Police in World War I', *Journal of Modern History*, 66 (1994), 34–78.

Levine, Philippa, *Prostitution, Race, and Politics: Policing Venereal Disease in the British Empire* (New York: Routledge, 2003).

Lewis, C. P. (ed.), *A History of the County of Sussex*, vol. 5, part 2, *Littlehampton and District (Arundel Rape, South-Eastern Part, Comprising Poling Hundred)*, The Victoria History of the Counties of England (London: Published for the Institute of Historical Research by Boydell and Brewer, 2009).

Lock, Joan, *The British Policewoman: Her Story* (London: Robert Hale, 1979).

McAleer, Joseph, *Popular Reading and Publishing in Britain, 1914–1950* (Oxford: Oxford University Press, 1992).

McBain, G. S., 'Abolishing Criminal Libel', *Australian Law Journal*, 84 (2010), 439–504.

McKeever, Kent, 'A Short History of Tontines', *Fordham Journal of Corporate and Financial Law*, 15 (2009), 491–521.

McKibbin, Ross, *The Ideologies of Class: Social Relations in Britain, 1880–1950* (Oxford: Clarendon Press, 1990).

McKibbin, Ross, *Classes and Cultures: England, 1918–1951* (Oxford: Oxford University Press, 1998).

Macrakis, Kristie, *Prisoners, Lovers, and Spies: The Story of Invisible Ink from Herodotus to al-Qaeda* (New Haven: Yale University Press, 2014).

Malcolmson, Patricia E., *English Laundresses: A Social History, 1850–1930* (Urbana: University of Illinois Press, 1986).

Manchester, Colin, 'A History of the Crime of Obscene Libel', *Journal of Legal History*, 12 (1991), 36–57.

Mandler, Peter (ed.), *Liberty and Authority in Victorian Britain* (Oxford: Oxford University Press, 2006).

Maza, Sarah, *Private Lives and Public Affairs: The Causes Célèbres of Prerevolutionary France* (Berkeley: University of California Press, 1993).

Maza, Sarah, 'Stories in History: Cultural Narratives in Recent Works in European History', *American Historical Review*, 101 (1996), 1493–515.

Millon, Theodore, et al., *Disorders of Personality: DSM-IV and Beyond*, 2nd edn (New York: John Wiley and Sons, 1996).

Mitchell, Paul, *The Making of the Modern Law of Defamation* (London: Hart, 2005).

Mnookin, Jennifer L., 'Scripting Expertise: The History of Handwriting Identification Evidence and the Judicial Construction of Reliability', *Virginia Law Review*, 87 (2001), 1723–845.

Mondimore, Francis Mark, and Patrick Kelly, *Borderline Personality Disorder: New Reasons for Hope* (Baltimore: Johns Hopkins University Press, 2011).

Mugglestone, Lynda, *'Talking Proper': The Rise of Accent as Social Symbol* (Oxford: Oxford University Press, 2003).

Mullan, John, 'The Strange Case of the Poison Pen Letters', *Guardian*, 28 June 2014.

Nairn, Ian and Nikolaus Pevsner, *The Buildings of England: Sussex* (Harmondsworth: Penguin, 1965).

O'Donnell, Bernard, *The Trials of Mr. Justice Avory* (London: Rich and Cowan, 1935).

Ogle, Vanessa, *The Global Transformation of Time, 1870–1950* (Cambridge, MA: Harvard University Press, 2015).

Ong, Walter J., *Orality and Literacy: The Technologizing of the Word* (London: Methuen, 1982).

Ong, Walter J., 'Writing Is a Technology that Restructures Thought', in Gerd Baumann (ed.), *The Written Word: Literacy in Transition* (Oxford: Clarendon Press, 1986), 23–50.

Partridge, Eric, *A Dictionary of Slang and Unconventional English: Slang—Including the Language of the Underworld, Colloquialisms and Catch-phrases, Solecisms and Catachreses, Nicknames, Vulgarisms and Such Americanisms as Have Been Naturalized* (London: George Routledge, 1937).

Pedersen, Susan, 'From National Crisis to "National Crisis": British Politics, 1914–1931', *Journal of British Studies*, 33 (1994), 322–35.

Peel, Mark, *Miss Cutler and the Case of the Resurrected Horse: Social Work and the Story of Poverty in America, Australia, and Britain* (Chicago: University of Chicago Press, 2012).

Poser, Norman S., *Lord Mansfield: Justice in the Age of Reason* (Montreal: McGill-Queen's University Press, 2013).

Pugh, Martin, 'Working-Class Experience and State Social Welfare, 1909–1914: Old Age Pensions Reconsidered', *Historical Journal*, 45 (2002), 775–96.

Rawlings, Mark, *Policing: A Short History* (Cullompton: Willan, 2002).

Reay, Barry, 'The Context and Meaning of Popular Literacy: Some Evidence from Nineteenth-Century Rural England', *Past and Present*, no. 131 (May 1991), 89–129.

Revel, Jacques, 'Micro-analyse et construction du social,' in Jacques Revel (ed.), *Jeux d'échelles: la micro-analyse à l'expérience* (Paris: Gallimard/Seuil, 1996), 15–36.

Roberts, Bechhofer, *Sir Travers Humphreys: His Career and Cases* (London: John Lane The Bodley Head, 1936).

Roberts, Elizabeth, *A Woman's Place: An Oral History of Working-Class Women, 1890–1940* (Oxford: Blackwell, 1984).

Rose, Jonathan, *The Intellectual Life of the British Working Classes* (New Haven: Yale University Press, 2001).

Ross, Ellen, *Love and Toil: Motherhood in Outcast London, 1870–1918* (New York: Oxford University Press, 1993).

Satia, Priya, 'Developing Iraq: Britain, India and the Redemption of Empire and Technology in the First World War', *Past and Present*, no. 197 (November 2007), 211–55.

Savage, Mike, 'Trade Unionism, Sex Segregation, and the State: Women's Employment in "New Industries" in Inter-War Britain', *Social History*, 13 (1988), 209–30.

Savage, Mike and Andrew Miles, *The Remaking of the British Working Class, 1840–1940* (London: Routledge, 1994).

Savage, Mike, *Identities and Social Change in Britain since 1940: The Politics of Method* (Oxford: Oxford University Press, 2010).

Scott, James C., *Seeing like a State: How Certain Schemes to Improve the Human Condition Have Failed* (New Haven: Yale University Press, 1998).

Scott, Joan Wallach, *Gender and the Politics of History*, rev. edn (New York: Columbia University Press, 1999).

Sheidlower, Jesse (ed.), *The F-Word* (New York: Oxford University Press, 2009).

Shpayer-Makov, Haia, *The Making of a Policeman: A Social History of a Labour Force in Metropolitan London, 1829–1914* (Aldershot: Ashgate, 2002).

Shpayer-Makov, Haia, 'Explaining the Rise and Success of Detective Memoirs in Britain', in Clive Emsley and Haia Shpayer-Makov (eds), *Police Detectives in History, 1750–1950* (Aldershot: Ashgate, 2006), 103–34.

Smith, Joan, *Misogynies* (London: Faber and Faber, 1989).

Smith, S. A., 'The Social Meanings of Swearing: Workers and Bad Language in Late Imperial and Early Soviet Russia', *Past and Present*, no. 160 (August 1998), 167–202.

Spencer, J. R., 'Criminal Libel—A Skeleton in the Cupboard', *Criminal Law Review* (1977), 383–94 (part 1), 464–74 (part 2).

Spivak, Gayatri Chakravorty, 'Can the Subaltern Speak?' in Cary Nelson and Lawrence Grossberg (eds), *Marxism and the Interpretation of Culture* (Urbana: University of Illinois Press, 1988), 271–313.

Steedman, Carolyn, 'A Lawyer's Letter: Everyday Uses of the Law in Early Nineteenth-Century England', *History Workshop Journal*, no. 81 (spring 2016), 62–83.

Strange, Julie-Marie, 'Reading Language as a Historical Source', in Simon Gunn and Lucy Faire (eds), *Research Methods for History* (Edinburgh: Edinburgh University Press, 2012), 167–83.

Strange, Julie-Marie, 'Fatherhood, Furniture and the Inter-Personal Dynamics of Working-Class Homes, c. 1870–1914', *Urban History*, 40 (2013), 271–86.

Supple, Barry, *1913–1946: The Political Economy of Decline*, vol. 4 of *The History of the British Coal Industry* (Oxford: Clarendon Press, 1987).

Symons, Julian, *Horatio Bottomley: A Biography* (London: Cresset Press, 1955).

Tebbutt, Melanie, *Making Ends Meet: Pawnbroking and Working-Class Credit* (1983; repr., London: Methuen, 1984).

Tebbutt, Melanie, *Women's Talk? A Social History of 'Gossip' in Working-Class Neighbourhoods, 1880–1960* (Aldershot: Scolar Press, 1995).

Thane, Pat, and Tanya Evans, *Sinners? Scroungers? Saints? Unmarried Motherhood in Twentieth-Century England* (Oxford: Oxford University Press, 2012).

Thompson, E. P., 'The Moral Economy of the English Crowd in the Eighteenth Century', *Past and Present*, no. 50 (February 1971), 76–136.

Todd, Selina, *Young Women, Work, and Family in England, 1918–1950* (Oxford: Oxford University Press, 2005).

Todd, Selina, *The People: The Rise and Fall of the Working Class, 1910–2010* (London: John Murray, 2014).

Tosh, John, *A Man's Place: Masculinity and the Middle-Class Home in Victorian England* (New Haven: Yale University Press, 1999).

Trivellato, Francesca, 'Microstoria/Microhistoire/Microhistory', *French Politics, Culture and Society*, 33 (2015), 122–34.

Ulrich, Laurel Thatcher, 'Vertuous Women Found: New England Ministerial Literature, 1668–1735', *American Quarterly*, 28 (spring 1976), 20–40.

Ulrich, Laurel Thatcher, *Well-Behaved Women Seldom Make History* (New York: Vintage Books, 2007).

Valiér, Claire, 'Psychoanalysis and Crime in Britain during the Inter-War Years', in *The British Criminology Conferences: Selected Proceedings*, vol. 1, *Emerging Themes in Criminology: Papers from the British Criminology Conference, Loughborough University, 18–21 July 1995*, ed. Jon Vagg and Tim Newburn (1998), www.britsoccrim.org/volume1/012.pdf (accessed 6 December 2015).

Vernon, James, *Distant Strangers: How Britain Became Modern* (Berkeley: University of California Press, 2014).

Vidler, Leopold A., 'The Rye River Barges', *Mariner's Mirror*, 21 (1935), 378–94.

Vincent, David, *Literacy and Popular Culture: England, 1750–1914* (Cambridge: Cambridge University Press, 1989).

Walkowitz, Judith R., *City of Dreadful Delight: Narratives of Sexual Danger in Late-Victorian London* (Chicago: University of Chicago Press, 1992).

Walkowitz, Judith R., 'The "Vision of Salome": Cosmopolitanism and Erotic Dancing in Central London, 1908–1918', *American Historical Review*, 108 (2003), 337–76.

Waller, P. J., *Town, City and Nation: England, 1850–1914* (Oxford: Clarendon Press, 1983).

Waller, P. J., 'Democracy and Dialect, Speech and Class', in P. J. Waller (ed.), *Politics and Social Change in Modern Britain: Essays Presented to A. F. Thompson* (Brighton: Harvester Press, 1987), 1–33.

Walton, John K., *The English Seaside Resort: A Social History, 1750–1914* (Leicester: Leicester University Press, 1983).

Walton, John K., *The British Seaside: Holidays and Resorts in the Twentieth Century* (Manchester: Manchester University Press, 2000).

Washer, George, comp., *A Complete Record of Sussex County Cricket, 1728 to 1957* (n.p.: Sussex County Cricket Club, 1958).

Wiener, Martin J., *Reconstructing the Criminal: Culture, Law, and Policy in England, 1830–1914* (Cambridge: Cambridge University Press, 1990).

Wiener, Martin J., 'Judges v. Jurors: Courtroom Tensions in Murder Trials and the Law of Criminal Responsibility in Nineteenth-Century England', *Law and History Review*, 17 (1999), 467–506.

Wild, Roland, *King's Counsel: The Life of Sir Henry Curtis-Bennett* (New York: Macmillan, 1938).

Winks, Robin W. (ed.), *The Historian as Detective: Essays on Evidence* (New York: Harper Colophon, 1969).

Wood, John Carter, *The Most Remarkable Woman in England: Poison, Celebrity, and the Trials of Beatrice Pace* (Manchester: Manchester University Press, 2012).

Wright, Joseph (ed.), *The English Dialect Dictionary: Being the Complete Vocabulary of All Dialect Words Still in Use, or Known to Have Been in Use during the Last Two Hundred Years*, 6 vols (London: Henry Frowde, 1898–1905).

Zeegers, Rolf, Juliet Nye, and Lucy Ashby, *Littlehampton Revisited* (Stroud: The History Press, 2007).

II. Report

Harris, Roland B., *Littlehampton: Historic Character Assessment Report*, Sussex Extensive Urban Survey (April 2009) https://www.westsussex.gov.uk/media/1734/littlehampton_eus_report_and_maps.pdf.

III. Websites

Ancestry.com (www.ancestry.com)

British Listed Buildings Online (www.britishlistedbuildings.co.uk)

British National Corpus (www.natcorp.ox.ac.uk)

Scotland's War (www.scotlandswar.ed.ac.uk)

Elizabeth Roberts' Working Class Oral History Archive, Regional Heritage Centre, Lancaster University (www.lancaster.ac.uk/users/cnwrs/resources/archive.htm)

Sussex Postcards (www.sussexpostcards.info)

UK Pub History and Historical Street Directory of London and the UK (pubshistory.com)

UK Census Online (www.ukcensusonline.com)

Wrecksite (www.wrecksite.eu)

Index

Page numbers in italics refer to illustrations.

The manufacturer's authorised representative in the EU for product safety is Oxford
University Press España S.A. of El Parque Empresarial San Fernando de Henares,
Avenida de Castilla, 2 – 28830 Madrid (www.oup.es/en or product.safety@oup.com).
OUP España S.A. also acts as importer into Spain of products made by the manufacturer.

Printed in the USA/Agawam, MA
December 20, 2024

879400.016